"If the ecological crisis is the greatest chall today, then Joanna Macy is the most important teacher of our time. For those who don't yet know her work, this anthology is an excellent place to start. For those of us who have already benefited from it, it provides an overview of an extraordinary woman and her remarkable career."—David Loy, author of *Ecodharma: Buddhist Teachings for the Ecological Crisis*

"How do we live in solidarity on this warming planet? This book captures a lifetime of grappling with this most important of questions—and invites readers into a thriving community of people who, like me, have been transformed by Joanna Macy's thought and practice." —Naomi Klein, author of *On Fire: The Burning Case For a Green New Deal*

"The conversation I had with Joanna Macy early in our tender, tumultuous century has shaped me ever after. I first discovered Joanna through her gorgeous translations of the poet Rilke, a voice of the last century's turnings that she has brought to accompany us in ours. I marvel at her many callings and adventures. She attended to the human trauma as Rilke's central European world disappeared in the aftermath of World War II—and in the exile from Tibet of a young Dalai Lama. She was an environmentalist before that term was on every tongue. And she became a great Buddhist teacher before anyone understood how this tradition would meet twenty-first-century people and potentialities. Through all of this, Joanna has come to embody a singular clarity of vision about the totality of what it means to be human—at this moment in time. Her wild love for the world is a beacon to us all—and an exuberant invitation—to join our passion to hers, whatever the lives we lead. This book is a precious offering toward life-giving possibility."—Krista Tippett, host of *On Being*

"Joanna Macy is one of the planet's treasures, not least for the remarkable cadre of people who have learned from and been inspired by her rooted and unstinting life. This fine book combines her insights and those who have learned from her, and it will be a joy to anyone who approaches it with an open heart."—Bill McKibben, author of *Falter: Has the Human Game Begun to Play Itself Out?*

"We can't save our world, we can only love our larger body, this living earth, and take the next healing step. To guide us, we have Joanna Macy, who embodies this active loving in her brilliant teachings, 'The Work That Reconnects,' and through her decades of serving our planet. This new book captures the great depth and breadth of Joanna's wisdom through her own stories, as well as through the richly shared stories of her colleagues—activists, thinkers, and teachers. Throughout, Joanna's understandings, group practices, and passionate heart offer us an urgently needed pathway of hope for this precious world."—Tara Brach, author of *Radical Acceptance* and *Radical Compassion*

"I am wildly in love with *A Wild Love for the World.* I can truly say that the stories in this book, and its life-transforming ideas and their practical applications, have changed me. The personal stories and focus on positive collaborative engagement offer a breath of energizing fresh air as we move forward. Joanna Macy's life, celebrated here in an engaging, inspiring, and practical compendium of approaches catalyzed by her 'Work That Reconnects,' offers each of us a light to cultivate resilience and illuminate the path ahead. Thank you to Stephanie Kaza and all the contributors, and to Joanna, for the love and brilliance that shine so brightly in this life's work of heart."—Daniel Siegel, author of *Aware* and *Mind*

A WILD LOVE
FOR THE WORLD

A
WILD
LOVE
for the
WORLD

JOANNA MACY
and the Work of Our Time

Edited by
STEPHANIE KAZA

Shambhala
Boulder · 2020

Frontispiece: Joanna Macy teaching in Bavaria in the 1990s
(photo by Klaus Kreuzer).

Shambhala Publications, Inc.
4720 Walnut Street
Boulder, Colorado 80301
www.shambhala.com

9 8 7 6 5 4 3 2

Printed in the United States of America

⊗This edition is printed on acid-free paper that meets the
American National Standards Institute z39.48 Standard.
♻This book is printed on 30% postconsumer recycled paper.
For more information please visit www.shambhala.com.
Shambhala Publications is distributed worldwide by
Penguin Random House, Inc., and its subsidiaries.

Designed by Kate E. White

LIBRARY OF CONGRESS CATALOGING-IN-PUBLICATION DATA
Names: Kaza, Stephanie, editor.
Title: A wild love for the world: Joanna Macy and
the work of our time / edited by Stephanie Kaza.
Description: First edition. | Boulder: Shambhala, 2020. |
Includes bibliographical references.
Identifiers: LCCN 2019034986 | ISBN 9781611807950 (paperback)
Subjects: LCSH: Macy, Joanna, 1929– | Environmentalists—United
States—Biography. | Environmentalism—Religious aspects—Buddhism. |
Environmental justice—Religious aspects—Buddhism.
Classification: LCC BQ4570.E58 W55 2020 | DDC 294.3/37092—dc23
LC record available at https://lccn.loc.gov/2019034986

Contents

PART TWO: SUSTAINING THE GAZE 69

PART THREE: THE INTERPLAY OF REALITY 145

Foreword

DAVID ABRAM

In the early 1980s I was driving along a poorly paved road in the outer suburbs of New York City, my right hand fiddling with the radio dial. As the sound skidded between the white fuzz of static and intermittent snatches of innocuous, overproduced music, I abruptly heard a clear and curious voice, not exactly singing but definitely singsong, lilting up and down. I stopped turning the dial and just listened. At a brief station break, the woman being interviewed was identified as Joanna Macy, a Buddhist scholar and activist. And then there was that unusual voice again, breathy, with a slightly nasal twang, saying something astonishingly simple:

"You know, the oxygen we need to breathe is precisely what all the green plants around us are breathing out. So what the plants breathe out, all of us are breathing in. And then what *we* breathe out is just what all those plants need to breathe in."

Wait a minute. I pulled the car off the road in order to think about this. Was this true? I knew well that the oxygen in our atmosphere is generated by the photosynthesis of plants. And I'd long understood that we and other animals breathe out carbon dioxide as a by-product of our own respiratory metabolism. But I had been taught about respiration and photosynthesis as two entirely separate, basically mechanical processes. Somehow I had never noticed how mutually entangled these two activities are.

And I had surely never thought of plants as *breathing.* I stepped out of the car to gaze at the leafing trees near the road. Plants just "give off" oxygen automatically, don't they? Yet the more I thought about it, the more I saw the perfectly analogous nature of these two processes, one zoological and one botanical. If we call our own uptake of oxygen from the air around us "breathing in" and the giving off of carbon dioxide from our lungs "breathing out," then surely we could say that all these green and rooted beings *inhale* carbon dioxide, and that they *exhale* the oxygen we animals need to live. I mean, *of course* they are breathing! I looked around me, my nostrils flaring. The broad-leafed maples lining the road, a beech scarred with someone's initials (the gray bark swollen with welts around the letters), even the clumped grasses underfoot—I remember how these all seemed oddly different, their foliage shimmering in the summer heat. They felt more *present*, somehow, more intensely alive. Or rather I was more present *to them*, my animal senses suddenly more open to these others as sensate beings in their own right, sensitive and sentient organisms vibrantly engaged in the same world as I.

Joanna's simple articulation in that radio broadcast has never left me. It was so dumbfoundingly obvious—something I already knew, although the mechanical jargon of college biology had blocked me from noticing the utter wonder of the thing: *What the plants are breathing out, all us animals are breathing in. And what we animals are breathing out, all the plants are breathing in.* The exquisite reciprocity remains astonishing to me even today—a magic pulse of interspecies generosity quietly unfurling itself in the depths of the present moment, hidden at the heart of all our experience.

Of course, many meditative practices central to the great spiritual traditions work to gently bring our skittish attention back to the quiet to-and-fro of our breathing. The very word *spirit* is cognate with *respiration*—both derived from the Latin *spiritus*, which originally meant a "breath" or a "gust of wind." Yet spiritual practice, in the West, is commonly framed as a path to personal fulfillment—as a way to find oneself or to transcend one's suffering, or simply as a way to open and deepen one's inner life. In the course of my own work as an ecologist and activist, I've often found myself teaching in tandem with Buddhist masters who skillfully draw practitioners to an awareness of the breath sliding in and out of their nostrils. Yet somehow these teachers rarely connect that breath to the birds swooping past, to the plants drinking sunlight all around us, to the whoosh of the wind along the walls of the zendo. Even when teaching outdoors, the most ostensibly awake spiritual teachers commonly fail to notice—much less make explicit for their students—the seamless continuity between our breath and the enveloping atmosphere, roiling with birdsong and clouds of pollen from the trees.

How remarkable, then, that this is where Joanna Macy begins. Her understanding of spiritual wisdom carries us not inside ourselves but out into the depths of the earthly sensuous. In one of the life-changing epiphanies that she describes in this book, Joanna recounts the uncanny experience of turning "inside out," a moment when her interior life became commingled with all she saw around her. For Joanna, the real "inner world" is the world we are *in,* the world *in which* we are bodily immersed along with all these other bodies—black bears, earthworms, sea turtles tangled in plastic, owl-haunted forests, and clearcut slopes strewn with debris.

And so it is here, in the collective depths of this world, where we grapple and struggle and gather to dance, where we grieve harrowing losses and then stand, shoulder to shoulder, to protect children and battered refugees and to safeguard the wild-flourishing beauty that remains. It is here, in the improvisational thick of the Real, that we must practice our spiritual work.

———

At the lustrous heart of Joanna's lifework and practice sits the Buddha's jewel-like insight into the truth of *pratityasamutpada*, a term that Joanna represents as "mutual causality" in her splendid doctoral dissertation on the dharma of natural systems. You will encounter many references to this principle in the pages that follow under a wide array of names—*dependent co-arising, emergent co-arising, reciprocal causality, dependent co-origination*, or even the deceptively simple notion that *everything leans* (that is, each apparently autonomous thing actually leans upon everything else).

Several decades ago, Joanna's spiritual brother, the Vietnamese Buddhist monk Thich Nhat Hanh, offered an eloquent translation of *pratityasamutpada* by coining the word *interbeing*. It is a luminous and indispensable term. Sometimes, when I'm unable to sleep—hounded by worries for my children, or for the whirling Earth at this teetering moment in its unfolding—I throw off the covers and slip naked out the back door to gaze up into the fathomless deep. Often the moon floats there, a slender crescent like a billowing sail, or a full round and radiant disk gliding in and out of the clouds. The moon's visage compels my gaze and reciprocates it; I cannot help but sense the moon gazing back at me, locating me just here, where I stand, gazing up. In Thich Nhat Hanh's sense, the moon and I *inter-are*.

As taught by many other Buddhist scholars and masters, however, the insight of emergent co-arising can seem a highly abstract concept, exceedingly difficult to grasp or perceive directly. Joanna's way, by contrast, is always to make such insights palpable, grounding them in our directly felt, bodily experience. What could be more visceral, more sensorially immediate, than breathing? Here is her pellucid translation (with Anita Barrows) of a stanza from one of Rainer Maria Rilke's *Sonnets to Orpheus*:

Breath, you invisible poem!
Pure, continuous exchange
with all that is, flow and counterflow
where rhythmically I come to be.[1]

The altered awareness of breathing as uttermost reciprocity—as a "pure, continuous exchange" between us furred or smooth-skinned animals and the numberless plants that surround us, each making possible the other—has become for me the most tangible, sensuous example of emergent co-arising. Interbeing as *interbreathing.*

Today, in late spring, I walk in the foothills near my home, allowing my footfalls to slow to the pace of my breath. All around me, mountains are conjuring clouds out of the fathomless blue. My ears drink in cricket rhythms and frog trills, while my nostrils inhale the scents of juniper and sagebrush. The fluted song of a hermit thrush quavers in the air. Drawn by a sweetness it can't resist, my nose nestles into the furrowed bark of one ponderosa pine after another, guzzling the scents of vanilla and butterscotch from the rising sap.

This holy Earth is far too wondrous to be fathomed or figured out by us. The erotic richness of the more-than-human world invites us always deeper into vital intimacy and participation with the rest of the Real—drawing forth our tears at the compounding wounds while engendering an astonished exaltation at finding ourselves immersed and participant in so much mystery, willing to risk everything for its continued flourishing.

A few years after hearing her voice on the radio I met Joanna face to face, and since then I've had the gift to learn from her, to break bread with her, and to teach alongside her under the tall red-woods of California and on islands dense with red cedars and Sitka spruces in the Salish Sea. The last time we saw each other, there were hardly any trees around. In the winter of 2017, we met in the high desert of northern New Mexico and went walking for an afternoon in the multihued canyons there, surrounded by stratified layers of ocher and beige, yellow-gold, and rust-red rock. As our voices glided in and out of the desert silence, we relaxed into the consummate pleasure of simply being oneself with a trusted other, sharing an almost drunken joy at the extravagant and shadowed beauty of the land. We soon found ourselves reciting poetry to each other, disparate verses echoing off the cliffs: Rilke, of course, and Tomas Tranströmer, and Gerard Manley Hopkins. But there was an inward trembling as well. For we knew that on the following day, a woefully callous and self-centered member of our species was to be inaugurated as the president of our country. And so, clasping hands and gazing into one another's eyes, we offered spoken spells of protection for the well-being of our bleeding world.

Which brings me to say a few words regarding why I think that Joanna's work will become ever more crucial in decades to come. I am writing in the late spring of 2019, almost two and a half years after our wander in those canyons. The damage wrought—not just within our nation but throughout the world—by the demagogue who was installed the next day is already immense. Still, many citizens are confident that within a couple years our battered country will return to normal. I am less sanguine. The multiple atrocities of the twentieth century provide abundant evidence of the human propensity—when economies falter for too long, when crops fail and famine spreads—for polarization and scapegoating, for ethnic cleansing and genocide. No matter how "civilized" the culture, whenever times get hard the most facile human response seems to be to locate some group to blame for all the troubles, and then try to eradicate that group or, failing that, to inflict upon them as much pain as possible.

It is now evident that things will be getting hard for a very long while. Due to our long forgetting of our human embedment within a much more-than-human biosphere, it now seems likely that never-before-seen hurricanes, smoke from runaway fires turning the midday sun blood red, surging floodwaters, and soil-cracking heat waves will be making things more and more difficult well beyond the foreseeable future, as our wombish world shivers into a bone-wrenching fever. In such a situation—wherein any of us may become refugees at any moment—should we not expect that the unconscious allurement toward demagoguery will swell and intensify? In such stressed-out times, those who wish to concentrate power have only to declare, with great certainty, whom the enemy is—have only to amp up fear and then escalate hatred—in order to swiftly amass countless followers. Such is the collective psychology at this moment in the world's unraveling, when the ecological strains on our civilization are poised to intensify by the year, by the month, and soon enough by the day. The polarizing rhetoric, the incitement to fits of rage, the bombast rattling so much of our current politics, may not at all be an aberration but an early glimpse of what is rolling toward us—not inevitably, no, yet a symptom, or sign, of what may soon show itself more fully as our most ready mass response to rapidly rising panic.

How can we short-circuit this reflexive recourse to scapegoating whenever adversity rolls like a great wave across numberless lives and fear rises like a tide within the populace? Surely this is one of the greatest riddles of our broken era, a koan that demands

our deepest and most attentive contemplation. If there exists anywhere a satisfactory reply to this conundrum, it resides in such
Earth-centered community practices as Joanna Macy's work has
engendered. It resides in the dawning recognition of our thorough
entanglement in this breathing biosphere, in the slow discovery
that our lives are hopelessly dependent upon one another—but also
upon the flourishing of earthworms, and humpback whales, and
the clouds that gather like a clamorous crowd above the rainforest. If we and the melting glaciers *inter-are* with one another, if the
life-giving atmosphere of this planet is born of the *interbreathing* of
us animals with the grasses and the forests, then it behooves us to
recognize that our two-legged forms are just our smaller bodies,
and that the animate Earth is our larger Flesh—a vast, spherical
metabolism in which our individual physiologies are all entwined.
Earth is the wider and much wilder Life in which our separate
lives all participate.

How fleeting is anyone's experience relative to the broad life
span of the planet! And yet we each partake of that whole. Indeed,
there are those who give themselves so deeply to this world, who
open their souls so fully to each chance encounter—who so thoroughly resolve not to shrink from any of the uncanny textures or
flavors or *feels* that this life offers—that from these many encounters their hearts distill a mysterious elixir, an invisible tonic that
streams out through their eyes to refresh all that they look upon,
waking a secret and long-slumbering sentience in things, quick-
ening a pulse deep within the ground wherever they wander.

Such a magical creature is Joanna Macy. When reading
through the various chapters that follow, you may find yourself
wondering how it is possible that a single human life can have
touched and transformed so many others, and in so many different
places. Yet this is hardly a mystery. By offering herself so uncondi-

tionally to each locale and situation wherein she finds herself, Joanna's life radiates out to touch and enliven every cell within our larger, spherical Body. By giving herself with such abandon to the very presence of the present moment, Joanna's tears and her joy— like those of any genuine bodhisattva—reverberate backward and forward through time to nourish all moments within the broad life of the breathing Earth.

NOTES

1. Anita Barrows and Joanna Macy, trans., *In Praise of Mortality: Selections from Rainer Maria Rilke's "Duino Elegies" and "Sonnets to Orpheus"* (Brattleboro, VT: Echo Point Books, 2016), 107.

Editor's Preface

STEPHANIE KAZA

Every book has a story, and this book started with a simple question: "Is anyone working on a collective tribute to honor Joanna Macy as she approaches her ninetieth birthday?" It seemed like an obvious thing to do for such a well-known and much beloved teacher. I asked because I wanted to contribute, to show my appreciation and gratitude for her tremendous gifts and influence on my life. As it turned out, I was far from alone in that desire.

Finding none in process, Kaye Jones and I approached Joanna with the idea of such a book. At first she hesitated. Already she had given the creative efforts of her life to any and all who wanted to use them for good works. What could one more book add to that generosity? Still, the stories began to emerge as we spoke out there by the grand sycamore tree on Kaye's homestead farm in Trout Lake, Washington. Before long, a list of names had materialized on the easel pad. Might there be something here? It was August 2018, when wildfires had blackened the western skies and breathing the smoky air was not so easy for any of us, especially Joanna.

I hesitated, too, humbled by the daunting scope of the project. I had known Joanna since my first systems theory class with her at Starr King School for the Ministry in 1988. I had taken her big ideas and creative exercises to the University of Vermont, where I taught impassioned students in environmental studies for twenty-four years. I had developed my own ideas in Buddhist environmental thought in books, articles, talks, and courses. Joanna's guiding foundations were with me every step of the way as

I carved an activist path through academia. Now I had a chance to make an offering to my teacher and hold up a mirror for her to see the great shining legacy of her life.

To test this bare seed of an idea, the three of us met again in Berkeley a month later, trusting the process of emergence to point the way. I offered to take the first steps of gaining support and commitment from Shambhala Publications. We laid out a rather challenging timeline, aiming to have the book in hand within the year following Joanna's ninetieth birthday. That meant that invites needed to go out immediately, giving writers barely three months to collect their thoughts. I agreed to accept the role of editor and shepherd the project from start to finish. Meanwhile, the stories continued to flow from Joanna during our monthly work sessions, and eventually, with Kaye's steady patience, these became refined into the eleven pieces Joanna contributed to the book.

While this volume began as a tribute, it quickly evolved into an opportunity to showcase the big ideas of Joanna's teaching. Many people know Joanna Macy for the dazzling array of transformative exercises she developed, tested thoroughly, and published for facilitators. They signify her work in the world as a teacher, a role she regards as one of the highest spiritual callings. But it is the big ideas that are central to her sense of self, for Joanna is a scholar at heart; she is a highly gifted and rigorous deep thinker. The five key sections of the book illuminate these big ideas—a planetary sense of self, the power of grief work, dependent causality, deep time, and taking up the work together. These are the gifts of a lifetime of reflection, insight, and thoughtful deliberation.

As we reviewed chapters and considered titles, we saw the book as a new infusion of energy for the ever more necessary work of our times. Joanna was adamant that the book serve those in the field now and in the future. New concepts emerged as chapters, and sections began to inform each other. In the year the book took shape, climate crises multiplied, and young people took to the streets to demand a livable future. As we began our sessions in silent meditation, the three of us sat with all of this, holding the griefs, the joys, and the not-so-distant outline of the future. This energy fills the book; every page calls us to be present to our beloved planet in distress.

Many, many people might have offered contributions to this book, and from every continent. We regret that we could not include all the writing that was prepared for this volume due to limits necessitated by publication. We are grateful for the efforts made by *all* writers to articulate their love and experience of Joanna Macy's work in their own projects and countries. It was no small challenge to manage communication with all the teachers, thinkers, writers, artists, and activists represented in this book as they headed off to lead retreats, speak at conferences, or take up the political urgencies of the world. As editor, I took every chance to express my gratitude for the important and dedicated work these contributors were engaged in. That they found time from their busy lives to write for this book is the measure of their love and appreciation for Joanna and her work, and their sense of good fortune in having met up with this prophetic and highly skilled teacher.

Finding the right order for these chapters, and making the right edits to align the content, required more than a little puzzle solving. In the end, the five themes dictated what would most effectively convey the broad legacy of Joanna Macy's work. Each section features reflections on the big ideas, examples of how Joanna's work has been applied in different contexts, and international histories and perspectives. Here you will find a wide range of voices from practitioners, scholars, Buddhist teachers, and long-time friends. Some writers worked from a first language other than English. Almost all drew on personal experience and insight. These are intimate pieces, born of a love for clear thinking and clear action.

Across the sections there are references to different iterations of Joanna's work. In the early days, soon after her own awakening to the state of the world, she called it *despair work*, and workshops were often titled, "Despair and Empowerment." As facilitators trained and took up the work, they self-organized into a support collective called Interhelp, which spread the ideas and exercises to activist circles around the world. From the start, the work was grounded in Buddhist philosophy and general systems theory. When I met Joanna in the early 1990s, she had been moved by the term *deep ecology*, and found that people appreciated the underlying philosophy that confirmed our belonging to something much larger than our small selves. Inspired by John Seed in Australia, she began using this name for her work when she returned to the US. We designed and taught a number of intensive Deep Ecology activist trainings in the US; the phrase caught fire as well in Germany and Russia, where it is still used today. In 1998, when Joanna and Molly Young Brown undertook a substantial revision of the facilitator manual, Joanna renamed the work and its spiral process to indicate its broad applicability. Thus was born the Work That Reconnects, a school of thought and practice that has found broad global resonance for the past two decades. In the last ten years, many also know the Work by the name of Active Hope, based on her book with Chris Johnstone by that title. Each new iteration of the work has reflected groundbreaking shifts in awareness and practice, in response to rising global challenges.

Though this book somewhat follows the form of a *Festschrift*, or collaborative celebration of a lifework, one unusual feature is the inclusion of Joanna Macy's own strong voice. Her stories frame each section, and her afterword gives her, literally, the last word in the book. Her thinking and pithy quotes enhance one chapter after another. The full measure of her scholarly contributions is tucked away in the back of the book, a complete bibliography of her books, articles, and interviews across forty-plus years of writing and speaking. There is a quiet delight in this compendium, a writer's record of engagement made public for the first time. This is the Joanna Macy I came to appreciate even more deeply through the process of completing this book. Her sharp mind, her exacting clarity, and her great love of words and story are rare treasures.

There are many people to thank for making this book possible. Let me begin with gratitude for the authors of these chapters and those that could not be included due to limited space; your words and dedication are much appreciated. For his early generosity and belief in the project, we thank Christopher Hormel, whose funding helped cover administrative and travel expenses. Joanna's assistant, Anne Symens-Bucher, provided invaluable aid facilitating communication and document review as needed. Our partners and families were remarkably kind in supporting me and Kaye to travel to Berkeley every month and make this project a top priority for the time that it took; our endless thanks to them. We were most fortunate in working with an outstanding team at Shambhala, with Matt Zepelin as lead editor and a well-coordinated team of copy editors, designers, marketers, and publicists. The book could not have been born without them, nor been as beautiful and appreciated.

My greatest thanks go to Kaye Jones and Joanna Macy herself. The teamwork on this project has been a marvelous wonder, filled with love and joy right in the midst of grave concern for the state of the planet, what Joanna calls *arbeitsfreudigkeit*, or "work joyfulness." We spent long hours around Joanna's dining table and ate many good salads to keep us going under the tight timeline. Kaye was a never-ending source of positive support, humor, and kindness, ever ready for the next task. Joanna was astonishing in her attention to detail, her meticulous fact-checking, her steady energy, and her commitment to the project.

As we worked, we were ever mindful of the photos on the wall of Joanna's teachers, family, and ancestors. They, too, carry our gratitude, for all that was transmitted to Joanna and is reflected back in this volume. We especially honor Fran Macy as Joanna's closest collaborator and beloved husband across the first three decades of this work. He believed deeply in the work and kept Joanna going across many challenges. Likewise, we thank Joanna's children—Peggy, Jack, and Chris—for all their support for the project and for helping sustain Joanna's life. While our working team bridged three generations, many more beings of the past and future are present in this book. Hummingbirds, dahlias, jasmine, and cherry tree offered their graceful spirits as part of the dance with us across the seasons.

It has been an honor and privilege to work with Joanna on this personal life review and to witness the remarkable scope of her legacy. Her work has been shaped by a formidable sense of commitment and motivation. She has modeled for so many the power of listening to the cries of the universe. I am one of these who have been invited to trust such calls of the heart. My deepest thanks to you, Joanna, dear dharma friend and teacher, for this ocean of blessing beyond measure.

Introducing Joanna's Stories

KAYE JONES

In this book you will find a series of reflections written by Joanna, stories of awakenings she experienced throughout the course of her life. They begin in 1945 when she was sixteen, then at age thirty-six in 1965, followed by a great concentration of ahas during a fertile period between 1974 and 1990. Two of Joanna's stories highlight each section of this book, thus weaving Joanna's voice and insights into the rich reflections offered by those whom she has touched.

What is an awakening? Here, it is a moment of penetrating insight coming up from the depths, when one perceives reality—seeing more clearly who and what we really are. When we meet the sixteen-year-old Joanna in "Trust in Life," we see that everything she needs and everything she will become is already there inside of her. Could the same be true for each of us?

As we worked on this book, Joanna explained, "An awakening is a full-body insight, an intuitive realization that you can't achieve by argument, persuasion, or thinking it through—you are delivered into it, held within its hands, like birth and death." In this book we experience these epiphanies—in quiet, in chaos, with mentors and spiritual teachers, in nature, in groups, in dark times, in times of not knowing, and in times of surrender. These stories speak to faith, to grace, to trust.

Joanna's stories bring to mind a metaphor from early Buddhist scriptures that she loves. One can see her slender hands dancing with each other in a mudra of mutual causality, as she explains the interplay of *panna* and *sila*. Panna is wisdom or insight, and sila is virtuous action. Our action in the world gives rise to wisdom, and wisdom gives rise to action, like two hands washing each other. For Joanna it was never just one or the other—a life on the cushion or a life in the world. As she says with feeling, "How could you wash with just one hand?"

In the last ten months, I've had the joy of serving as Joanna's scribe for these stories. Since fall of 2018, we have been in a seemingly continuous conversation via phone calls, emails, texts, and monthly visits. Collaborating with Joanna has been like being in the mind of Gaia herself. Her awakening stories were culled from recordings, previous writings, and memories; from our conversations, our silences, and from the ether. Some of Joanna's stories came slowly and iteratively, while others tumbled out quickly in a graceful flow. We brought our drafts to Stephanie, who with her editor's eye and fine Zen mind helped us lift up what was essential.

As we put our friendship in service of the work, no part of life was left out. The aches and pains of a ninety-year-old body, sleepless nights, dishes to wash, the chaos of my young family and old farm were all woven into the draft documents and revelations. Across our fifty-three-year age difference, I share with Joanna the dharma and systems thinking; we are each wife and mother of three children. Some of our most profound transmissions came when we were doing the dishes together or speaking by phone at sunset for an evening work session. With Joanna, there is no separation between the joys and struggles of daily life, the work, and the spiritual journey. This is what she teaches us—to take life as our field of practice.

After each monthly work session in Berkeley, I would dash out the door to catch an evening plane home. My young children 650 miles to the north were getting into pajamas, and the farm animals were bedding down for the night. There, on Cherry Street, Joanna would stand on her steps, hand on the railing, seeing me to my taxi. How often I would turn back and hold her face in my hands for a moment!

In her struggles, her fears, her joy, and her humanness, Joanna's awakenings are a model for our own. And yet one can't help but wonder if perhaps Joanna Rogers Macy has had a few more awakenings than the rest of us. Over the years I've observed that Joanna is uniquely suited for an adventurous life of awakenings and transmissions. She trusts. She is Taurus, rooted in the earth, the form maker. Moon in Aquarius, the creative mind, always investigating and innovating. Neptune on the ascendant, spiritual by nature, anything is possible. Joanna was made to open to something vaster than her, to offer herself up, to give Earth a voice.

In Joanna's bedroom, between her bed and the altar in the corner, hangs a picture painted by her beloved monk Choegyal Rinpoche. It depicts a bodhisattva joyously leaping off a cliff, arms spread wide. This is how I think of Joanna, with her own unique quality of fearlessness. She leaps.

As we've examined the span of Joanna's work for this book—with scholarly analyses, stories, and reflections pouring in from contributors—her life has come together before us like a tapestry. It is a breathtaking confluence of timing, geography, political and evolutionary unfolding, and spiritual synergy. She has often seemed to be in just the right place at the right time, opening to and working on behalf of her world. This life of ninety years reveals to us that our lives co-evolve with the time in which we live: Joanna shaped this last century, even as it was shaping her. Like the two hands of panna and sila washing each other, Joanna's life exemplifies reciprocity in so many ways.

Let these stories inspire our own awakenings. May all of us have the courage to open ourselves to the time that we live in, to let it shape us as we, in turn, shape it. May we perceive what is being asked of us. May we awaken here, on this sharp edge of uncertainty.

Joanna, Fran, Christopher, Jack, and Peggy Macy in a
Christmas photo, 1963, just before they left for India and their
travels as a family during Fran's years in the Peace Corps.

PART ONE

OUR PLANET, OUR SELF

At the root of Joanna Macy's work and legacy is an unshakable love for Earth, a profound sense of belonging to our home planet. This living planet is our larger self. By widening our sense of relationship with all of life, we open to what Joanna refers to as *the ecological self.* This way of thinking and perceiving can be called "Gaian consciousness," a gateway to liberation from the limited views of the small self. It is this consciousness that provides a tonifying correction to the blinding impacts of anthropocentrism that have so crippled human action in response to the climate crisis. In her first story of awakening, Joanna reveals her sense of "trust in life," a sense that has matured over the decades into a deep knowing of the richness, mystery, and complexity of this living Earth, our home.

From the very beginning, Joanna has made a link between inner and outer work, drawing on Buddhist practices to transform emotional energy and calm the mind in the midst of chaos. This work is not to be done alone but rather in groups with other deeply concerned Earth citizens. This is a critical point: This work takes all of us waking up together. It cannot be done alone, one person at a time. In this section we hear testimony to the many ways in which Joanna's teachings cultivate great joy through giving attention to gratitude and beauty, even while acknowledging the pain of immense loss and destruction on the planet.

Much of Joanna's work was developed and tested in the United Kingdom amid tense preparations for war, and then in Australia, where peace and environmental activists were resisting nuclear weapons and rainforest destruction. Across the early and extensive international workshop tours, Joanna in concert with others came up with many of the powerful teaching exercises that have now spread around the world. Her earliest publications on despair work were circulated rapidly, influencing thousands of people in movement politics and activism for decades to follow. Today, such teachings are applied in government policy forums, activist trainings, and sustainability efforts at all levels. Climate change activists in the growing Extinction Rebellion movement are the latest in this generational legacy of those whose worldviews have been shaped by exposure to Joanna's key ideas.

The writers in this section identify the foundations of Joanna's thinking as they are drawn from Buddhist philosophy and Western systems thinking. Here we see how dependent co-arising and relational practice provide a platform for sustained social and environmental work. What appears to be a deceptively simple shift in perspective from small self to ecological self can be a profound experience in awakening. These stories and reflections reveal key aspects of this remarkable person as well as the power of her work around the world. Collectively they offer an invitation to intimacy and possibility, when so much seems distant and overwhelming. Above all, they demonstrate the power of mutual belonging within this Earth planet-home.

—Stephanie Kaza

TRUST IN LIFE

Joanna Macy

IN 1945, THE YEAR I TURNED SIXTEEN, I began the summer at a weeklong religious conference for Presbyterian youth. Church was a steady, unquestioned part of my growing up, between summers near my grandfather's and great-grandfather's churches in western New York and school-year weekly attendance at the Fifth Avenue Presbyterian Church. By sixteen I was pretty thoroughly imbued with liberal Protestant Christianity. That June conference was a welcome break from our city apartment, where waves of tension and anxiety characterized our home life. Although my brothers seemed less bothered, I lived in fear of my father's verbal abuse and in anguish over his manipulation and humiliation of my mother.

One of our youth conference teachers was a US Air Force chaplain just back from the war in Europe. Mustached and solidly built, he wore no uniform and would have looked like a businessman if he hadn't been so raw and serious. Each morning in our sunny classroom full of teenagers, he paced back and forth, turning frequently to look into our faces, as if the words he wanted were somewhere in our eyes. It seemed the war had stripped him of the comfortable ideas that make life easier for people.

He didn't bring us stories about patriotism or the faith of the pilots he served; instead he brought us a way of looking at things that were hard to look at. They weren't so much the horrors of war as the kind of world that makes war possible—the way we treat one another, the injustices and betrayals in our own society. He spoke of poverty and prejudice, war profiteering, and squalor in migrant worker camps and Indian reservations. He spoke about a kind of God who can be there for us in spite of the mess we make of our world, a God who shows us the hell we make for ourselves and one another and meets us there.

Carefully and thoroughly, like the good lycée student I was, I took notes in my notebook. But inside I felt a shuddering deeper than the fears and resentments of life at home. Something in me was riveted. I thought, "If we're all connected enough to belong to one another," as I sensed in the hymns we sang, "then we're connected enough to hurt one another—a lot."

Now the chaplain was speaking the words I first heard from my grandmother Daidee: "And Jesus said, *In as much as ye have done unto the least of these my brethren, ye have done unto me.*" The chaplain confronted us with what Jesus had gone on to say, challenging us to look not so much at our occasional acts of compassion as at our more habitual indifference: "*I was hungry and you gave me no food; I was thirsty and you gave me no drink; I was a stranger and you took me not in; naked and you clothed me not; sick and in prison and you visited me not.* And those who heard him said, 'Lord, when did we ever see you hungry or thirsty, a stranger or sick or imprisoned, and did not minister to you?' Then Jesus said, *Inasmuch as you did it not unto the least of these, you did it not unto me.*" By that logic I could see that we were *all* there with Jesus at the end of his life, doing our part to put him on the cross. We were Pontius Pilate washing our hands to avoid involvement; we were the crowd watching; we were the Roman soldiers hammering in the nails.

Near the end of our week, I found myself slipping away from the others, overwhelmed by feeling. I fled for solitude to the far side of campus. My throat and chest were constricted; I could hardly breathe. The guilt I felt was not for hating Papa—which seemed too natural and inevitable to get upset about—but for what I had let that hatred do to me. I had allowed it to close me in and cut off my heart. The resentful self-enclosure was such a denial of life that ultimately it made me an accomplice to the world's suffering. We were *all* involved; there was no way to stand on the sidelines. And if this were so, as the almost intolerable pressure in my chest seemed to confirm, then how could we ever get free from our complicity? No judgment of God could be greater than my own self-judgment, right then and there. I could not imagine how to live with it.

I asked for a moment alone with the chaplain, and the next morning, the last of the week, he met me in the chapel during "quiet time." I wanted to know how to go on living with the knowledge that if Jesus was being crucified every day, I was letting it happen. My words stumbled over one another. The chaplain leaned forward, listening intently. He paused to draw a deep breath. "Look!" he said, pointing above the altar. "Look up, the cross is empty. He is not still nailed on it; he is down here at your side." He quoted the verse where Jesus says, *Lo, I am with you always.* "It is the risen Christ who says that, Joanna, and he is risen into the openness of your own heart." I felt his words cut through the impasse, carving open a space I could walk through.

Then the chaplain spoke the words of the Communion service: "This is my body broken for you, Joanna. This is my blood, shed for you." The phrases from the Last Supper I'd heard so often were suddenly filled with new meaning. I felt an acceptance so deep that my mind could hardly grasp it. If I were willing to let Jesus's crucifixion become so real to me, so powerful and compelling, then I could receive as well the hugeness of his trust in life.

The next morning, waking up at home, I could hardly wait to tell Mama about what had unfolded in the chapel. We sat in a shaft of sun amid half-packed suitcases, bound for our summer at my grandfather's farm. "Oh, Mama, what happened with Jesus and the disciples is happening right now!" Her eyes never moved from my face as I told her what had happened for me with the chaplain. She almost hated to tell me that Papa had orders for me; I was to help in his Wall Street office instead of spending summer at the farm.

For a moment I felt the old fear grip my stomach, but that evening I said, "Papa, I'm going up to the farm. We can talk about my working in your office in the fall." As those words came out of me, I began to feel the courage I had discovered at camp, and I knew there was ultimately nothing to fear.

NO SEPARATE SELF

Joanna Macy

IN MAY 1965, DURING THE SECOND YEAR of living in India with my young family, I knew it was time to ask for meditation instruction, and Freda Bedi, or Mummy, as the Tibetan lamas all called her, was the one to ask. Mummy, a British-born Tibetan nun, had adopted our family, along with all the Tibetan *tulkus* in exile. By then I had been working with the Tibetan refugees for over a year and had become increasingly fascinated with the Buddha Dharma that illumined their lives. Still, I was reluctant to ask for instruction from the lamas, overburdened and exhausted as they were in those early years in exile caring for their flock. Mummy instantly agreed to my request and invited me to come to Dalhousie, a Himalayan hill station where she had established the Young Lamas Home School to prepare young tulkus to teach in the West.

The only way up to the railhead nearest Dalhousie was by night train. I felt, after almost two years in the subcontinent, that I was a seasoned Indian *wallah*, and so, without three children to manage, I booked a berth on a third-class coach. The departure from home went smoothly. Menus had been written, carpools and after-school activities arranged, and promises secured from my husband, Fran, to come straight home after work at the Peace Corps office. Now it was just a question of getting me, my backpack, bedroll, and water jug onto the Pathankot Express before its 10:00 p.m. departure from the Old Delhi station.

The train station was a madhouse; half of north India's population must have poured onto that one platform for my train. When the coach doors to the nearest third-class coach finally opened, the crowds at each door were ten or twenty bodies deep, each person hell-bent on getting aboard. The crush pressed me so tightly I could barely breathe. I feared I would suffocate, yet the surging push left no option for escape. My arm with the water jug, caught between bodies as they shoved ahead, seemed to separate from me; I was sure I'd be dismembered. As I was rammed through the door, I started to panic. Over the shouts and din I heard someone screaming. It was me. In the narrow aisle between the three-tiered wooden berths, I started to cry. Then, from the maelstrom of bodies below, hands pushed me up onto a topmost shelf, like jetsam tossed from the sea. Other hands threw up my bag and bedroll. Weak with relief and drenched with sweat, I cowered there under the ceiling.

Directly beneath me, a large, garrulous family, unpacking an endless series of containers, generously thrust up wads of rice, curry, and melting banana. Accepting a chapati, I drew up my feet and disappeared behind a book. I wanted to effect as total a withdrawal as possible while the lights still permitted me to read. I wanted to banish from my mind the whole teeming carriage with its jabber and clamor and smells. A pencil marked my place in a chapter on Buddhism in a collection by Huston Smith that I found in the Peace Corps book locker for volunteers. The subject was the second noble truth, the cause of suffering, held to be *tanha*, or craving. Grateful that I could concentrate at all, I reread a paragraph that tugged at my attention.

"*Tanha* is a specific form of desire, the desire to pull apart from the rest of life and seek fulfillment through those bottled-up segments of being we call ourselves," I read. "It is the will to private fulfillment, the ego oozing like a secret sore . . ." To let the words sink in, I would lift my eyes every few lines and let my gaze wander down the packed coach. "We strap our faith and love and destiny to the puny burros of our separate selves which are certain to stumble and give out. . . . Prizing our egos, coddling them, we lock ourselves inside."

My breathing deepened, each breath filling more of my body, as if to steady me for a physical challenge. My mind stilled in wonder, for the thing that then occurred seemed outside its control. Suddenly I was no longer enclosed inside my own body. I wasn't outside it either. My body seemed to be silently exploding, expanding to the point where everything else was inside it too. Everything out there—each gesticulating, chewing, sleeping form; each crying baby and coughing heap of rags; and the flickering, swaying carriage itself—was as intimately my body as I was. I had turned inside out, like a kernel of popcorn shaken over the fire. My interior was now on the outside, inextricably mixed up with the rest of the world, and what I had tried to exclude was now at its core.

The book fell aside. Some primordial tension dissolved, letting self-righteousness and self-blame cancel each other out. The self was neither to be vaunted or overcome, neither to be punished or improved. It only needed to be seen through, like a bubble that would eventually pop. The world from which I could not protect myself became a world that I was free to enter, free to be. My mind, when it could think, repeated one thing over and over: *Released into action, now we can be released into action.*

As the lights switched off, I stretched out on the wooden shelf while the swaying coach rattled northward on to Pathankot. I let the experience hold me till dawn, then slowly fade as I scrambled off the train and onto the bus to Dalhousie. There, I made my way up the mountain to the Young Lamas Home School and Mummy,

tasting that experience every now and then. I didn't fret at its going, because I didn't expect it to last. I was just glad for this taste
of freedom—and the awe that it left in its wake.

Later that day, Mummy began to teach me a basic meditation.
She wanted me to use *satipatthana* (as we called it then) as my foundation for the teachings of Tibetan Tantra, just as she had. Then
she escorted me up to the nuns' hermitage, perched up under the
sky above Dalhousie's weather, where I would practice alone. To try
to focus on the mind itself proved difficult. My mind was slippery
as an eel. Continually it escaped my grasp, slithering into memories and conjectures. I was shocked and appalled to discover how
little I stayed in the present moment—had I always lived my life in
absentia?

When Mummy came up after two days, I spoke of this, my
voice rusty from disuse: "I am so dispersed! I am amazed how
inattentive and lazy I am!" She cut me short: "Stop saying 'I' in
that way when talking about your experience." She explained that
using the first-person pronoun to categorize yourself works like
cement, anchoring passing feelings into a kind of permanence. It
is more accurate, Mummy pointed out, to say "judgment is happening" or "sloth is occurring" or "fears are arising." Her admo-
nitions helped me recognize the burden of a solidified self and of
its everlasting carping and goading. Soon that burden, like the
clouds outside the window of my hermitage, began to lift.

GAIA CONSCIOUSNESS IN THE GREAT TURNING

Stephan Harding

WE MUST BEGIN BY TRYING to give some sort of idea about what a Gaian consciousness might be. The concept of Gaia itself has many levels, from the mythological to the ultramodern and scientific. Right from the start, Gaian consciousness is a style of being and understanding deeply rooted in the mysteries of the psyche as well as in the vibrant and exuberant ecological reality of our living Earth. This is Gaia. We feel her ancient myths alive in us, and also her immense age, since we are in her heart and psyche.[1]

We feel the presences of her forests, oceans, deserts, mountains, and plains in our blood, in our hearts and minds. We care for her, we love her, and we know all the more that we belong to her because that is what our very best science tells us. The Gaia theory of James Lovelock and Lynn Margulis shows us that Gaia is a vast being who has regulated key aspects of her surface conditions such as temperature and acidity over huge spans of geological time, reflecting the manifold, richly interlayered interactions between her living beings, rocks, waters, and atmosphere.

Within a Gaian consciousness, we are in Earth and we are of Earth. Her body is our wider body, our psyche is her psyche. Modern yet ancient, this noble view of our living planet brings wisdom, inspiring us to act ethically and beautifully in pro-Gaian ways without need for any coercion or external force. Those of us developing educational styles that foster Gaian consciousness, as I have been doing at Schumacher College for the last twenty-seven years, feel that this style of awareness must spread quickly from mind to mind and from soul to soul before our suicidal, growth-obsessed industrial society inflicts more irreversible damage to our planet. There is perhaps not much time left.

One of the key pioneers in the effort to develop and spread Gaian consciousness is Joanna Macy, the accomplished Buddhist scholar, systems thinker, educator, and social activist whom I had the immense joy of meeting with her husband, Fran, in the late 1990s. Joanna truly is a Western bodhisattva—it takes just a brief time with her to know that.

Over many years of deep practice, Joanna has developed her own Gaian consciousness to such a great extent that she is a beacon of inspiration to all those who wish to work peacefully to remedy the appalling harm we are inflicting on this marvelous living planet of ours. She has helped many thousands of people around the world discover and cultivate Gaian consciousness through her immensely effective Work That Reconnects. The Work is based on her synthesis of two key principles of great importance to her: the enlightened understanding of the Buddha; and general systems theory put forward by Gregory Bateson, Ervin Laszlo, and others, enriched later on with strands from deep ecology and Gaia theory. Through a lifetime dedicated to developing the Work That Reconnects, Joanna and her collaborators have given us many ideas, meditations, and group practices that also serve to greatly accelerate the development of Gaian consciousness.

BUDDHIST FOUNDATIONS

In her book *World as Lover, World as Self,* Joanna tells how, one day, after seven years of intense spiritual seeking and practice, the meaning of the Buddha's central insight of *pratityasamutpada*, or "dependent co-arising," dawned on him. When the Buddha recognized it as the foundational character of reality, he had the sense of "coming upon an ancient forgotten city, overgrown by jungle and awaiting re-discovery and restoration."[2] Joanna writes, "No philosophic tenet has had more impact on me than the Buddha's central teaching of *paticca samuppada*."[3]

The Buddha taught that everything arises in our psyche and in the world, thanks to a dependently co-arising, flowing network of events and processes that, like all things, are impermanent. They come to be and pass away. The Buddha showed how the self we cherish and think of as permanent is in reality quite perishable. He also taught that, although impermanent, the self is capable of powerful transformative experiences that open us to vast new horizons of meaning and understanding, transforming us into people truly capable of working for the benefit of all beings—or bodhisattvas.

Joanna skillfully draws on pratityasamutpada in the Work That Reconnects to help people discover the open horizon of consciousness in which the "absence of a permanent separate self erupts as a reality that changes the face of a life,"[4] giving us insight and freedom to interact with the flow of events around us in life-sustaining ways.

GENERAL SYSTEMS THEORY

During her graduate studies, Joanna was excited to discover the convergences between pratityasamutpada and general systems theory, a branch of science dealing with the interdependent, self-organizing nature of open systems. Historically, most religious scholars drew on linear logic to try to understand the Buddha's teaching, which made it difficult for them to fully grasp the complexity of dependent co-arising. By contrast, pratityasamut-pada suddenly became comprehensible to Joanna through the nonlinear lens of systems theory. Joanna saw how these two major schools of nonlinear thought could mutually elucidate each other and offer tools for understanding and interpreting each other's views. She recognized this potential despite the fact that they deal with different kinds of data and are two and a half millennia apart in their time of arising. Their common ground is that systems theory as well as Buddhist views see mind throughout all reality in various gradations and expressions.

Systems theory offers a coherent set of principles that apply to all irreducible wholes, be they molecule, cell, organism, personality, or social body. In the systems view, the world is a set of interconnected, interacting components linked together through feedback. The dynamic interplay permitted by feedback enables a system to sense and choose how to respond to influences from the rest of the network. Feedback happens when a change in one component in a system travels back to that same component through its network of relationships, causing that original component to either dampen or amplify the very change it has wrought upon itself. Systems self-organize and learn as they interact openly with the world via complex expressions of these two kinds of feedback.

In both the Buddha's teaching and in general systems thinking, a system's capacity for self-organizing and evolving resides in its relationships and actions. Freedom of choice arises here, in actions that are not predetermined, with a wide scope for future options. Therefore we are not bound to the past but can choose to cultivate Gaian consciousness now. This can set off chains of effects and events that will strengthen the development of Gaian consciousness, leading to new levels of systemic mind in which we belong mutually to the human community, to our local ecology, and to Gaia.

Combining Buddha's teaching of dependent co-arising with an understanding of general systems theory has helped Joanna develop her own Gaian consciousness. "Even my pain for the world is a function of this mutual belonging like a cell experiencing the larger body. . . . Causality or power resides in relationships rather than persons or institutions, it offers the courage to resist conformity and to act in new ways to change the situation."[5] Thus, lotus-like, does Gaian consciousness open and flower through participation in the Work That Reconnects, empowering us to help solve the immense global ecological crisis impacting this lustrous sacred planet of ours, our contemporary Gaia.

THE WORK THAT RECONNECTS

The Work That Reconnects offers practices to help participants experience periods approaching Gaian consciousness during which the feedback between our mental states and the body of Earth can be felt and become self-evident. In such moments we encounter huge potential for creating what Joanna calls a "life-sustaining society," for as we create the world through our particular style of consciousness (world as matter to exploit, or world as self?), so does the world create us. Joanna again: "Sometimes, as I behold the ways we attune and support each other in cooperative efforts on behalf of Earth, I imagine that we ourselves are like nerve cells in a larger brain—and that brain is starting to think."[6]

Details of many of these practices can be found in *Coming Back to Life*, Joanna's book co-authored with Molly Young Brown, in which the Work That Reconnects is conceptualized as a spiral that maps the journey to Gaian consciousness in four stages. The first is *gratitude*, in which we experience our love for life. Next is *honoring our pain*, in which we learn how to suffer the pain of the world with others and with the world itself. Then, in *seeing with new eyes*, we experience our connection with life in all its forms through all the ages. Finally, in the last stage we *go forth into action* in the world as open human beings, aware of our mutual belonging in the web of life, learning through feedback in our social and ecological domains.

One of the many practices in *Coming Back to Life* is Widening Circles, which supports the third part of the spiral but can also be used as a stand-alone exercise.[7] Widening Circles expands each participant's sense of self, moving them into their Gaian consciousness by allowing them to speak in four different voices about an ecological or social issue that deeply matters to them. Participants are carefully guided by an experienced facilitator as they go through the process in a relaxed way in groups of three or four, giving each person the opportunity to concentrate as much as possible on what comes up when the various voices speak out.

With their first voice, participants share their own personal views on the issue that concerns them. In the second voice, they are invited to speak about the issue from the perspective of an adversary, trying very hard not to stereotype them but rather to enter as much as possible into the opponent's lived experience of how the issue impacts them. Then they are invited to widen their sense of identification beyond the human realm by speaking in the voice of a nonhuman being directly affected by the issue of concern. This could be the voice of another species, a river, a mountain, or a large-scale Gaian process such as the cycling of carbon through the ancient body of Earth. Lastly, they are encouraged to speak from the point of view of a future human being seven generations from now helping us see our present situation from a deep time perspective.

DEEP TIME

An expanded sense of time is an absolutely vital component of Gaian consciousness. We need to feel our planet's vast sense of time. We need to feel and know something of the radical transformations and revolutions she has experienced during her long and quite astonishing evolutionary journey. In the early 1990s, my partner, Julia, and I were members of a group being guided by Joanna in a slow meditative walk along a hundred-meter cord laid out on an English summer lawn. It represented the almost 4.6-billion-year journey that is our planet's story. At various points we stopped and contemplated key evolutionary events in the story as narrated by Joanna. I remember feeling a wonderfully liberating expansion of consciousness. Despite all my scientific training in evolutionary biology, this may have been the first time I properly experienced and embraced our planet's deep trajectory through the fabric of time. It was perhaps the first time I truly felt her wonderfully huge bulk, her vast age, her almost timeless being. This was my moment of Gaian consciousness.

Many years later, Joanna's walk inspired the geologist and Schumacher master's of science student Sergio Maraschin and myself to create what we call the Deep Time Walk. Rather than a hundred-meter stretch, our student group walked a 4.6-kilometer section of the coastal path in South Devon near the college, representing the age of our Earth. On this scale, every millimeter embodies one thousand years of Gaia's ancient story, every footstep five hundred thousand years. I have led this walk here over a hundred times for well over a thousand people since 2008 when we created it. Sergio leads the walk in Portugal where he now lives. A few years ago, a group of us created the Deep Time Walk app for smartphones, so you can be guided on the walk anywhere you choose. After hours of walking we conclude by showing on a ruler how the industrial revolution took off two hundred years ago, a mere one-fifth of a millimeter from the very tip of the ruler, which represents the present day.

It is at this point that the power of Gaian consciousness sometimes bursts upon our walkers. Open jaws, speechlessness, and tears are all quite normal in such moments of what Joanna calls "the Great Turning," when we deeply and truly open to the reality of the sacred cosmic jewel that is our spinning planet.

NOTES

1. Gaia is gendered as feminine because she comes to us as image and myth from the ancient Greeks. The Homeric "Hymn to Gaia" was written down around 500 B.C.E. from preliterate sources that stretch back much further in time. Here are the first lines of the hymn: "Gaia, mother of all, the oldest one, the foundation, I shall sing to Earth. She feeds everyone in the world." Jules Cashford, trans., *The Homeric Hymns* (New York: Penguin Classics, 2003).
2. Joanna Macy, *World as Lover, World as Self* (Berkeley, CA: Parallax Press, 1991), 55.
3. Macy, *World as Lover*, 63.
4. Macy, *World as Lover*, 71.
5. Macy, *World as Lover*, 63.
6. Macy, *World as Lover*, 84.
7. Joanna Macy and Molly Brown, *Coming Back to Life* (Gabriola Island, BC: New Society Publishers, 2014), 146.

SARVODAYA MEANS
EVERYBODY WAKES UP

A. T. Ariyaratne

IT WAS IN THE MID-1970S WHEN I first came across Professor Joanna Macy. When I learned that she was a Buddhist scholar and
practicing Buddhist, I invited her to come and participate in our
Sarvodaya Shramadana movement in Sri Lanka, so that we could
learn from her vast experience in both the theory and practice
of Buddhism. The movement had grown quickly from an educational initiative and service learning program to a full community
development movement supporting self-reliance in hundreds of
villages. From the start, the program was based on principles of
nonviolent social transformation.[1] We were delighted when Joanna
accepted our request and returned to be a part of our movement
for one full year from June 1979 to June 1980.

When Joanna joined us, she was no longer a young volunteer. She was a quite matured personality of around fifty years.
She was well versed not only in Buddhist philosophy but also in
her native Judeo-Christian heritage and other forms of religious
teachings, such as Islam and Hinduism. She was also a social and
political scientist. In her pursuit of knowledge, she had traveled
all over the world, staying in meditation centers, Himalayan temples, churches, hermitages, and convents. She had met numerous
theologians and philosophers. She had worked with many volunteer organizations and served with her husband in the US Peace
Corps.

Being an accomplished scholar, reputed teacher, internationally known speaker, and popular writer, we could not believe that
Joanna would be so humble as to conduct herself as an ordinary
young learner living in a humble village hut. In meeting the young
and the old, the educated and the illiterate, she treated all of them
with love and kindness. In no time, our village folk affectionately
named her Sudu Akka, "white elder sister." On her motorcycle,
Joanna was a common sight in work camps, family gatherings,
schools, temples, and all kinds of village ceremonies. Her humility
and keenness to learn like a small child enabled her to have access to the great scholar monks in our villages and cities. With her
knowledge of Sanskrit and Pali, she was able to master the difficult
Sinhala language in no time, which allowed her to get close to every level of the community.

Sarvodaya was never short of local and foreign volunteers,
interns, evaluators, researchers, and other such persons. Joanna
Macy was an exception to all of them. She never tried to evaluate
or assess what Sarvodaya was doing in over four thousand villages
at that time. Neither did her agenda include any exercise to fulfill
a requirement for a master's or doctoral thesis for a university.
Her main objective was to understand the secret behind the fact
that thousands were drawn to Shramadana camps and other community development activities of the Sarvodaya movement. "Why
were they attracted to Sarvodaya and how?"—this is what she set
out to find out.

Joanna never tried to teach us anything. Instead, her humble conduct as one of us made her sit even at training courses
for young preschool teachers, community health workers, community leaders, and so on. Through her example she taught us
something we still remember after almost forty years. At the end
of her stay in Sri Lanka, we were gifted with a very honest and

clear publication released by Kumarian Press in 1983 under the title *Dharma and Development*. Even today this book is used by all those who are seriously interested in the study of Sarvodaya and its significance to modern Sri Lankan society.

Joanna traced the Sarvodaya thought to the ancient Buddhist civilization going back over twenty-six centuries. She vividly described the evolution of Sri Lankan village communities from the water tank to the stupa, from the village to the temple. Numerous foreign invasions from South Indian kings and then Western powers, culminating in total surrender to the British in 1815, changed this national scenario completely. Sri Lanka regained independence in 1948, and from 1958 on, the Sarvodaya Shramadana movement attempted to revitalize the community spirit hidden in our customs and traditions. This history is chronicled by Joanna in her classic book. Her brilliant insight into the way monks and other religious dignitaries, women, and government servants—land-owning as well as landless people—were drawn into the movement is well described in her narrative, the first of its kind in today's now vast Sarvodaya literature.

Four decades have passed since Joanna was physically present as part of the movement. But in addition to a few short follow-up visits she made to us, in all her subsequent teachings and writings Joanna Macy continued to be one of our great supporters and inspirers. Her later scholarly works, such as *World as Lover, World as Self* and *Coming Back to Life*, each at some point or another refer to her Sarvodaya experiences, thus further contributing to our Vishvodaya program.

Throughout its sixty-year history, Sarvodaya evolved not by trying to implement in the field a theory preconceived in an air-conditioned office. Instead, Sarvodaya workers closely studied social, economic, and political problems that communities face from time to time, and through a variety of consultations, decided on their remedies, putting them to test at the grassroots. Accepting these as a part of our methodology and giving them theoretical validity came later, after we found that they did not conflict with our basic spiritual, moral, and cultural value systems. It is at this stage the teachings of the Buddha gave us confidence to go to the community with a message already existing in the local religious heritage.

Professor Joanna Macy has closely followed the development of the Sarvodaya Shramadana movement since the year she spent with us. In the midst of chaotic world political and economic crises, one after the other impacting on our local politico-economic situation, we had to find a way to realize our goals of awakening people, families, village and urban communities, nations, and the world. In short, we had a common ideal of releasing spiritual, ethical, cultural, social, and economic forces to connect not only all of humanity in peace and well-being but also to live in harmony with the rest of the living world, including fauna and flora. A life of simplicity and highest possible spiritual awakening for all humans was our common ideal.

At this moment, my country is facing an unprecedented moral, social, economic, and political crisis. Seventy years of imitating materialistic party politics and exploitative economic systems have created an almost anarchic situation in our country. Now what Sarvodaya has to face is that challenge for which we have launched the Deshodaya, or National Awakening movement, to look for a new sociopolitical economic order based on the teachings of the Buddha. As Buddha taught nondiscrimination between humans and all living beings in his all-embracing compassion, we are proposing a solution based on Buddhist philosophy that can work for all who inhabit our country. How great if we can have Professor Joanna Macy by our side at this challenging time.

May I wish Joanna a healthy and long life with the blessings of the Buddha.

NOTES

1. See www.sarvodaya.org/history for a full history of the organization's development from the 1960s across many decades of self-organizing and community building to serve people's basic needs through volunteer efforts.

DEVELOPING A SOCIALLY ENGAGED BUDDHISM

Donald Rothberg

THE TERM *ENGAGED BUDDHISM* was first coined by the Vietnamese monk, teacher, and activist Thich Nhat Hanh. He used this phrase to stress the importance of Buddhists being involved with the larger issues of their societies. In his case, this included both the anti-colonial struggle against the French as well as what Vietnamese call the "American war." Western engaged Buddhists were initially inspired by Thich Nhat Hanh's work and by the work of other Asian engaged Buddhists such as A. T. Ariyaratne, the founder of the Sarvodaya movement; Sulak Sivaraksa of Thailand, cofounder of the International Network of Engaged Buddhists; and Aung San Suu Kyi of Burma. As the number of Western engaged Buddhists grew, we began developing our own approaches, initially linking Buddhist principles and practices with social service and social action, and later creating new models of activism and Buddhist practice, interweaving the social dimension with both individual and relational practice.[1]

As this new movement began to develop in the 1970s, I was drawn to its integration of Buddhist practice and social action, the two main passions of my young life. In the 1980s, I learned of Joanna's own initial contribution to this area through her workshops and through her book *Despair and Personal Power in the Nuclear Age.*[2] When I moved to Berkeley, California, in 1988, I joined Joanna and her husband, Fran, in a neighborhood Buddhist practice network of some ten households. I became a board member of the Buddhist Peace Fellowship (BPF) and began to organize socially engaged Buddhist workshops through Spirit Rock Meditation Center in California and BPF. Soon I was attending Joanna's trainings and, with her guidance, incorporating her teachings and practices into my own work.

For more than forty years, Joanna has been intimately connected with the various streams of socially engaged Buddhism, both in Asia and in the West. She has worked with some of the early leaders of the movement and has guided, mentored, and befriended many of its recent Western leaders. She has offered powerful perspectives and practices that have deeply informed the movement's evolution. Within this creative and evolving movement of socially engaged Buddhism, Joanna's core work in the last few decades, the Work That Reconnects, continues to thrive. Two elements are central to her contributions: her understanding of spiritually grounded social transformation; and her skillful use of group practices for waking up together, particularly through accessing and transforming practitioners' pain for the world.

THE NATURE OF SOCIAL TRANSFORMATION

In her trainings and writings, Joanna has articulated three broad ways that lasting social change occurs in the "Great Turning" to a life-sustaining world.[3] First, she says, we need *holding actions* that prevent further damage from occurring, or slow it down. This is the usual province of activism—protests, campaigns, and attempts to change policies. Second, we need ways to *dismantle old structures and build alternative ones.* Central social institutions must be analyzed and changed—economically, politically, socially, ecologically, educationally, and culturally. Third, we need ways of *changing consciousness.* Consciousness itself must shift in appropriate ways that correspond to the institutional shifts, through various practices such as meditating; developing embodied awareness; relating to the earth; and inquiring into race, gender, and sexuality.

Through this model Joanna conveys a broad map of social change, drawing on two important elements of socially engaged Buddhism. The first is the importance of *both* protest *and* movement toward the "good society." For Gandhi, the good society was his aspiration for a "constructive program" to complement nonviolent civil disobedience. For Dr. Martin Luther King Jr., that element was the vision and practice of the "beloved community." Unfortunately, many activists often focus only on the negative, protesting *against* something without a clear sense of what they are *for.* A second element that Joanna emphasizes is the development of the internal correlates of institutional transformation through the transformation of awareness (and the resultant behavior) on personal, relational, and collective levels. Without integration of inner and outer transformation at every level, the outer transformation will not be supported and will not ultimately "stick."

In the last few years, the Buddhist Peace Fellowship has organized its primary trainings inspired by this three-part model, expressed as "Block. Build. Be." Likewise, in my own teaching, I use the model to introduce a broad sense of how to connect inner and outer transformation.[4] I also use the model in asking students to reflect on their next steps as socially engaged Buddhist practitioners. This helps me point out the variety of ways they can respond to social concerns that align with their own particular gifts and inspirations. I often tell the story of how the great African American theologian and activist Howard Thurman responded to a young man's heartfelt question. "What shall I do?" he asked. Thurman replied, "Don't ask what the world needs.

Ask what makes you come alive and go do that, because what the world needs is people who have come alive."[5] Students commonly respond with palpable relief, as they realize that they don't have to be the world's foremost activists or spend their lives continually on the front lines. Working steadfastly in one of the three broad areas of transformation *and*, very importantly, continuing to experience their interconnection is all that is required.

Also core to Joanna's training model is an important balance in transformative training and practice. We must attend *both* to what nourishes and inspires the practitioner *and* to the interconnected painful dimensions of experience, including one's personal pain and one's pain for the world. We find a similar balance in traditional Buddhist practice, as we open *both* to various aspects of *dukkha* (including reactivity, and what is unpleasant, difficult, or leading to suffering) *and* to more awakened qualities such as mindfulness, equanimity, kindness, and wisdom. This understanding can also be found in many other transformative modalities including psychotherapy and trauma work. To encounter what is difficult and painful, especially over a sustained period, one needs resources, supports, and ways of finding balance when triggered, overwhelmed, or otherwise out of balance. Such an understanding is absent in many contemporary approaches to activism, where a continued focus on the negative, as well as a lack of attention to inner and outer resources, often leads to burnout.

Attention to gratitude and beauty—to what, in the words of the Buddha, "gladdens the mind"—helps one unfreeze reactivity and attend to what is painful, based on a rhythm of moving back and forth between relaxed or joyous states and painful states. The trauma worker Peter Levine calls this "pendulation."[6] Being able to experience and hold difficult emotions both individually and in groups is helpful in moving out of repetitive, reactive patterns (linked with some activist strategies), rooted in often unconscious emotions. Later in the progression of the Work, Joanna more explicitly brings in Buddhist principles, such as dependent co-arising, as well as the four heart qualities, or *brahmaviharas*, of loving kindness, compassion, joy, and equanimity. Those addressing the needs of the world begin to be able to take up their work from an increasingly stabilized experience of awakened mind and heart. Action and next steps increasingly come out of the freshness and creativity of having been on a transformative journey, awakening awareness and moving beyond conditioned and often unconscious modes of thinking and emotion.

THE IMPORTANCE OF GROUP WORK

At the heart of Joanna's work, and perhaps her most important contribution to socially engaged Buddhist practice, is the development of powerful group practices such as the Truth Mandala, the Council of All Beings, and the deep time practices with ancestors and future beings. Joanna has developed a form of *relational* spiritual practice that complements individual spiritual practice and is particularly useful in addressing both social and cultural conditioning and larger social issues. Group or relational practice helps mitigate tendencies to isolation and powerlessness and generate creative responses to large-scale challenges. Groups can play a crucial role in furnishing the training grounds and seeds for the evolution of culture and a future society, as well as providing what Joanna calls "rough weather networks" in difficult times.[7]

These practices especially help individuals, organizations, and communities access, work with, and transform difficult cognitive and emotional material related to community and social experiences. These may include fixated mental narratives and "frozen" emotions. Such narratives and emotions related to social experiences are generally hard to access in individual Buddhist practice or even in psychotherapy. Meditation teachers and some therapists may not know how to work skillfully with material such as deep fear about a future altered beyond recognition by climate disruption. Socially triggered emotions and thoughts are often better accessed in group or social settings. Many indigenous societies, for example, work with grief or loss within the collective body of the community.

The Work That Reconnects offers both a relational mode of transformative practice and facilitators skilled, as much as possible, in helping participants navigate such material (as well as helping participants access their own deeper understandings and aspirations).[8] Such practice is particularly important in the context of the nonstop difficult news and new horrors or atrocities of our times. For those who are engaged, it may be difficult not to be dominated by reactivity, albeit reactivity seemingly in the service of moving toward justice and the good society.

The heart of Buddhist practice is cultivating nonreactivity. The Buddha says that he teaches "dukkha and the cessation of dukkha."[9] We may interpret the deep meaning of dukkha as reactivity, as in the teaching of the Two Arrows. In that teaching, the Buddha says that everyone at times is, as it were, shot by an arrow, the arrow of the unpleasant; this is the first arrow. We all at times have unpleasant physical sensations as well as unpleasant thoughts, emotions, or interactions with others. Upon experiencing the pain of the first arrow, the nonpractitioner often automatically and semiconsciously shoots a second arrow in reaction, as if it would help the situation. This can generate further unpleasant physical sensations, thoughts, and emotions, manifesting, for example, in blame of self or other, negative narratives, or reactive

speech. The practitioner, in contrast, learns to be with the unpleasant experience without reacting, yet while being skillful and
responsive moment to moment. This approach is also at the heart
of Gandhian and Kingian nonviolence, with the emphasis on, as
King says, the means being as pure as the ends, coming from
love, and refusing to injure one's opponents.[10] The deepest value
of group practice in the Work That Reconnects is developing this
capacity for nonreactivity and responsive action, in part through
opening to and working through one's pain for the world.

Through these crucial contributions to the evolution of socially engaged Buddhism, and to the broader Great Turning to a
life-sustaining, just society, Joanna and her colleagues have given
us important perspectives and practices, vital for our times of crisis and opportunity. Joanna once summarized her approach in a
simple, powerful way: "The most radical thing any of us can do at
this time is to be fully present to what is happening in the world."[11]
We can hear again in this guidance the core link between engagement and the great presence cultivated in Buddhist practice.

NOTES

1. See, for example, Christopher S. Queen, ed., *Engaged Buddhism in the West* (Boston: Wisdom Publications, 2000).
2. Joanna Rogers Macy, *Despair and Personal Power in the Nuclear Age* (Philadelphia: New Society Publishers, 1983).
3. See Joanna Macy and Molly Young Brown, *Coming Back to Life: Practices to Reconnect Our Lives, Our World* (Gabriola Island, BC: New Society Publishers, 1998), 17–24.
4. Donald Rothberg, "Socially Engaged Buddhist Contemplative Practices: Past and Potential Future Contributions at a Time of Cultural Transition and Crisis," in *Contemplation Nation*, ed. Mirabai Bush (Kalamazoo, MI: Fetzer Institute, 2011), 109–30.

5. Howard Thurman, cited in Gil Bailie, *Violence Unveiled: Humanity at the Crossroads* (New York: Crossroad, 1997), xv.

6. See Peter A. Levine, *In an Unspoken Voice: How the Body Releases Trauma and Restores Goodness* (Berkeley, CA: North Atlantic Books, 2010).

7. Donald Rothberg and Joanna Macy, "Facing the Violence of Our Times," *ReVision* 20, no. 2 (Fall 1997): 48.

8. Two of the current connected growing edges of this work would increase the skill of facilitators through (1) integrating understanding of and work with trauma; and (2) transforming the work so that it is more accessible to people of color and members of other marginalized groups, and expressive of their perspectives.

9. Bhikkhu Bodhi, ed., *The Connected Discourses of the Buddha: A New Translation of the Samyutta Nikaya*, vol. 1 (Boston: Wisdom Publications, 2000), 938.

10. See James M. Washington, ed., *A Testament of Hope: The Essential Writings and Speeches of Martin Luther King Jr.* (San Francisco: HarperSanFrancisco, 1986), 45–46.

11. Dahr Jamail, "Learning to See in the Dark Amid Catastrophe: An Interview with Deep Ecologist Joanna Macy," Truthout, February 13, 2017.

WIDENING THE CIRCLE

Philip Novak

I MET JOANNA IN 1973 AT Syracuse University, where we had come, she a year earlier, to earn doctorates in the Department of Religion. I was twenty-three and just a year out of college. Joanna was forty-four and at a very different stage of life.

She and her husband, Fran, had already lived on four continents and raised three children, then eleven, fifteen, and nineteen years old. Twenty-five years earlier, Joanna had been a star student and campus leader at Wellesley College. Fluent in French, she took a post-undergraduate Fulbright year in France studying European Marxism and Jacques Ellul's seminal work in technology. At that point she thought perhaps her career path would follow those of her grandfather, his father, and his father, in service to the liberal Protestant church. But that vocation would soon slip underground for two decades until, via Syracuse, it resurfaced quite transformed as the inspired, trailblazing, and globetrotting Buddhist ecological and social justice activism of the second half of her life.

But there were a few other stops along the way. The Central Intelligence Agency had spotted the twenty-two-ish Joanna on their perpetual scan for American brainiacs. She accepted their job offer but knew within eighteen months that it wasn't for her. When she married Fran in 1953, she agreed to support his career in Soviet affairs, which took them to Munich where he worked for Radio Liberty. Joanna learned German well enough that twenty years later she could score a perfect eight hundred on her graduate German exam and, later, publish translations of Rilke's poetry. American democratic idealists to their core, Joanna and Fran would soon experience the building of the Berlin Wall in 1961 as a personal blow, confirming their Cold War concerns. Present at Kennedy's 1960 inaugural and moved by his charge to "ask what you can do for your country," they were ready when Fran was recruited to help run the American Peace Corps in India. Deputyships and directorships took them to successive two-year stints in India, Tunisia, and Nigeria. In India, friendships with Tibetan refugees led to Joanna's first serious encounters with the Buddhist ideas that would play an inestimably important role in her life.

At Syracuse, Joanna and I were classmates in Huston Smith's Buddhist Philosophy seminar—fortuitously, since the Dharma was destined to be our deepest bond. As our friendship developed, Joanna asked if I might babysit the kids for a couple of nights when she and Fran were out of town. I was honored but, lacking experience, a tad daunted. Needlessly. My delightful charges that weekend were sixteen-year-old Jack and twelve-year-old Peggy who, not really needing supervision, welcomed me warmly nonetheless. We too became friends.

I didn't know then that Joanna and Fran had been thinking about merging their family into a larger communal living situation. Inspired by the nascent American ecological movement and in the habit of walking their talk, they were hoping to live more simply and also to creatively disrupt their nuclear family roles. Joanna had another motive as well. She knew from direct experience how all too often the unwritten job description of the nuclear-family mom is to mastermind the universe on a daily basis. Communal living might redefine her role in a way that gave her more uninterrupted time to dedicate to her precious years of graduate study.

But Joanna and Fran would do none of this without Jack's and Peggy's consent. (Christopher, their eldest, was already living communally on The Farm in Tennessee.) A March weekend in 1975 marked, says Joanna, "a turning point in our lives." The Macys drove to Philadelphia to attend a Movement for a New Society workshop dedicated to "living more frugally and with less of an impact on the earth." Joanna was impressed to see from a distance that Jack and Peggy, separated from their parents and each other, were comfortable in "managing their own time and contacts and being treated as competent and interesting people in their own right." The workshop's content enthused them all. On the way back to Syracuse the four agreed: "Let's do it!" Two months later they sold their tidy single-family house in Dewitt to purchase 600 Allen Street, a sprawling, eight-bedroom fixer-upper near the university.

The Macys initially considered inviting a second family of parents and two children to join them, but Peggy vetoed this on grounds of insufficiently diverse generations. Much better, they eventually decided to bring in four singles—two men and two women—in their twenties and thirties. Thanks to my famous one-night stand of babysitting, I was one of them. All eight of us dove in gleefully, little suspecting that a distinctive era of our lives would forever after be dubbed "600 Allen." Joanna has called these days the dawn of one of the happiest adventures of Macy family life.

We did not pool income or assets, but we did share food costs and household responsibilities, setting up rosters for cleaning, shopping, and cooking dinner. We regularly checked the communication notebook at the back door to read or scrawl messages to one another. All of us joined Syracuse's New Environmental Association and the food co-op, where, in exchange for a few monthly hours of service, we enjoyed excellent produce. And we held a weekly house meeting, the agenda for which always began with a wise little practice called Feeling Dealing, a chance to share as-yet-unshared feelings about our interactions. No one was required to share a feeling, and if one did, it might be simply to express thanks: "The mushroom gravy you made for Tuesday's mashed potatoes made me feel downright loved." But Feeling Dealing's killer app was helping us deal with hurts that, if ignored, could poison our life in common. The reporter adhered to a simple verbal structure: "I felt X when you said (or did) Y." For example, "I felt ignored when you said we didn't need the heat turned up." The reporter owned their feeling from the get-go instead of beginning with the typical and predictably counterproductive "You ignored me . . ." type of accusation. It made a world of difference and usually set the stage for swift and satisfying resolutions via clarifications or apologies. No small thanks to Feeling Dealing, 600 Allen was a happy and harmonious house.

How did Joanna and Fran balance relating to Peggy and Jack as their own incomparably beloved children and as two of eight equal housemates? During house meetings they never interfered with Jack's or Peggy's autonomy, even in those difficult moments when the teens might have been tempted to let their parents speak for them. Nor did Joanna and Fran ever even hint that Peggy's or Jack's responsibilities ought to be any different from everyone else's. Yet I never witnessed a moment when they could doubt the reality of their parents' special concern for them. Even within the communal dynamic there was plenty of opportunity for Peggy and Jack, as students and maturing teenagers, to enjoy their parents' special solicitude, encouragement, and quality time. The Macys continued to hit the ski slopes together each winter, vacation together in the summer, and enjoy their familiar rituals and traditions throughout the year. Joanna and Fran hugged and kissed their children and laughed with them. Not too surprisingly, the children's love for their parents has always been palpable.

An unforeseen opportunity to study abroad would limit my own time at 600 Allen to one year. Yet within the next seven years, unpredictably and for very different reasons, I and most of the Macys had relocated to the San Francisco Bay area. Here we and other Syracuse pals have remained in warm touch for nearly forty years, often congregating around the Macy dinner table, as we did after Huston Smith's 2017 memorial service. I like to think that nothing less than dharmic currents pulled Joanna and me out West and kept us there. After all, the great Buddhist scholar Edward Conze, concluding his late-1970s visit to the San Francisco Zen Center, cheekily proclaimed his discovery that Buddhism actually comprised not just two great schools but three: Theravada, Mahayana, and Bay Area.

Joanna mentions a time in her life, before I knew her, when an unskillful tendency for "everlasting seriousness" was bearing some unpleasant fruit. Yet my experience of Joanna's basic vibe has always been quite different, one of spacious love. It's safe to say that the Dhamma (Dharma) had something to do with this difference. "Who sees dependent arising sees the Dhamma; who sees the Dhamma sees dependent arising," said Gautama. No idea would be more foundational for Joanna's work, her thought, or her life than what she rightly calls the Buddha's central teaching, the dependent co-arising of all phenomena. It revealed to her "the awesome coherence of everything the Buddha thought and did," and in those words we hear her own recognition that would inspire everything else she would henceforth think and do. Its psychological entailment, of course, is that the separate self, also dependently arisen and thus empty of own-being, is a fiction, an insight matchlessly handy for sanding down even the gnarliest edges of our "everlasting seriousness." But let me be clear—dependent co-arising did *not* make Joanna any less serious about the bodhisattva vow that would guide the rest of her life; rather, it allowed her access to that incomparable, selfless seriousness classically etched in the *Diamond Sutra*—working ceaselessly to save all beings from suffering while never forgetting that ultimately there are neither beings to save nor bodhisattvas to save them.

For many aspiring to walk along the Buddha's eightfold path, the practice of meditation appears indispensable—as in the T-shirt imperative "Don't just do something, sit there!" But Joanna's self-described "innate itch for action and passion for justice," while not dismissing sitting, have always tilted her dharma work in the direction of the imperative's standard form: "Don't just sit there, do something!" Even during her initiation into the Vajrayana some forty-five years ago, when she learned that one of her new Tibetan names meant "meditation," she admitted having hoped for "something more active!" So much for names: active she has been!—in half a lifetime more than enough for ten. In her own way the ancient archetypal tension riddling every heart that aspires toward the good—how to balance the great ways of contemplation and action—was strikingly resolved. And her resolution of it, favoring the way of action, is to me as impressive and consequential as Thomas Merton's famous resolution a generation earlier, favoring contemplation. Joanna's activist writing and teaching have made an immeasurably great contribution to the American creation of socially engaged Buddhism, sending numberless waves of *dukkha* antidotes rippling across vast stretches of time and space. Countless present beings already are, and countless future beings surely will be, deeply grateful.

THE WORK TAKES
ROOT IN THE UK

Pat Fleming[*]

IN SPRING 2019 IN THE UNITED KINGDOM, powerful change was in the air. We witnessed mass civil disobedience in London and elsewhere as an unprecedented groundswell of protest took place in response to our government's lack of action over climate change. Traffic-filled Waterloo Bridge was temporarily transformed into a plant-lined people's park. Amid busy streets filled with shoppers, hundreds of protestors occupied Oxford Circus for days. Courageous activists formed a superglued human chain to halt business at the London Stock Exchange. Others enacted a mass die-in at the famous Natural History Museum.

This peaceful series of protests, organized by Extinction Rebellion (XR), was undoubtedly influenced by Joanna Macy's work. Introduced thirty-six years ago in the United Kingdom, her work and its seeds are now blossoming in a thousand ways. A number of the protestors and organizers active in the current movement have trained in the Work That Reconnects (WTR). Their songs of the Great Turning were a key part of the climate strike protests.

[*] Authored by Pat Fleming, this piece also includes written contributions from Chris Johnstone, Jenny Mackewn, Lesley Joy Quilty, and Jane Reed, with further assistance from Liz Hosken, Justin Kenrick, Peter Reason, Helen Sieroda, and Kathleen Sullivan.

ARRIVAL OF THE WORK

It was spring 1983 when Joanna first visited the United Kingdom, carrying freshly published copies of her first and widely influential book, *Despair and Personal Empowerment in the Nuclear Age.* American peace activist Paul Cienfuegos, who had worked with Joanna, organized a ten-stop tour for Joanna around the UK. She arrived to a country in the grip of Prime Minister Margaret Thatcher, the Iron Lady, who had just triumphed militarily in the Falkland Islands. The Cold War was casting deep shadows of potential nuclear war across Europe. We had growing concerns about the effects of nuclear power accidents and waste dumping by the UK's nuclear-power/weapons program. Thatcher and US President Ronald Reagan made an agreement to cooperate on the Trident nuclear program. US troops and cruise missiles had arrived on UK soil the previous year, sparking multiple peace protest camps, including the women's camp at Greenham Common. We were certainly in need of Joanna's work to support us in expressing our socially unacceptable feelings of despair about a scary and uncertain future.

On the tour, Joanna started in Glasgow and traveled southward, giving a series of talks and workshops, including at the Manjushri Institute at Conishead Priory where she offered her first UK intensive. This invitation to immerse in her work drew thirty-five of us, including educators, antinuclear activists, mental health counselors, Quakers, and Buddhists. A vibrant, clearheaded, articulate woman in her fifties, Joanna skillfully led us through some of the most profound inner work we had encountered, linking this to our actions in the world. In speaking of our fears, rage, numbness, and utter despair, we uncovered powerful joy and an extraordinary elation of meeting one another within this work. Joanna's influence in the UK had begun. Fertile seeds were sown and Interhelp UK took root, with Paul Cienfuegos, Maria Brown, me, and others giving talks and workshops in many different circles long after Joanna had returned home.

In 1986, Joanna gave the Schumacher Lecture in Bath, a great honor for her. Afterward she joined the Brazilian environmentalist José Lutzenberger, a fiercely outspoken defender of the Amazon rainforests, on a four-hundred-mile drive to northeast Scotland to the Findhorn Foundation community. Thus began a long relationship between Joanna and Findhorn.

In the fall of 1987, Joanna was invited by Liz Hosken and Ed Posey, who had recently set up the Gaia Foundation, to lead "For the Healing of Our World," an experiential intensive training held again at Conishead Priory. This time she was assisted by her husband, Fran, just back from meeting with Soviet psychologists, as well as Justin Kenrick and me, both rainforest activists. I'd recently returned from helping set up Interhelp in Australia, and Joanna had flown in from Tibet, where she continued her Buddhist engagement. This Conishead training involved a powerful sense of international cross-fertilization, which was evident in the breadth and creativity of the work we explored.

The UK was developing its huge nuclear-powered Vanguard submarine, to be armed with US-supplied Trident II nuclear missiles. By chance, the first of these was being built for the Royal Navy at nearby Barrow-in-Furness, a small town where we went to interview people living in the shadow of the massive Trident shipbuilding hall. We ventured nervously along rows of terraced houses where workers lived, knocking on doors and speaking with workers and their families. Time after time, they shared their fears, including mushroom-cloud nightmares, and thanked us for the chance to talk about how very wrong it felt to be building such powerful machines of mass destruction. We learned that some workers had acted on their concerns, installing equipment upside down within the submarines to slow production.

This particular week was exceptionally vivid and fertile, with long-reaching impacts. The activist Jane Reed, inspired to take Joanna's work into educational settings in England, describes her Conishead experience: "Participating in this intensive turned my life unexpectedly on its axis with new experiences of power, purpose, and comradeship that reframed almost everything. *Waking up* was an understatement. Joanna warned us that 'increasing our felt connectedness with life on Earth would not always bring us ease and harmony,' which was certainly true for me. But what a journey it was!" Mary Inglis, from the Findhorn community, felt determined to offer a longer immersion of Joanna's work at Findhorn and impulsively offered her an invitation. Joanna jumped at the chance to return.

TEACHING AT FINDHORN

As an intentional community, eco-village, and education center, the Findhorn Foundation community became internationally famous in the early 1970s. Community member Lesley Joy Quilty reflects on the center's growth and on Joanna's participation: "The Findhorn village gained international attention when residents were shown growing enormous vegetables in very poor sandy soil. When asked how this was possible, the founders explained that they drew on three principles: inner listening, co-creation with the intelligence of nature, and work as love in action. Paul Hawken's book *The Magic of Findhorn* and Louis Malle's film *My Dinner with Andre* added to the community's fame, drawing seekers to this day who are interested in new ways of living."

As Lesley describes, "Joanna has enjoyed a long and abiding relationship with the Findhorn community, and for over thirty years has participated in numerous films and online summits produced by Findhorn. She is a Fellow of the Findhorn Foundation, a group of more than one hundred individuals with deep connections to the community, who are honored and appreciated for their transformative work in the world. Our relationship began in 1986, when she presented despair and empowerment work to two hundred and forty delegates at Findhorn's international conference on the world's ecological crisis, 'One Earth: A Call to Action.' This took place soon after the tragic Chernobyl accident, so we had a strong focus on nuclear issues and Joanna's trailblazing work at this conference."

In April 1989, Joanna returned to Findhorn with rainforest activist John Seed, where I joined them and an international team of facilitators to offer a weeklong intensive, "The Power of Our Deep Ecology," an event considered a watershed for the Findhorn community. Planning sessions ran late into the night, often accompanied by wine, music, and much hilarity. It was a life-changing week for participants from all over the world, beginning with daily poetic teachings from Joanna, followed by experiential exercises and collective rituals. As the work opened us to our deeper truths, we touched into our individual and collective pain around gender issues. What emerged was the shadow side of Scotland's cruel history of witch-burning and misogyny. Some of the workshops took place at Cluny Hill, where nearby in the 1500s, witches were brutally punished by being rolled down the hill in wooden barrels stuck through with spikes and then burned at the bottom. In their memory, some workshop participants enacted a ritual of asking forgiveness, offering a peace blessing to all those who had suffered.

In 1991, the year of the first Gulf War, as smoke from burning oil wells engulfed the cradle of our civilization, an unforgettable "Easter Mysteries" event unfolded at Findhorn. Joanna had been deeply affected by her friend Matthew Fox and his book *The Coming of the Cosmic Christ.* In it, he prophesied that the Pascal Mysteries of the third millennium would have to do with the death and resurrection of Earth, where Earth plays the role of Christ crucified.[1]

"Knowing that the anguish of our planet's peoples cried out for acknowledgment and ritual," recalls Joanna, "and that all faith traditions deserved to take part, Matthew and I, helped by an international team, orchestrated a Passion week that included a Buddhist Day of Mindfulness on the Four Noble Truths, a Jewish Passover, Sufi circle dances, pagan Celtic sweat lodges, deep mourning of the burning times, and the stations of the cross."

Two hundred participants were organized into ten home groups that met daily. For one of their tasks, the groups were asked to represent different stations of the cross, in whatever way the suffering of Earth spoke to them. They improvised props and roles, setting up the stations around the wild edges of the community, ending in the sandy dunes of the nearby beach. On Good Friday, participants processed slowly from one station to the next, chanting a Russian Kyrie eleison as they paused to honor each manifestation of Earth's suffering—the AIDS epidemic, deforestation, proliferating waste, nuclear contamination, Chernobyl, homelessness, species loss, the burning Amazon rainforests. As Joanna said later, "Whilst on the beach waiting for dawn on Easter Sunday, I stood there bleakly, not knowing what would, or even could, resurrect from Earth's suffering and pain. As the sun rose, it came to me suddenly: *It is the reawakening of the ecological self that can save us and the life of our planet.*

In 2000, Joanna and a large team of facilitators developed a mass group role play to experience her new work in deep time. It took the form of a pilgrimage to a nuclear guardian site in the future. Two-thirds of the participants became "pilgrims" and one-third became "guardians." Together, using their collective imagining, they contacted future beings who had somehow survived, despite the perils of present times. They also called on the beings of the past—long lineages of survivor ancestors upon whose shoulders they stood, to offer a source of strength in the present.

Joanna returned to teach at Findhorn many times, always offering profound teachings to the community and workshop participants. Her last visit, in 2013, gave birth to a Work That Reconnects practice group for people living in the local area, peer-facilitated by Chris Johnstone and others. Later, a weeklong Findhorn program was created by Chris and community member Margot van Greta based on the concept of active hope, which Margot continues to offer at Findhorn.

ACTIVE HOPE

The inspirational retreats and facilitator trainings at Findhorn and elsewhere in the UK led Chris Johnstone and Joanna to co-author the now widely appreciated book *Active Hope: How to Face the Mess We're In without Going Crazy*.[2] This publication offers a new expression of the Work That Reconnects, where the book itself acts as a co-facilitator, guiding readers around the spiral with stories, insights, and exercises designed to strengthen our capacity to make a difference in the world. Chris, a well-being and resilience trainer, tells us, "Within *Active Hope*, we encourage readers to seek company to co-explore what we've written, trying out together the practices we describe. Trainees in the work may find leading an intensive workshop daunting, so this process offers easier first steps to develop their confidence in facilitation."

Active Hope book groups have now taken off in many countries. The book is used as a core text in both mainstream and alternative educational settings. Hundreds of people from many countries have now engaged with this process, organizing informal gatherings with friends and family members, or setting up programs of mini-workshops.[3] Transition Network groups, religious communities, the Pachamama Alliance, and sustainability networks worldwide have all run *Active Hope* journey groups. These groups follow the journey mapped out in the book, having conversations that support them in being fully present to the world while building community and fellowship through sustaining Active Hope practices. The book is now on the key text list compiled by UK Extinction Rebellion (XR), who recently ordered hundreds of copies to support XR groups around the UK.

TAKING ROOT

Over the past three and a half decades, it is extraordinary that so many thousands of people in the UK have experienced the life-changing effects of Joanna's work. I've witnessed a steady stream of people whose lives have been profoundly impacted, who have then carried the seeds of this work to many organizations and communities around the UK and Europe.

Given this widespread interest, it has never been more vital to have a pool of experienced and trained WTR leaders. For over a decade, social and business change educators Jenny Mackewn, Chris Johnstone, and Kirsti Norris have offered the innovative Facilitator Development Adventure program, a residential nature-connected WTR leadership training, attracting participants internationally.[4]

Jenny comments, "Twenty years ago, nature connection work was not particularly fashionable or sought after. But now with the sea change in awareness of our planet's issues, combined with the wider collective awakening of our sense of responsibility, new programs are drawing in a wide range of people."

The Institute of Deep Ecology Education was set up by pioneers Jane Reed, Chris Johnstone, Peter Evans, and Kathleen Sullivan in 1992 to promote Joanna's work in the UK. Jane also helped develop Leading Sustainable Schools, a project that brought together school leaders to identify the practices, vision, and leadership required to become a sustainable school.[5] This program defined the essential leadership quality of *courageous agency*—the power to act on behalf of the whole of life—and shared common themes with active hope—a wider sense of self, a different kind of power, and a richer experience of community.[6]

The work became part of the curriculum of a radical master's degree in responsibility and business practice set up by Peter Reason at the Centre for Action Research in Professional Practice, University of Bath. Here he promoted Joanna's five motivating guidelines for social change: come from gratitude, don't be afraid of the dark, dare to vision, link arms with others, and act your age. Peter also published an inspiring book, *Stories of the Great Turning*, with his colleague Melanie Newman.[7]

Many other positive-change organizations within the UK have been deeply influenced by Joanna's work, including the Transition Network, which has inspired transition towns and communities worldwide. This is also true of the Permaculture Association, now a major global movement and influence. Ongoing Deep Ecology work is offered at Schumacher College on the historic Dartington Estate, where Joanna has taught residential courses on systems theory and spiritual transformation. I continue to teach

there with Toni Spencer on the "Call of the Wild," and Chris Johnstone teaches resilience and well-being residential courses.

NEW ARISINGS

We are currently in a fresh and evolving wave of peaceful mass activism and protest in the UK, amid social and political ferment as
we try to exit the European Union. Climate change is increasingly
featured in the mainstream news and media, with ground-shifting
documentaries including the BBC's *Climate Change: The Facts*, narrated by David Attenborough, watched by millions. In store check-
out lines, ordinary people now talk about rejecting plastics and the
damage being done to our beautiful Earth by our carelessness.

The impacts of the protests continue to reverberate. There is
a surge of younger people speaking out and taking action, empowered by social media. Tens of thousands of school children practice
nonviolent "Fridays for Future" strikes, expressing their climate
and biodiversity crisis fears on streets around the UK and Europe.
Over 1.3 million school children around the world took part in a
day of action in March 2019 in more than one hundred countries.

Extinction Rebellion activists are holding nonviolent direct
actions all over the planet. Within the UK XR movement, members continue to train as leaders within the Facilitation Development Adventure program. They work with *Active Hope* to empower
each other to speak out, building personal and social resilience
while acting from compassion and love for the Earth.

The UK's Parliament declared a state of climate emergency
in May 2019, while Mark Carney, the head of the Bank of England,
told global banks and businesses forcefully that they cannot ignore
climate change. Never before has our mainstream and social media been so focused on what's happening to the planet's climate

and ecosystems, the rapid loss of biodiversity, and the mass impacts of human activity across this planet, especially as they are now measured from orbiting space satellites.

So, are we witnessing a critical mass tipping point as the Great Turning gains traction? It is heartening to those of us who have been doing this work for decades to hear so many others around us asking, "How can we urgently repair and reverse our species' destructive impacts on this precious shared planet?" At last, our global ecological self is posing these questions on a wider stage, with a collective louder voice!

NOTES

1. Matthew Fox, *The Coming of the Cosmic Christ: The Healing of Mother Earth and the Birth of a Global Renaissance* (San Francisco: HarperOne, 1998).
2. Joanna Macy and Chris Johnstone, *Active Hope: How to Face the Mess We're in without Going Crazy* (Novato, CA: New World Library, 2012).
3. The Active Hope website offers a range of resources at www.active hope.info, with book group resources at https://app.ruzuku.com /courses/4355/about.
4. See more at the Facilitation for Life on Earth website, www.facilita-tionforlifeonearth.org.
5. National College for School Leadership (NCSL). The UK government was the contractor for the project. Leading Sustainable Schools, Nottingham, UK, 2007–10.
6. Anna Birney and Jane Reed, *Sustainability and Renewal: Findings from the Leading Sustainable Schools Research Project* (Nottingham, UK: National College for School Leadership, 2009).
7. Peter Reason and Melanie Newman, eds., *Stories of the Great Turning* (London: Jessica Kingsley, 2017).

THE RAINFOREST
PROTECTING ITSELF

Australia Rising

Bobbi Allan[*]

WE ARE STANDING, SOME OF US with babes in arms, on what re-
sembles a bomb site in the midst of the most extraordinarily beautiful subtropical rainforest. Our bodies reverberate with shock and
tears. It is 1979 and Terania Creek rainforest, a few kilometers from
our homes in northern New South Wales, is being logged.[1] We are
here to stop the logging, and we will soon succeed, but today the
forest is as shocked and sad as we are. What should be dappled
shade filled with birdsong is a blaze of hot sun on shattered "collat-
eral damage" trees. Giant pink brush box logs, once the guardians
of the rainforest, bleed bloodred sap into the scoured earth. The
birds are silent.

Many hundreds of us have come to this region to build intentional communities. We are drawn together by visions of positive futures, sharing skills and resources, living lightly and more
harmoniously with the earth. We want to bring up our children
cooperatively, in a peaceful world. We have traveled, opening to
wider perspectives on the world and encountering in our neighboring countries the great spiritual traditions of Asia. We have

[*] With contributions from Inna Alex, Rachel Benmayor, Eshana Bragg, Simon
Clough, John Croft, Claire Wren Dunn, Pat Fleming, Juli Glasson, Stuart Hill,
Sue Lennox, Kathryn McCabe, Ken McLeod, Emma Pittaway, Katrina Shields,
Lisa Siegel, Jo Vallentine, David Wright, and Ruth Yeatman.

returned with meditation and yoga practices, and a hunger for continuing spiritual inquiry beyond the bounds of churches and religious dogmas.

Two of our intentional communities are Dharmananda and Bodhi Farm, bonded in engaged Buddhist practices, sharing care of the Forest Meditation Centre, built in 1975–76 above the Terania Creek Valley. People from both communities are among the two hundred and fifty or more responding to the call to stop the logging in the head of the valley. Among us is John Seed, emerging from the successful Terania blockade with the epiphany: "I am not a separate human protecting the rainforest. I am the rainforest, recently evolved into human intelligence, protecting itself.[2]

DESPAIR WORK ARRIVES

Two people from Bodhi Farm, Gai Longmuir and Ian Gaillard, joined the 1981 voyage of the 56-foot yacht *Pacific Peacemaker* sailing eleven thousand miles across the Pacific to Seattle, Washington, to be part of a blockade to prevent the launching of the first Trident submarine. Tridents were also planned to be built in Australia—their powerful missiles launched via signals from US bases here. What could we do?

In 1983, John and Greta Seed received a copy of Joanna's booklet titled *Despairwork*, mailed to them by a US friend. They gathered a group of forest and antinuclear activists from Dharmananda and Bodhi Farm to discuss its profound insights. Could releasing the emotional horror of nuclear annihilation cut across Australia's political divisions? Could it be empowering? We thought so, but we didn't know how to proceed.

Later that year I was about to go to the Forest Meditation Centre for a ten-day Insight meditation retreat with the Buddhist teacher Christopher Titmuss when my husband, John Allan, came home with a copy of *Despair and Personal Power in the Nuclear Age.* Despite the prohibition on reading during the retreat, I read it by torchlight in my tent, crying with relief at Joanna's elegant articulation of what had been deeply troubling yet inexpressible murmurs and inklings in my heart; and marveling at the amazing processes that so profoundly brought Buddhist spirituality and activism together with scientific general systems theory! Late in the retreat, I told Christopher I was reading the book. "Oh," he said, "I know Joanna Macy—why don't you invite her to come to Australia?"

Within the week, the activist Simon Clough had donated seed funding and we had an organizing team from our two communities. Joanna soon accepted our invitation, and the tour date was set for January 1985. In my files is a folder of all the "snail mail" that took ten days to fly back and forth across the Pacific to organize this extraordinary tour.

We were joined and enormously assisted by Pat Fleming from the UK, who had worked as a mental health counselor in Sydney before returning to the UK, where she trained intensively with Joanna beginning in 1983. While we planned the megatour, we formed Interhelp Australia to support Joanna's work and build networks around the country. Pat mentored and trained several of us to prepare and co-lead Joanna's work. By the time Joanna arrived, our small team had already led five "Despair to Empowerment" workshops in Sydney, Canberra, and regional centers, as well as hosted talks and written articles to spread the word.

We still have the handwritten schedule of Joanna's first trip. She arrived on January 31, 1985, and flew out on March 3, then flying on to New Zealand, where Rex McCann and Vivian Hutchinson trained others to spread the work. In that month she led one-day and two-day workshops and gave public talks in all the major Australian cities—Sydney, Brisbane, Lismore, Canberra, Melbourne, Adelaide, and Perth. Hundreds of activists, professionals, therapists, artists, media people, Quakers, Buddhists, and Christians attended.[3] We had press conferences, and television and radio coverage for Joanna all over Australia.

Immediately, the power of Joanna's work was apparent. The systems work cut through old divisions, putting major issues in a larger context. Doing the deep emotional work to deal with our grief and anger allowed us to see the people behind the polarized stereotypes, bringing a previously absent openness and compassionate understanding to politics. We could now begin to build relationships across previously impassable divides. This was soon extended to conscious work across diversities in the annual Heart Politics conferences, inspired by the 1986 book *Heart Politics* by Joanna's Interhelp colleague Fran Peavey.[4]

Lessons were learned from the divisions between "old" and "new" settlers during the Terania Creek protests in another local blockade to prevent coal seam gas drilling on valuable farmland. The campaign was organized systematically, neighbor by neighbor, with great support for inclusiveness, based in shared caring for the land, respect for diversity, and clear lines of communication with all parties.[5]

THE COUNCIL OF ALL BEINGS IS BORN

Joanna's tour culminated in a final four-day training intensive with over fifty participants at Elanora Heights, Sydney. It was there that Joanna and John Seed, with input from Pat, created the first-ever Council of All Beings, developed as a regeneration ritual for activists and others to experience a nonanthropocentric worldview. On an ancient sandstone plateau, surrounded by rock pools, cliffs, and forest, while the didgeridoo[6] summoned ancestral beings to join us, Joanna and John invited each of us to identify with an other-than-human being—plant, animal, or element—and to create a mask representing it. Gathering in council, our masked creatures found powerful voices bearing witness to the destruction of habitats and ecosystems. We took turns unmasking to become undefended humans, just listening, feeling. After the masked beings shook our anthropocentric worldviews to the core, they gifted us with strengths we hadn't thought humans could claim. Mosses that survived the Ice Age became ground we could stand on, while ancient rocks had our backs. Now we all knew what it was to be "the rainforest protecting itself." Here was a powerful new authority from which to act!

In 1987, Joanna, John, and Pat met up again at an Interhelp conference in San Francisco. It was there that the book *Thinking Like a Mountain*, with contributions from the Norwegian deep ecologist Arne Naess, was conceived as an inspirational reader for Deep Ecology work and as a workshop manual for leading the Council of All Beings. Joanna then headed off to Tibet, Pat returned to England, and John came back to Australia. It was the very early days of using the internet, and they all had to find the necessary technical support to write, exchange, and co-edit various chapters of the book electronically. Eventually published by New Society Publishers, it was possibly one of the earliest books to be written collaboratively via the internet. Since then, John Seed, joined by many others, has run Council of All Beings workshops and Deep Ecology road shows around Australia, in New Zealand, and in many other countries, continuing tirelessly right up to 2019, when ill health enforced a break.

DEEP ECOLOGY ACTION

People who attended Joanna's 1985 workshops took up all three of Joanna's domains of activism—holding actions, institutional change, and shifts in consciousness—on a broad front of issues.[7]

While some groups protested land clearing and uranium mining, there were also more unusual actions.

In 1986, Sydney Harbour was the major venue for the Australian Navy's seventy-fifth anniversary, which saw the largest international assembly of allied vessels in a foreign port since World War II, including nuclear-armed destroyers. The protests were spectacular. Ian Cohen, later to become the first New South Wales Greens Party senator, jumped off a zodiac with his surfboard, grabbed the prow of the USS *Oldendorf*, and surfed the bow wave up the harbor as the cameras clicked.

In the same year, Pat Fleming, Ken Golding, and Patrick Anderson held the "Cafe Anti-Boom-Boom," occupying the lawns of the French Embassy in Canberra, to protest the French nuclear bomb testing at Mururoa Atoll in the Pacific Ocean. A local French bakery donated croissants and pastries served to the public at small tables. Early customers were undercover police officers who came for coffee. One of the officers surreptitiously lifted his lapel to show an antinuclear badge! Tourist coaches stopped to join, writing lists of what they appreciated about the French while signing petitions against atmospheric nuclear testing.

A few years later, five of us attended a hearing about a rare earth processing plant, proposed to be built not far from Terania Creek. Based on the Council of All Beings, we spoke for the Wilson River, a cow (this was prime dairy country), a native duck, a platypus, and a human of the seventh generation to come. The commissioner of the hearing had tears in his eyes as we spoke. In the end, permission to build the plant was denied.

One of the many impacts of Deep Ecology work was on the forest campaigns in the state of Western Australia. Joanna's work had come to Western Australia in 1987 after Vivienne Elanta read *Thinking Like a Mountain*. The Gaia Foundation of Western Australia brought John Seed to Western Australia for two workshops and a road show, to help save the Western Australian jarrah and karri forests from wood chipping. A Council of All Beings was held in the threatened Giblett forest of the southwest of the state. For the next sixteen years, Vivienne Elanta and John Croft led an average of three Council of All Beings each year, while mentoring others who continue to lead the work today. In 1994, Joanna held a forest workshop for one hundred activists, empowering their campaign that led to the creation of eight new national parks in Western Australia.

Despair and Personal Power in the Nuclear Age sent its ripples far and wide. In 1985, Western Australians elected to the Australian Senate Jo Vallentine,[8] representing the Nuclear Disarmament Party. Jo had been profoundly inspired by reading the book in 1984; as she traveled to Canberra, she and Joanna met in a Sydney train station for an hourlong conversation that would cement Joanna as Jo's guiding light in her work as a senator, and in her ongoing antinuclear work. In 2007, Jo and Scott Ludlam, who had both attended workshops with Joanna and been arrested at forest blockades, were influential in the formation of the Western Australia Greens Party. In 2008, Scott was elected as a federal senator and served through 2017.[9] In their political work, Jo and Scott frequently used systems theory as it relates to change making, particularly the cross-party networking the Greens achieved within the rigidly adversarial parliamentary structures. They reminded each other to "touch the earth" every day.

Joanna returned to lead more trainings around the country in 1997, 1998, 2001, and 2005, exploring her deep time work in the context of Australia's ancient cultures, and inspiring the idea of social action as spiritual practice. Her work found natural allies in the social ecology course at the University of Western Sydney and in the teaching of permaculture. Shambhala warriors dispersed from each of these trainings to beaver away in all sectors of government, in frontline activism and long-term structural change making, religious and spiritual settings, schools and universities, local food cooperatives and gardens, earth repair systems, refugee and social justice organizations, greener technologies, participatory democracy, and more.

STILLNESS IN ACTION RETREATS

Joanna's "Social Action as Spiritual Practice" tour encouraged me to partner with Simon Clough to develop four-day "Stillness in Action" retreats. Over forty retreats have been held in Australia and New Zealand to support activists from all domains to sustain and deepen the insights gained from the Work That Reconnects by situating it within a reflective retreat setting and teaching simple meditation practices. The retreats follow the four-part spiral of the work. Silent mornings include a WTR-themed dharma talk, followed by significant reflection and meditation time in nature. After lunch we break the silence and enter the spiral, assisted by WTR facilitators.[10]

Over the years we modified processes and added new ones. By combining Buddhist practices with deep time work, we added new dimensions to both. Sitting silently, as a drum beat the rhythm of our hearts, we heard our ancestral human journey expressed in the geological and human time frames of this ancient continent. Opening our eyes, we beheld other modern human faces of Gaia, honoring their presence with loving kindness, compassion, appreciative joy, and depths of timeless equanimity. Finally, face to face with nature—a rock, a tree, a bird—we inquired: "Who am I without my names and labels? What is constraining, what has benefited me? What might I be ready to let go of, or at least hold less tightly?" In the silence that followed, we heard a beautiful Aboriginal-inspired call to simply "Remember you are as beautiful as all this. Stand up alive and be committed!"[11]

"STOP URANIUM, RECLAIM THE FUTURE"— A PILGRIMAGE PROJECT[12]

In early 1997, after a training with Joanna in beautiful Denmark, Western Australia, I remember sitting in front of the fire with a small group of people including John Croft, Vivienne Elanta, and Jo Vallentine, tossing around an "impossible idea." We would invite to Australia two of Joanna's friends from the Chernobyl-contaminated Ukrainian town of Novozybkov and bus them around the country to meet the Aboriginal traditional owners of uranium deposits and sacred sites, to share experiences of living on contaminated land.

Miraculously, money was raised, a bus purchased and decorated, airfares and visas arranged. On Hiroshima Day 1997, a small band of pilgrims including Natalia Dikun and Andrei Kryshtop from Novozybkov set out from Perth. The bus was to travel 18,000 kilometers on a 55-day journey, with 31 "pilgrims," including me, joining and leaving at intervals. The learning and sharing were mutual. In every Aboriginal language, arising from this land at least 80,000 years ago,[13] there was a word for uranium; the land holding the deposits was known as *sickness* or *poison country*. The elders in each community held the responsibility for ensuring "the poison" was left undisturbed, to prevent it from causing harm.

The pilgrims sat down with traditional owners of six uranium deposits across the country. They shared stories and drawings by the children of Novozybkov, some sick and dying, now removed from contaminated land to live in high-rise concrete flats, barred from their beloved forests. In Aboriginal culture, stories and drawing are traditional modes of communication. The pilgrims heard from children whose grandparents had been blinded and sickened by Maralinga bombs—a series of atmospheric nuclear bomb detonations and other nuclear tests conducted by Britain on the land of the Anangu peoples of Maralinga in the Central Desert of Australia during the 1950s and 1960s. They heard the dilemmas of weary elders, pressured to allow uranium mining on their land: "Even though we say no, they keep on asking. I'm sick and tired of it . . . all the lawyer mob, the mining mob. They don't listen to me."

At the end of each day everyone circled up for the Elm Dance, a Lithuanian circle dance Joanna had taught to the people of Novozybkov during a workshop there in 1992, then continued to teach everywhere, so their story would not be forgotten. One smiling elder said, "We hear so many words, some say dig it up, some say leave it in the ground . . . but you fellas must know something real if you dancing!" The pilgrims took messages from the elders to Adelaide, Sydney, Canberra, and Melbourne before crossing the Nullarbor Desert back to Perth. The Elm Dance accompanied them everywhere and was even danced inside Parliament House, Canberra.

SEEDS FOR THE FUTURE

Joanna was keen to devote a full lunar cycle to deep time work, in the context of Aboriginal Tjukurpa in which past, present, and future continuously interact, co-creating the world. Vivienne Elanta, John Croft, Joanna, and Fran dreamed up a thirty-day event, "Seeds for the Future: Training for the Great Turning." Held in January 2005, it was attended by forty-three people from around Australia, the US, Germany, the UK, and Canada. Tragically, Vivienne Elanta died from a brain tumor less than a month before the workshop, absolutely insistent we proceed, her spirit palpably present throughout.

The workshop opened with a "welcome to country" out in the bush by the local Noongar elders. Joanna later wrote:

> There, under the wheeling stars by the southern sea, we felt the power of this planet-time. In our silence, rituals, and role play, we sensed the ancestors and the future ones moving in our midst, encouraging us in the work that is ours to do. In our discussions, we felt the presence of those living now and the magnitude of their manifold efforts on behalf of life. Earth Community became for us not only a promise, but a present reality.
>
> Returned to our daily lives, we call each other *seedlings*. That's what the Great Turning makes of us: seedlings of the future. How can I falter now, with so many hands and hearts at work, and all generations lending their support?[14]

At least one-third of the participants at "Seeds for the Future" were under thirty, assisted to attend by generous scholarships. They included former Wilderness Society and Greenpeace activists Claire Wren Dunn and Emma Pittaway, who took their bodhisattva vows seriously, creating dozens of "Earthworks" workshops over the next five years. Here new generations of people encountered Joanna's work, and younger people joined our "Stillness in Action" retreats.

Young people are still finding the Work That Reconnects though the OzGreen's "Youth Leading the World" workshops, inspired and influenced by both Joanna and Fran Peavey, and through the Deep Ecology work of Bellingen EYE (Environmental Youth Experience), mentored by John Seed and Lisa Siegel. In

2016, the Joyality Program was co-created by Eshana Bragg and the young US activist Rachel Taylor in response to the rates of depression and anxiety experienced by young adults coming of age at this point in human history. There are now twelve accredited facilitators in six countries, sharing these WTR-influenced processes in online and in-person circles.

Joanna's work has been part of most activist training in Australia, including training run by the Australian Student Environmental Network and the Change Agency. Her work was cited as a support for school students in the recent Australian student climate strikes.[15] Tens of thousands of students left their classrooms to participate in these marches around the country, calling for a future for themselves, their children, and the earth.

Joanna's teachings now have even greater significance and are more necessary than ever, as our continent, as with all life on planet Earth, faces a more profound existential crisis in which all our previous challenges—environmental, nuclear, political—are melding into a global perfect storm. At the "Seeds for the Future" training, we made three beautiful ceremonial masks for the archetypes: ancestor, future being, and nonhuman creature from planet Earth. On occasions when our fragile human egos slipped back into the delusion of separate selves, generating conflict, we held circles to talk things through. We took turns stepping out to don one of the three masks. The archetypes watched silently and compassionately as we found our way through and back into connectedness with what really matters. They then spoke with objective, stern kindness of the struggles and courage they had witnessed.

What if these three archetypes could bear witness to every public forum from local halls to parliaments, to the UN, and above all, to climate change negotiations? Could they help us see beyond the hard borders and boundaries we have drawn on the flowing Earth? Could we release the full potency of our human intelligence by learning to think not just like a mountain but like a planet?[16] Perhaps these precious archetypal companions would say to us, "Remember, you are as beautiful—and as smart—as all this. Stand up alive and be committed!"

NOTES

1. Vanessa Bible, *Terania Creek and the Forging of Modern Environmental Activism* (London: Palgrave Pivot, 2018).

2. After securing the Nightcap National Park, he and others went on to take part in protection of the Franklin-Gordon River wilderness in Tasmania and the Daintree Rainforest in northern Queensland, and started the Rainforest Information Centre, https://www.rain forestinfo.org.au.

3. In particular, this drew Christians who had encountered Matthew Fox's writings on Creation Spirituality. Their work continues today among the Sisters of Mercy and Sophia Spring groups within the Uniting Church of Australia.

4. Fran Peavey, *Heart Politics* (Philadelphia: New Society Publishers, 1986), and Fran Peavey, *Heart Politics Revisited* (Australia: Pluto Press, 2000).

5. See *The Bentley Effect*, directed by Brian Shoebridge (Half Smile Productions, 2016), https://www.thebentleyeffect.com.

6. The didgeridoo, or Yidaki, is an Aboriginal wind instrument with a deep and resonant drone sound created by circular breathing.

7. Although examples here are mainly environmental, Australia has always had numerous and diverse activist groups. To see more: http://www.ecoshout.org.au/green-environmental-social-justice-active-groups.

8. In 1995, after a campaign largely run by young mothers and their children, Jo Vallentine was elected as a Nuclear Disarmament Party senator but sat in the Senate as an independent (1985–90), then later as a Western Australia's Greens representative (1990–92).

9. You can feel Joanna's deep time/Deep Ecology work coming through in his memorable Senate speech: https://greensmps.org.au/articles/adjournment-speech-abbott-well-see-you-wa.

10. The first retreats were designed and facilitated by Bobbi, Simon Clough, Isabelle Rogers, Wendy MacRae, and Rohan Stewart. Wendy Macrae, Subhana Barzaghi, and Gilly Coote were the meditation/dharma teachers for the first two years, before Bobbi stepped into that role in 2001. Over the years, other facilitators included Ken McLeod, Glenda Lindsay, Ruth Yeatman, Tathra Street, Leith Maddock, Joan McVilly, Wil Bulmer, Claire Wren Dunn, Emma Pittaway, and Olivia Bernardini. See more at www.stillnessinaction.net.

11. Adapted from David Mowaljarlai and Malnik Jutta, *Yorro Yorro: Everything Standing Up Alive* (Broome, Australia: Magabala Books, 1993), 105.

12. Janet Ristic, ed., *A Journey in Connectedness: A Pilgrimage Project* (London: Gaia Foundation, 2002). Book design by Scott Ludlam, also a gifted graphic and film artist.

13. Recent discoveries are likely to push back the evidence of Aboriginal life on the continent to 120,000 years. Bruce R. Fenton, "Archaeology Places Humans in Australia 120,000 Years Ago," Ancient News, March 11, 2019, http://ancientnews.net/2019/03/11/archaeology-places-humans-in-australia-120000-years-ago.

14. Joanna Macy, "The Great Turning as Compass and Lens," *Yes! A Journal of Positive Futures* (Summer 2006): 44–46.

15. Adrienne Hunt, "Political Change, Not Climate Change: How Australians Can Overcome Climate Denial," *Sydney Environment Institute* (blog), University of Sydney, March 15, 2019, http://sydney.edu.au/environment-institute/blog/political-change-not-climate-change-australians-can-overcome-climate-denial.

16. Ken McLeod, formerly a facilitator on Stillness in Action retreats and now convenor of the Anthropocene Project, https://iiraorg.com/2018/10/21/learning-to-think-like-a-planet.

HOUSEGUEST

Catherine Johnson

SHE INVITED HERSELF, AT LEAST that's what I remember. It was during a spring phone call that Joanna proposed she stay with us for a few days in August in between workshops she had scheduled here in the Northwest. "Yes, yes," we said. "Of course," and "We can't wait." At the time, her visit seemed a long way off, but it arrived in a blink, and we found ourselves madly preparing.

For us, summer is a time devoted more to the needs of the garden than the home. Planting, weeding, thinning, and harvesting take priority over laundry, dishes, and housecleaning. However, on behalf of Joanna, the garden would wait.

We started by cleaning the house as if the queen of some mystical and verdant land were on the way. We beat the rugs and scrubbed the floors, which hadn't seen a mop in months. We fluffed and buffed, aired and washed everything, both in and out of sight. This was in part because of Joanna's respiratory sensitivities, in part to honor the gift of her presence in our home, and because the place simply needed it.

Just when it seemed we were ready to welcome her, we realized our bathhouse posed a serious hazard. For five years we had been entering and exiting the small outbuilding by stepping on a tottering stack of rotting wooden pallets. While this is not a good idea for two women in their sixties, it is definitely not a good idea for a woman in her eighties. We called a carpenter friend and begged the favor. "Steps and railing, tomorrow, before noon?"

After explaining who Joanna was (queen of a mystical and verdant land) and why we were so urgent, (she's arriving—tomorrow!) our friend agreed. He showed up as promised, early the next morning, with coffee in hand. As we left to pick up Joanna at the ferry, he was finishing a nice set of cedar steps with a sturdy railing.

Dana and I live on a rural island in the central basin of the Salish Sea. Our house is situated on two acres. Half of it is open, planted in vegetable gardens, the other half is forested. It's a beautiful and quiet place. Once a workman paused at his truck, looked around and said, "I got me some peace here." We hoped Joanna would too. It is a privilege to offer hospitality to another, especially to one, who through her work, her teaching, and her person has given me and many others so much. (Hospitality comes from the Latin *hospes*, which recognizes the natural reciprocity of the host-guest relationship.)

When the ferry docked, Joanna walked off smiling broadly. She wore a wide-brimmed canvas hat tipped at a rakish angle. In one hand she grasped a walking stick, in the other she pulled a small roller bag. She could have been any elder traveling, but she was our Joanna! We were thrilled to see her. As I hugged her I could feel both her fragile frame and her surprising strength, and although she is often cold, I felt her great warmth as well. After the hug, Joanna stepped back and simply looked at me, her smile softer, her gaze steady. This was not a workshop exercise—this was Joanna the woman, seeing in the other their suffering, their courage, their failings, and their potential. To be greeted and recognized in such a way is a blessing, a call to remember our shared humanity, our deep interconnectedness with each other and all things. The moment between us lasted only a couple of seconds, but it felt timeless. Then we piled into our (also very clean) car and drove down the island toward home.

When I remember that August visit, Joanna is most often outside. I recall her sitting contentedly on a bench by the bathhouse with our small flock of chickens curiously clucking and scratching around her. She, in turn, spoke to them in a delighted and slightly bemused voice—a deep interspecies conversation, no doubt. At other times we saw her out in the old orchard where the late summer light was dappled, the grass golden, and the fruit just beginning to blush. She often had a book open in her lap, alternating between fits of note scribbling and long moments of staring into the distance. Was she thinking, or listening, maybe meditating? Who knows? And on more than one occasion, we glimpsed her there with head slightly bowed, napping. Joanna was indeed at peace here.

We shared wonderful meals together, Joanna always praising the bounty gleaned from the garden, and talked at length about her work and the state of the world. She brought copies of an academic paper (she often does) for us to read and then talk over. Joanna has a brilliant mind. You can almost see the wheels inside her head turn as she talks her way toward a more thorough understanding of an idea. Sometimes these conversations would last for a couple of hours, with Joanna doing most of the talking. Then, when the conversations were finished, she would sincerely thank us for our "help," which I always found dear, because she is the one who did all the heavy lifting.

When we taught Joanna our favorite card game, a funny and very irreverent side of her emerged. She picked up the game instantly and started beating us with glee. Our card game involves card names. Joanna chose her own—Sweet Mouth. And since our card game also includes permission to swear with gusto, her name choice may have been prescient. I don't remember hearing Sweet Mouth swear, but I do remember her playing with ruthless cunning, literally sweeping up the tricks and the points. It appears that Shambhala warriors not only wield the swords of compassion and insight but also carry the concealed dagger of card-playing acumen.

Joanna was the easiest of houseguests. She needed no entertaining, no special treatment, although we longed to give her some. A little breakfast (cereal or soft-boiled egg), a place to read (garden bench or easy chair), an occasional walk (beach or forest), a bed for rest, and a simple supper with time for conversation was all she wanted. Those few days together that summer will stay with me always. While I have learned a great deal from Joanna the teacher, I have been most deeply moved by Joanna the person. Over the years I have witnessed her delight in small children, her generous sharing of her work, her loyalty to her family and friends, and most of all, to Earth herself. Whenever I am with Joanna, I feel nourished in some deep place that I didn't know was hungry.

Our planet is in dire straits. Sometimes I feel lost, impotent, and very sad. But if I go outside and allow the mystery and beauty of creation to fill me, I am comforted. We are all Earth beings who need one another, and we especially need those teachers and elders who can help us navigate these desperate times. If joy is the other side of the coin of sorrow, then wonder must be the other side of despair. Joanna Macy is both a wonder and a joy.

After the 2016 presidential election, Dana and I were, like at least half the American electorate, stunned by the outcome. As the days passed, our incredulousness gave way to righteous anger. We discussed moving to Canada. We wrote letters to our representatives in Congress, complaining bitterly and urging their resistance. We truly feared we were losing everything we had gained.

One night, in a fit of postelection desperation, Dana called Joanna to commiserate. Joanna listened patiently as this went on for some time. Then finally she responded, "Well, you wouldn't want your loved ones to go through this without you, would you?" Bingo! Pure Joanna: smart, funny, practical, yet offering a star to steer by, or at least a way to "sustain the gaze," as she often says, in the face of hopelessness and despair. Dana scribbled Joanna's words on a piece of scratch paper and stuck it with a magnet to the refrigerator door, where it still hangs. It helps us keep our bearings.

Joanna Macy near her home in Berkeley in 1987.

PART TWO

SUSTAINING THE GAZE

The practice field of grief and despair is wide and unending in this era of climate change, consumerism, species extinction, poverty, and environmental injustice of all scales. For Joanna, grief and despair are constant companions in facing the world as it is. In being with the pain and suffering, we see what it asks of us. We see, as Joanna says, that "we only mourn what we love," and thus the depths of our dark emotions reveal the depths of our longing for intimacy and healing. By honoring these strong feeling states, we find a path of transformation, allowing the energy that has been stuck to move toward action.

In her stories of awakening, Joanna takes us to her own darkest moments and how she finds a path forward through sharing that anguish with others. At a workshop in Germany, she invents on the spot a powerful exercise to allow the full expression of fear, anger, grief, and despair. She speaks of "sustaining the gaze" and voicing the truth of what we see unfolding, disturbing as it is—from climate disasters to toxic pollution. As writer after writer testifies, by working with others we experience our collective nature—what Joanna says is "the only thing that can save us."

This powerful work gained early traction in Germany just as the Berlin Wall was coming down. What became known as Deep Ecology work took hold in the midst of nuclear threats and a divided culture. Joanna came to appreciate the sober realism of a country that had experienced extremist fascism and an unimaginable holocaust. Her work catalyzed a response to counter the pressure to keep silent and not resist. In Colombia such silence is reinforced by linked oppression of land and people, and Joanna's work has become a tool for liberation from tremendous suffering.

The writing in this section is vivid, personal, inspirational, and sometimes difficult to read. Climate scientist Susi Moser and climate journalist Dahr Jamail testify to their experiences in the field, facing denial and repudiation of well-proven facts. Installation artist Beverly Naidus uses participatory art to draw people in to express their fears related to nuclear waste and weapons. Anita Barrows brings forth the timeless beauty and wisdom in thought-provoking words from Rainer Maria Rilke, a beloved favorite of Macy's. In Colombia, Helena ter Ellen invites the voices of indigenous elders into the circle of reconciliation, calling on ancestral knowledge for these challenging times.

For Joanna, this legacy of facing pain with courage and honesty is all part of building a network of resilience. She draws on a Buddhist understanding of emotions as impermanent expressions of strong energy, available for transformation into positive action. Through ceremony, ritual, and reflection, the work leads people to speak what must be spoken, and to remember at the deepest levels the "thrumming relationality of all things."

—STEPHANIE KAZA

THUNDERCLAP

Joanna Macy

IN FALL 1976, JACK LEFT FOR Tufts University to study environmental engineering. When he came home for the holiday break at the end of his first semester, he handed me a term paper he had written for a freshmen course. The title was "Thermal Pollution from Nuclear Reactors." I embarked upon it dutifully, wading through statistics and footnotes about the volumes of water being cycled continuously through American nuclear power stations to cool their cores. Then sheer fascination took over, as Jack detailed the impacts of the heated water when it is pumped back into our rivers, lakes, and offshore waters. "This can't be true," I protested in disbelief. "Fishermen and marine biologists would be taking to the streets!" "And Mom, those are only the *thermal* effects of nuclear power. I didn't mention the radioactivity." I began then and there to receive from Jack an education in nuclear power that would change my life.

The following spring, in May 1977, I drove to Boston with Peggy, now a sophomore in high school, for a weekend visit with Jack. He showed us around the Tufts campus, took us to his favorite Indian restaurant, and told us that he had gotten us tickets for a big event the next day. The Cousteau Society was staging an all-day symposium on threats to the biosphere. We gulped down breakfast and caught the T in Cambridge, crossing the Charles River in time for the morning program at the Boston Coliseum. All morning we listened to a dizzying array of speakers, including Jacques-Yves

71

Cousteau himself, interspersed with the music of John Denver. We spent the afternoon moving from one exhibit to another, from briefings and workshops to panel discussions by scientists and activists. It was an immense bazaar of apocalyptic information, backed up with firsthand reports, film clips, and volumes of data.

By late afternoon I was exhausted, my feet hurt. Peggy and Jack were staying on for an evening concert, and before heading back I slipped off to sink into a chair in a darkened alcove. No one else was there, but on the screen a film about the fur trade was playing over and over. I watched in a daze as a man in a cowboy hat, a baby seal wedged tight between his boots, slowly and methodically clubbed it to death. It was horrifying, but part of the horror of it was his skill and care in aiming his blows to keep the blood from staining the fur while staying relaxed enough to stop for a cigarette. I leaned forward to try to see the mouth and eyes of this Marlboro man under his broad-brimmed hat. I peered at his features as if to catch my own reflection in some kind of collective mirror. For, I thought, he was *all* of us. Weren't we all, in the ways we lived and consumed, complicit in wasting our world?

As I headed back on the T to Cambridge, I gazed past the passengers on the opposite bench to the windows behind them and watched the train emerge into evening light as it crossed the bridge. It was an idyllic scene, the sunset gleaming on the broad expanse of the Charles, sailboats heeling into the wind and light. At that moment something gave way inside me. I found myself looking at the faces across the aisle through tears I was powerless to hide or stop.

It felt like the collapse of some inner scaffolding that for years had been holding the kind of information that I had been hearing all day. As that scaffolding crumbled, years of stored knowledge about what we humans are doing to our planet and

to ourselves cascaded into my heart and body, bringing a realization I could no longer keep at bay. *Yes—we can do it now, we can
destroy our world.* Hadn't every exhibit of the day demonstrated
that? Hadn't that knowledge been lurking all along in every sight
of streaming smokestacks and clearcut forests? That knowledge
came out of hiding now, and I had no idea how to live with it.

Over the coming weeks and months, it would return at odd
moments, like a blow to the solar plexus. The most ordinary
things—the slamming of a screen door, the smell of mown grass—
made tears blur my eyes. After the dark epiphany on the T, I hid
my despair from my family, afraid they would worry about me.
When I tried to share it with my colleagues in the Syracuse religion department, their responses were both avoiding and patron-
izing. I felt like the sole victim of a unique and nameless disease
with no one to share and compare symptoms. *What do I do with
this suffering? What good is it?* Later, of course, I learned that I was
far from alone. Others, too, carried this dread-filled grief like a
hidden ulcer, this sorrow for our world.

The summer of the following year, 1978, my dissertation completed and defended, Fran joined me to attend a conference at Notre Dame in Indiana. I had been asked to chair a working group
at a meeting of the Society for Values in Higher Education. The
name of the group was "The Human Prospect." Preparing for it
helped me focus on the planetary perils that had silently gripped
me since that day at the Cousteau symposium.

Some thirty or so men and women, faculty and administrators in higher education, gathered for that first morning of our
weeklong group. Because I could not bear to hear people identify
themselves by their rank and academic credentials, I broke with
convention and said, "Please introduce yourself by sharing an image or an experience of a moment when you felt the planetary crisis

impinge on your own life." The brief introductions that followed were potent as those present spoke simply, poignantly of what they saw happening to their world, of their fears and discouragement, of their children. That brief sharing transformed the seminar. It came to me like a thunderclap—"Oh my God, the suffering can be spoken!"

This breakthrough brought us close together, unleashing creative energy and mutual caring. Sessions went overtime, laced with hilarity and punctuated with plans for future projects. Some kind of magic had happened. Late one night, as a group of us talked, a name for that magic emerged: despair work. That night in the dormitory basement, next to a humming soda machine, while Fran was asleep in our bed, I stayed up for hours writing, the words flowing through me as I opened to what despair work could be: "Just as grief work is a process by which bereaved persons un-block their numbed energies by acknowledging and grieving the loss of a loved one, so do we all need to unblock our feelings about our threatened planet and the possible demise of our species. Un-til we do, our power of creative response will be crippled."

The dark passage that had begun over a year before, that I'd suffered in silence, had brought me to the discovery that our de-spair, when shared, delivers us to a new kind of humanity. It gives us new eyes to be able to look at what is happening in our world *together*. I knew then that my grief and despair would be my close companions and gateway to my work for decades to come.

THE FIRST TRUTH MANDALA

Joanna Macy

EARLY IN THE FALL OF 1990, I returned to Germany, to the hill town of Kronberg not far from Frankfurt, for an intensive in Deep Ecology work, as it was known then. I loved this land; its language and people evoked something deep in me. For four years in the 1950s we had lived in Munich, where our second son, Jack, was born, and where the poetry of Rilke began to infuse my life.

In 1983, the year the US installed nuclear warheads and missiles on West German soil, it galvanized a vigorous peace movement. Bea Fröhlich, a peace activist and psychotherapist in Hamburg, translated my first despair work article. She began making a hundred copies at a time, which she took with her to the many meetings and conferences she attended. She also took them into Soviet-controlled East Germany by way of subway from West Berlin. It was an auspicious introduction of despair work to this land cut in half by the Iron Curtain. I found a strong response when I came in 1986 on a workshop tour of West German cities, including West Berlin. I remember one former SS officer voicing his shame and guilt, and I recall my own response to his words: "It is easier for me to respect people who know they produced a Hitler than a nation so convinced of its innocence it imagines it could never produce one."

From the beginning of my work with the Germans I respected their readiness to face their moral pain over their Nazi past. Our despair work was an antidote to the avoidance and silence of the previous generation, and they responded with their deepest feelings. As a result, I seem to have been more creative in Germany than almost anywhere else, inventing processes as grave as the Death Walk and as silly as the Bodhisattva Competition for overcoming excessive modesty.

Four years later in Kronberg, 1990, a robust group from my first tour came to assist me in a ten-day intensive. Among the eighty participants, a half dozen had come from East Germany where they had lived under the most repressive of the Soviet satellite regimes. As we got going, I could see the East Germans found it hard to relax, tense and tighter than the West Germans who had been exposed to New Age thinking in the West. What did open them up was a Council of All Beings, where they could talk more freely in the voice of another life form.

It so happened that partway through the intensive, the night skies lit up and resounded with fireworks to celebrate the first anniversary of the reunification of East and West Germany. The next morning, I had prepared carefully and was eager to get started. However, as I walked into the room, I found everyone in a clamor, talking loudly at each other and too upset to proceed in our customary way. The official celebrations of reunification had triggered painful feelings and resentments. I saw pretty quickly that we all needed to find a way to deal with feelings of bitterness and disappointment without turning on one another. For that we needed some kind of ritual.

Out of the corner of my eye, I saw someone walk in with an unusual object—a large tuft of grass growing out of a cement block. Instantly I heard myself say, "Objects for the feelings . . . *wahrheit* mandala . . . a truth mandala." I announced to the group that we would be doing a Truth Mandala, speaking the formal name as if it were something venerable that had existed prior to that very moment.

I had everyone sit in a small circle several people thick, enclosing a round, open space. "We will make thick walls like the walls of a containment vessel of a nuclear reactor to hold the sacred space, and we will make this space sacred by truth-telling. Here we will enter a new dimension, made sacred by truth-telling, assisted by objects we will place in this circle." In the quadrants formed by two intersecting invisible lines, I placed a stone for fear, a pile of dead leaves for grief, a stick for anger, and the grass for hope. I explained that we will support one another as we enter one at a time, take an object, and let it speak through us to express our thoughts and feelings.

In that moment, Mummy's teachings were there for me. I knew our feelings were strong yet impermanent, and as they are openly expressed, we have less need to hang on to them. Rapidly I invented guidelines. "Only enter the mandala if you want to. Keep it brief. Speak for yourself only. To show you are listening, you can murmur in refrain after each person has spoken. *Ich höre dich, ich bin mit dir* [I hear you, I am with you]."

After chanting the seed syllable AH, representing all that has not yet been spoken, we opened our Truth Mandala. As it was new for each of us, I expected there would be quite a spell before things got under way, but with hardly a pause there they were, rising and stepping into the circle to take up an object. One veteran facilitator of the Work grabbed the chance to speak, eager to release his anger: "I have been working for reunification my whole damn life . . . and now that it has happened, it looks like the triumph of capitalism. Where does a socialist like me go? I feel I don't belong in this country anymore."

I remember the words of an East German woman, born under the Soviet regime. She had spoken in the Council of All Beings as a dolphin in a tank of water, with people watching her and no place to escape: "I have been organizing for years, risking my life in hopes of reunification, to tear down the curtain . . . but I certainly didn't want my village to become a golf course."

Though I had invited this ritual, I could in no way have anticipated the power and beauty I experienced in these men and women after forty years of separation and hostility. We discovered that not only could we tolerate but we even welcomed the intensity of one another's feelings. I drew the ritual to a close, naming the source or tantric side of each painful emotion expressed in the mandala. "Our sorrow is in equal measure our love," I said, picking up some dead leaves, "for we only mourn what we love." Similarly, I spoke of courage as the tantric side of fear and passion for justice as the tantric expression of anger. In subsequent rituals, we replaced the concrete block with an empty bowl, its emptiness permitting us to speak to our inadequacy and allow space for the new to arise. Hope in its turn became the very ground on which we practice.

Today, thirty years now after that morning in Kronberg, the ritual spreads ever more swiftly through different countries and cultures. I cannot hear the voices, but I can imagine the faces, their rapt attention around the circle, and I can feel the listeners' deepening patience and respect. I can sense the relief of being heard and of hearing, at last, one's own voice speak what only it can speak.

TO BEHOLD WORLDS ENDING

Susanne Moser

THE YEAR I SETTLED INTO THE CIRCLE of my first Truth Mandala, Joanna Macy had long since published her first book of Rilke poems, translated with Anita Barrows. Reciting from heart, Joanna invoked one of his poems, "Go to the limits of your longing," and thus led us into what was to become one of the most profound experiences of my life. She spoke it not in English but in the original German. I imagine that my fellow workshop participants sitting there cross-legged on the floor heard her intoning a guttural sense of what was to come. A foreboding, sensed somewhere in the body.

Little did she know she was speaking in my mother tongue. I understood every word she was saying, in German and in a language older than words:

> *Laß dir alles geschehen: Schönheit und Schrecken.*
> *Man muß nur gehen. Kein Gefühl ist das fernste.*
> Let everything happen to you: beauty and terror.
> Just keep going. No feeling is final.[1]

What unfolded in the next hour and a half was just that—beauty and terror. The beauty of some thirty people speaking their truths, expressing their emotions in stance, body, gesture, and voice; in tears, agony, silence, and wailing. The beauty, also, of finding myself no longer alone with the immensity of my visceral experience of the dying world. And yes, the terror of saying

79

that out loud. The terror of hearing so much unspeakable truth being expressed. That day was the one-year anniversary of 9/11.

Truth be told, little even did I know she was speaking in my mother tongue—that deeper language. I only sensed the most superficial level of what she was saying that day. But here I was, a scientist trained in the ways of the planet and the ways of humans treading on it, still in the early days of my professional becoming, yet well socialized into the dissociation of our feelings from facts that we scientists call "objectivity." And here was someone arguing that this dismissal and suppression of our feelings about the state of the world is as sick and disastrous and consequential as any blind dissociation. Here was someone utterly believable suggesting that experiencing our pain for the world—however grievous— would free us and reconnect us to our innate ability to work more energetically and effectively for the preservation of what we loved.

> Nearby is the country they call life.
> You will know it by its seriousness.[2]

Her invitation was nothing short of a lure off the cliff. The "safety" I thought I had a firm foothold in was my professional identity, my only "capital" in science and policy debates (namely, untainted, unassailable, allegedly value-free credibility), and some notion of what I thought I could bear without losing my sanity.

I don't recall much else about the Truth Mandala that day. I remember there being a stick, a rock, some leaves, and an empty bowl at the center. I remember that terrible silence before it all began. And then it did. For some, it was the crushing of human bodies under the weight of two toppled towers; for others, it was the carpet-bombing of Baghdad; for yet others, it was the corruption underpinning deforestation. For me, it was climate change.

Not just because as a geographer and climate communication expert it was my field of study, but because to me it encompassed and epitomized practically all other forms of human destruction of the environment. At the heart of my grief was the nearly inconceivable degree of suffering we are creating for ourselves and the more-than-human beings on Earth. *Give me your hand,* implored Joanna. And I did. My heart's imagination of all that was ending by our hand was coming unhinged. That day, I cried over a plate of dry leaves until they nearly dissolved.

WORLDS ENDING

Joanna Macy's life of nine decades on planet Earth has spanned so many endings, but none so grave and ultimate as the threat of nuclear annihilation and the destruction of Earth's life-support system—its biota, climate, waters, and soils. She entered the public sphere through the door of the nuclear threat and remains a ringing bell tower on climate change. At a time when the *Bulletin of Atomic Scientists'* doomsday clock is set to two minutes before midnight precisely because of those two existential threats, the specter of not just our one world but of oh-so-many worlds ending is as or even more acute than it was when Joanna first began looking these threats straight in the eye.

But even a symbol as ominous as the hands of a clock approaching midnight barely conveys the gravity of what it is saying. In some ways, only naming the real thing in its horrendous factuality will do. And maybe calling the unfolding grim reality by new names, as the journalist David Wallace-Wells does in *The Uninhabitable Earth,* has a similar effect. He calls us to pay attention by introducing words to describe a heretofore unfamiliar, climate-altered world, such as *hidden hunger* for food that has lost essential micronutrients due to too much carbon dioxide in the atmosphere, or *airpocalypse* for deadly air pollution in mega-cities around the world. Joanna insists—with a faith and clarity that only comes from lived wisdom—that our human hearts are indeed big enough and strong enough to bear witness to these endings.

As a daily consumer of science, I've had to consider that, whether or not we ultimately cause the end of our own species, we are already responsible for the endings of so many of our brother and sister species on Earth. We are fundamentally altering the climate system and thus the living conditions on our planet. Already we hear so much less birdsong than when I was born. (Rachel Carson's *Silent Spring* is indeed unfolding.) Already, due to climatic shifts, habitat destruction and pesticide use, there is a drastic diminishment of insects, and I myself regularly shun consideration of how precarious, in their absence, is the food system that results in meals on my table. How long has it been since last we paid attention to the list of critically endangered species, made longer every year by changed seasons, temperature extremes, and too much or too little rain? How many cities can I bear being burned to the ground? How ready am I really to imagine the end of meltwater from Himalayan glaciers for the one billion people downstream in China, India, Bangladesh, and Pakistan?

In my work on emotional responses to climate change, and also as a conscientious consumer, I have had to consider the ending of entire landscapes as mountains are flattened, as scars the size of small countries are carved into plains whose oil riches we extract. In my work on climate adaptation, I face some new story nearly every day: shorelines vanishing under the ocean, homeowners realizing their life's biggest investment will soon be worthless, ancestral burial grounds being lost as coastal erosion takes the bones and throws them into the rising sea. And all of us who believe ourselves protected at a safe distance, on higher ground, will come to learn what Joanna has taught all along—the radical interrelatedness of all beings and all things. We will find that whatever safety—real or imagined—we thought would guard us from the physics of reality, will fall away and leave us naked.

As a communication expert attempting to support communities moving forward, I continue to struggle to find ways to say that the endings won't stop there, because they are not only physical, visible, audible, and tangible. A growing number of writers now suggest that the endings will also include the end of our sense of power over our fates, the end of our sense of control over much of anything. They will encompass the end of our heretofore unshaken belief that there will be a future, that lineages of family will go on unbroken into the future, forever.

None of us are guaranteed to be spared any of these endings, and certainly none—ultimately—will be spared profoundly personal, even existential questions. For many years, the question I carried was: *What is meaningful work on the way down?* I have witnessed others struggle with whether to bring children into the world we are creating. While some have arrived at a solid no, concluding that it's too late to prevent abysmal changes on Earth, others proceed with caution, honoring new life in the face of enormous risk and uncertainty. They all, one way or another, ask the penultimate moral questions: *How then shall we live? And how have we lived?*

Joanna Macy never pretends that these endings—and the questions they raise—won't break our hearts. Instead, she calls it the great wisdom of the heart to break under the weight of such knowing. In 2016, in an interview with *On Being* host Krista

Tippett, Joanna reassured us, "It is okay for our hearts to be broken over the world. What else are hearts for? There is great intelligence in that."

THE INTELLIGENCE OF GRIEF

"Flare up like a flame," Rilke demands, because it creates a shadowed space big enough for God to move in. It creates a space big enough for all of us to move in—that is, to move again after the paralysis caused by suppressed emotions. At the most basic level, Joanna Macy's insistence on and mastery of despair work can be seen as a contribution to movement building and movement sustenance in the literal and metaphorical sense. In responses to my own writing, to my speeches, and in the climate dialogues I have facilitated, I see over and over again that truth-telling—and the honorable embrace of our emotional responses to this unfolding truth—helps individuals, groups, and entire movements maintain their psychological well-being and energy. This frees their powers to persist in the three dimensions of the Great Turning—holding actions that prevent further loss and destruction, dismantling old structures and building alternative ones, and doing the deep work of changing consciousness.

From this perspective, the practices and rituals Joanna offers are instrumental: they help us release the internal energy pent up in avoidance and suppression and make it available to the external work that needs to be done. What's more, they help us reconnect with our love for the world and open us to grief. As a researcher of the psychological responses to climate change, I am observing a rapidly rising interest among researchers and others in *climate grief*—the reactive and anticipatory mourning of all we are losing due to the disruption of our climate. It is as if the losses directly or vicariously experienced from the growing number of devastating disasters is a terrible wake-up call, the gateway into the difficult process of reconnecting with the larger body of Earth from which we have become so estranged. Grief in this way brings us alive again; grief of our climate-driven losses returns us to the treasure of life itself. From this place, we see with new eyes and go forth to do what we can with renewed energy and appreciation for whatever time we have left.

Yet there is a deeper intelligence in grief and despair work that Joanna embodies in her own self. Over the years, I have come to view this intelligence as countercultural and profoundly courageous. Courage is what it takes to honor psyche in a world—and not only in a world of science but certainly there!—that diminishes, dismisses, silences, pathologizes, or ignores earnest emotional responses to existential risk. Three hundred years after the Enlightenment, which gave reason primacy over all forms of human expressions, we scientists still take pride in distancing ourselves from our objects of study; we claim that our work is free of values and traits chauvinistically associated with the feminine. Feelings clearly do not belong in such an enterprise, even though such insistence ignores the findings of neuroscience, which show how cognition and emotion are *functionally* implicated in each other. Traditional positivist science insists that knowing can only come by way of frontal-cortex activity, and only by using tangible data turned into meaning by logic, and logic alone. This science has declared itself the holder of Truth, even if that truth consists only of part—the smaller part—of the whole picture.

Joanna Macy—trained in systems science *and* the humanities—insists on the wholeness and indivisibility of reality and thus knows emotion to be a matter of concern to science and to the humans conducting that science. This is remedial not just in an additive sense but in a confrontational sense, demanding that we revisit the question of *how* we know the world and *what* and *whose* knowledge counts. As such, it is countercultural to the core of the Western mind-set (and probably beyond), and we ignore it at our peril!

In my own work—in part dedicated to disturbing traditional science with these insights—I have brought the importance of emotions in response to climate change to the fore of social scientific debates about why individuals and society fail to respond adequately to the overwhelming reality of human-caused climate change. In peer-reviewed publications, keynote addresses, communication trainings, and most recently in efforts to build psychosocial support for individuals working to serve climate-impacted communities, I have insisted on grief work because I see the need for it growing everywhere. Overwhelm, numbing, apathy, and burnout are spreading just at the moment when we most need people to be present to one another and take life-saving action. What some call an "irrational" response and thus relegate to the shadows of societally (and particularly professionally) acceptable experience is in fact an utterly rational, appropriate, and vital sign that we humans are aware of what is happening. We are afraid, in grief, and in despair. Underneath is our love for this planet, even if we have become estranged, and we do not want to lose it. Writers across the social sciences are finally now recognizing the mobilizing force of grief, and not a moment too soon.

In this way, Joanna's work with grief and other dark emotions is, finally, and maybe most importantly, transformational. In my ear's memory, I can hear her incant the Rilke poem that begins with the quiet, darkly spoken words *Du dunkelnder Grund*— "Dear darkening ground." The poem is a plea for patience with us humans:

Just give me a little more time!
I want to love the things
As no one has thought to love them,
Until they're real and ripe and worthy of you.[3]

If grief is a measure of our love for life, then grief work at this late hour is the entry point into the deeper transformational work, the redemptive work we humans must undertake. It is far from guaranteed that we will save much, or ourselves, but grief work is inviting us into a new way of being with the world, an intimacy we have forsaken for far too long.

Whether this is a return to a bygone intimacy or an arrival at a heretofore unknown intimacy with one another, our planet, even the cosmos—as Thomas Berry has suggested—is not irrelevant but it may be unanswerable. More importantly, we must embrace this reckoning with the ways we have been, the pain we have inflicted, the harm we have caused in order to come into such intimacy. In that intimacy we will have to confront our personal and collective past with all the traumas we have experienced and imposed on nonhuman nature and one another, including the collective "climate trauma" we are both victims and perpetrators of. This will force us to face our deepest fears, anger, shame, and despair; it will also make us grapple to find a hope and love strong enough for the times ahead. Through it, we may come to appreciate grief work as an opportunity for reconciliation and healing thousands of years overdue, and as such, a grace we scarcely deserve. As ancient cultures, mythologists, theologians, depth psychologists, and, yes, Joanna Macy have long known, it is through such a collective dark night of the soul that we may come to discover humanity's truer purpose here on Earth.

GOING TO THE LIMITS OF OUR LONGING

A year after that first Truth Mandala, I returned to Joanna to be trained in the Work That Reconnects. One evening, after a session I and two other trainees had co-led, she came up to me, looked me in the eyes, and said, more as a command than a question, "Promise me you will do this work!" Speaking to me in a tongue my deeper self understood better than my conscious mind, I answered in the only way I knew how to honor her. It has taken me years to understand what my deeper self knew right away: doing grief and despair work—in whatever ways I have found to do—is love work, is the work of going to the limits of *my* longing.

There is no point in arguing over what Joanna Macy's greatest contribution to our time, to this kairos, has been. But putting her finger on the fact that we have—almost—lost it, and how unspeakably painful that is, must be among them. She would ask us not to stop here but to keep going. To go to the limits of our longing.

NOTES

1. Rainer Maria Rilke, *Die gedichte* (Frankfurt am Main: Insel Verlag, 1986), 240. The English translation is from Anita Barrows and Joanna Macy, *Rilke's Book of Hours: Love Poems to God* (New York: Riverhead Books, 1996), 88.
2. Rilke, *Die gedichte*, 88.
3. Rilke, *Die gedichte*, 91.

THE THRUMMING RELATIONALITY OF ALL THINGS

Andy Fisher

IN ECOPSYCHOLOGICAL CIRCLES, Joanna Macy's presence is everywhere; it is hard to imagine the field without her. My own reflections on her place in ecopsychology cannot be anything other than one of many possible story lines. For me, she has been a key source of sharp and courageous ideas exactly attuned to our perilous times. But more than this, she has been a major role model and living inspiration, walking with the likes of Rachel Carson and Gautama Buddha—all those wise ones who have gone before, teaching the noble things we still urgently need to learn today.

I can't remember just how I came upon Joanna's work, but I do remember the first thing of hers that I read: "Buddhist Resources for Confronting Nuclear Death."[1] I had recently left a career in environmental engineering. I was quite depressed and found myself looking for something deeper in life than helping developers get past environmental regulations. I figured that someone teaching us how to keep breathing while facing nuclear annihilation would be an important source for whatever it was that I was trying to develop.

What I was trying to develop, in my own fumbling way, was ecopsychology. I began graduate work in environmental studies in 1990, having discovered the radical ecology movement and then committing myself to building up its psychological wing. Indeed, the idea of ecopsychology was much in the air around this time. Theodore Roszak's book *The Voice of the Earth: An Exploration of Ecopsychology* came out in 1992, introducing this new *eco*-word to the world. Shortly thereafter, in 1995, the *Ecopsychology* primer, edited by Roszak, Mary E. Gomes, and Allen D. Kanner, spread it even more widely. These were heady days for ecopsychology—"a new beginning for the environmental movement and a revolution in modern psychology," Roszak called it—but what, precisely, was it?

In trying to get a handle on this nebulous new field, the editors of the *Ecopsychology* primer looked around for authors already doing something akin to what ecopsychology might be. This was ecopsychology as a cast of characters, Joanna being one of the main players, along with others such as Paul Shepard, David Abram, Sarah Conn, Carl Anthony, Jeannette Armstrong, James Hillman, Robert Greenway, and Chellis Glendinning. In Joanna's chapter in *Ecopsychology*, drawn from her 1983 book *Despair and Personal Power in the Nuclear Age*, she calls the loss of certainty in the ongoingness of life on Earth "the pivotal psychological reality of our time"[2]—a line that made it inevitable her work would be part of the body of ecopsychology. Tellingly, this chapter was one of the most popular readings in a course on ecopsychology I taught for a number of years at the University of Vermont. It spoke so directly and truthfully to the emotional and spiritual reality the students were experiencing. "Why," they asked, "haven't we heard anything like this before now?"

The answer, of course, lay in Joanna's ideas themselves. As she has been saying for decades, our society pathologizes and numbs painful emotion, most especially our pain for the world. It is no wonder university professors aren't talking about it—nobody is. This is an important area where I think Joanna's work reflects a defining characteristic of ecopsychology: the recollection of modes of experience that connect us to nature. Every society shapes its members into a personality structure congruent with the continuation of that society. In an eco-destructive society, this means we are forced to repress or marginalize the wrenching pain we feel over the wasting of the earth in order to be the cheerful consumers of it. But other modes of experience must be marginalized as well—such as the earth-loving, ritualistic, and heart-centered ways of being that are cultivated by the practices in the Work That Reconnects. By recollecting such ways, we are "coming back to life"—as good a basic definition of ecopsychology as any. In my ecopsychology course, I learned to make more space for students to have just these kinds of experiences, not because of any particular wisdom on my part but because the students themselves often told me they got more from this aspect of the course than they did from my big ideas.

There is another line from Joanna's chapter in *Ecopsychology* that has stood the test of time: "As a society we are caught between a sense of impending apocalypse and the fear of acknowledging it."[3] Today, climate chaos, mass extinction, plastic insanity, and other signs of impending apocalypse are that much more real. And the dilemma Joanna identified is now being framed as that between either developing "*pre*-traumatic stress disorder" from facing reality (to use the psychiatrist Lise Van Susteren's term) or using various forms of psychological protection, such as denial or magical thinking, in order to block reality. Though awareness of this dilemma is growing, it remains true that, as Joanna put it three decades ago, "Unless you have some roots in a spiritual practice that holds life sacred and encourages joyful communion with all your fellow beings, facing the enormous challenges ahead becomes nearly impossible."[4] This is crucial. The little-recognized answer to the grave emotional dilemma of our times, in other words, is ecospiritual development. Building the capacity within our society to face the mess we're in, to do this without going crazy, indeed to find the deepest possible meaning and joy in it, is something that ecopsychology, too, must stand for—and I think the example Joanna provides with her own life gives us much to go on.

What Joanna's life shows us is a rich model of worldly rather than otherworldly spirituality. If spirituality means escaping or transcending the earth, then it is no spirituality at all. That is why the description of Joanna's work as a synthesis of spirituality and activism doesn't seem quite right to me, for it maintains the implication that spirituality is something necessarily done at a remove from politics. Rather, Joanna has lived a life that makes space for translating poetry and for spiritual education while not retreating from the world—indeed, that views these activities as necessary for a skillful turning toward it. As the poet Rainer Maria Rilke teaches, God is not separate from the world.

Joanna's spirituality is fully in love with the sensuous divinity of earthly life. Because of this, hers is a spirituality unafraid to use terms such as *political economy* and *late capitalist war-making states* in order to identify the forces destroying this sacred earth. Coming back to life, it seems, includes speaking truth to power. Pain for the world is a political phenomenon calling us back to this earth, not a divine punishment prompting us to escape it. I have described ecopsychology as a politics to develop the subjective conditions for an ecological society—to foster, in other words, a new-old kind of subject or human being, one with sufficient psychological, ecological, and political literacy to act as the social agent needed at this epochal moment in history. I can think of no better example of such subjectivity than that given by Joanna's life and her earthbound spiritual politics.

Something else Joanna's work shows us is the radicalness of an ecological understanding of reality. Ecopsychology doesn't always manage to do this, especially when it takes the form of conventional psychology. Joanna's work is emblematic, in this regard, of the first wave of ecopsychology, which maintained more of a connection to the radical traditions in ecology than have later developments in the field aimed at aligning with mainstream psychology. As one of the most eloquent voices in the ecology movement for recognizing the interdependent nature of reality, and as someone whose very being radiates the "thrumming relationality of all things,"[5] Joanna represents for me a constant reminder to keep ecopsychology close to the kind of radical edge she herself has spent a lifetime on. Look into the gleaming eyes of another being, human or other-than-human, she says, look and see: "We're in this great mystery!"

She reminds us to keep bringing it back to this—to the simple, beautiful, profound, radical mutuality of all things. In doing so, she demonstrates the tremendous value of Buddhist psychology as a basis for ecopsychology. In her training DVD, she calls the central Buddhist teaching of dependent co-arising "a teaching for our time." It teaches, for instance, that the "colossal anguish" we all feel is "not an individual matter," and that we must all, with our different gifts, act together for the sake of the Great Turning. When I was trying in the late 1990s to define the practice of ecopsychology, I chose Joanna's work as one of my prime examples precisely because it displays this inherent togetherness of psychospiritual practice and ecological politics.

The practice of ecopsychology can, in one sense, be seen as a program of human development toward the kind of ecologically mature selfhood that will build a more life-centered society. A key way the field envisions and pursues this development is through tending the human life cycle, such that each stage of human *un*folding is simultaneously an *en*folding into the body of this earthly cosmos. As the human ecologist Paul Shepard argued, the failure of this kind of development has much to do with the ecological crisis. The teenage, school-striking Swedish activist Greta Thunberg seems to agree when she says that today's world leaders are acting like children. Not surprisingly, Joanna has made her own remarks along these lines. In my favorite video on her work, she chuckles as she tells us that "if you want to get anywhere, honey, if you want grow up, if you want to open to life, if you want to be enlightened, then you have to learn to befriend suffering." Yes, the ability to thrive while holding and working through dark emotion is a grown-up, ecopsychological skill that Joanna teaches over and over again. But there are two other areas of life-cycle practice that, again, I think she teaches best through the example of her own life.

Perhaps the central task of adolescence is to discern the unique gifts, powers, or genius, the soul-level image or question, that we will incorporate into our adult selves. Knowing our dharma or spiritual duty—to use still other language for this task—is to give our adult life its compass, worth, depth, and place. It is to know how we belong to and serve the whole in our own particular way. Need it be said, very little effort is made in the modern world to help adolescents arrive at this soulful adult place. Quite the opposite, in fact, given how the capitalist system requires that we remain wounded children with limitless desires. Such soul discernment, then, is another crucial life-connecting mode of human experiencing that requires recollection. Like the rest of us, Joanna was not given a hand with this task in her youth. She nonetheless found her own way to complete it, offering us an astonishing example of the power of knowing your dharma. In her life it came as an insistent question: How can I be fully present to my world—present enough to rejoice and be useful while we as a species are engaged in destroying it? The great force of Joanna's life, the reason she has had such enormous influence, comes, we could say, from this courageous question. Imagine a world in which all adolescents were mentored by elders into such a state of spiritual clarity.

Indeed, elderhood is the other pole of the adolescent-elder axis, and here Joanna is our role model one more time. In his book *Nature and the Human Soul*, Bill Plotkin presents an eight-stage model of the human life cycle that incorporates the natural world at each stage—a kind of ecologizing of developmental psychology. Among the small handful of candidates he identified to use as examples for the stage of early elderhood, Plotkin chose Joanna, not only because she fully expresses (then in her late seventies) the qualities of this life stage but also because she holds out to the world the inspiring image of the Great Turning. From my own perspective, the fact that Joanna so exemplifies an ecologically mature, fully lived life would all by itself give her a special place in ecopsychology.

One last place I would like to tie Joanna's lifework to ecopsychology is in her recent comments about anti-oppression work within the Work That Reconnects. Because I wrote a book called *Radical Ecopsychology*, I make a point when I am teaching to clarify just what I mean by the word *radical*. I underscore, in particular, that the least recognized dimension of radicalism is probably the practice of *reflexivity*, which means reflecting on how our own social position, biases, interests, and personality are implicated in our ideas and actions. It means being open to critical feedback from others about how we are not sufficiently awake, accountable, historically informed, or in solidarity. Joanna has openly welcomed and herself given voice to this process: "I myself acknowledge that my privilege has impacted the formation and facilitation of [the Work That Reconnects]. I deeply regret any harm that has ensued. I apologize to each person who has been hurt by my facilitation and/or by the practices I have created."[6] Here, too, then, I turn to Joanna for a living example of what I hope ecopsychology could look like.

Ecopsychology's subject matter is the human-nature relationship, but this relationship does not occur in some pure space. Rather, it is complexly entwined with all the intersecting social issues—white supremacy, heteropatriarchy, classism, colonialism, Eurocentrism, and so on—that form the unfinished business of human history. Perhaps the recent deepening of a reflexive practice within the Work That Reconnects, a movement so close to ecopsychology, will be paralleled by a productive unsettling of ecopsychology more broadly considered.

I will finish with a brief story. As I was leading a training in ecopsychology a few months ago, my grief for the earth, for the enormous pain we all carry, suddenly came pouring out of me. Some of the participants looked concerned. But I was able to say, "Don't be fooled; I'm okay. This is simply me showing you my pain for the world." In writing this chapter I have come to realize how much the teachings and person of Joanna Macy have seeped into me, how much she was present in that moment. I see better now the reasons for her remarkable omnipresence in ecopsychology. Thank you, Joanna.

NOTES

1. In *Heal or Die: Psychotherapists Confront Nuclear Annihilation*, ed. Kenneth Porter, Deborah Rinzler, and Paul Olsen (New York: Psychohistory Press, 1987), 111–23.

2. Joanna Macy, "Working Through Environmental Despair," in *Ecopsychology: Restoring the Earth, Healing the Mind*, ed. Theodore Roszak, Mary E. Gomes, Allen D. Kanner (San Francisco: Sierra Club Books, 1995), 241.

3. Macy, "Working Through Environmental Despair," 242.

4. Joanna Macy, *World as Lover, World as Self* (Berkeley, CA: Parallax Press, 1991), 185.

5. Anita Barrows and Joanna Macy, trans., *Rilke's Book of Hours: Love Poems to God* (New York: Riverhead Books, 1996), 3.

6. Joanna Macy, "Letter from Joanna Macy," *Deep Times: A Journal of the Work that Reconnects* (February 2018): https://journal.workthat reconnects.org/2018/01/30/letter-from-joanna-macy.

GRIEVING MY WAY INTO LOVING THE PLANET

Dahr Jamail

IT WAS FEBRUARY 2005, and after several months of frontline reporting from Iraq, I had returned to the US a human time bomb of rage, my temper ticking shorter each day. Walking through morgues in Baghdad left scenes in my mind I remember even now. I can still smell the decaying bodies as I write this, more than a decade later. Watching young Iraqi children, shot by US military snipers, bleed to death on operating tables left a deep and lasting imprint.

My rage toward those responsible in the Bush administration bled outward to engulf all those participating in the military and anyone who supported the ongoing atrocity in Iraq. My solution was to fantasize about hanging all of the aforementioned from the nearest group of light poles. Consumed by post-traumatic stress disorder, I was unable to go any deeper emotionally than my rage and numbness. I stood precariously atop my self-righteous anger about what I was writing, for it was the cork in the bottle of my bottomless grief. To release that meant risking engulfment in black despair that would surely erupt if I were to step aside, so I thought.

My dear friend Anita Barrows translated Rilke poetry with a woman named Joanna Macy, whom I'd met briefly once before. Anita, who is a psychologist, had taken one look at me and shortly thereafter let me know Joanna wanted to have tea with me. I made my way over to Joanna's home in Berkeley, driving through the chilled, foggy morning, unaware of how much help I needed at the time. I remember seeing only fog, no trees.

I knew Joanna was an ecophilosopher and a scholar of Buddhism, general systems theory, and deep ecology. I knew she and her husband, Fran, had been antinuclear activists for longer than I'd been alive, and that she ran workshops for artists, writers, and activists. Beyond that, I had no idea what I was about to get myself into.

Joanna invited me in, and we went upstairs to her kitchen table while she prepared our tea. After quietly filling our mugs, she looked me straight in the eyes and said slowly, "You've seen so much." With my own grief beginning to be witnessed, tears welled up in my eyes, as they did in hers.

Thus began my learning about what those of us on the front lines of the atrocities against the planet, and those living amid what she calls "the industrial growth society," must do, if we are to sustain ourselves, both within and without, as the future rushes toward us with ever-increasing speed.

Six months after having tea with Joanna, I found myself with her and a few dozen others in the redwoods of coastal California, where for ten days we dove deeply into the violence that was happening to the planet, what it meant to humans and all other species, and how dire our situation really was. (Today, more than a decade later, it is, of course, far, far worse.)

I allowed myself to plunge into my grief around all I had witnessed in Iraq—school children being shot at by US soldiers, refugee tents filled with widows weeping for their husbands, car bombs detonating near me and the carnage on the streets in the aftermath. As an Arab American, the sadness about what happened in Iraq was akin to having it happen to my own brothers and sisters. I began to weep and was unable to stop for several days. At one point in the circle, I sat weeping next to Joanna. She paused, looked over at me, and placed her hand on my shoulder, smiled, and said, "You're just my little water faucet." I laughed and kept on crying.

During one of Joanna's discussions, she said, "The most radical thing any of us can do at this time is to be fully present to what is happening in the world." For me, the price of admission into that present was allowing my heart to break. But then I saw how, in the face of overwhelming social and ecological crises, despair transforms into clarity of vision, then into constructive, collaborative action. "It brings a new way of seeing the world, freeing us from the assumptions and attitudes that now threaten the continuity of life on earth," Joanna said.

Her lifelong body of work encompasses the psychological and spiritual issues of living in the nuclear age and is grounded in a deepening of ecological awareness that has become all the more poignant as the inherently malefic industrial growth society of today's corporate capitalism continues on its trajectory of annihilation.

"I look at the path we're on to the future as having a ditch on either side," she told me. "We have to hold on to each other in order not to fall into the ditch on the right or left. On one side lies panic and hysteria, on the other, paralysis and shutting down. You see this rampantly in the US. There is more and more social hysteria, greatly aided by the corporate media and its finger-pointing and scapegoating. On one hand, you have the mass shootings, and on the other, a deathlike closing down under the pressures of the moment when you need to just get food on the table."

Joanna believes that those who "are still on the path and not in one of the ditches" are seeing with clarity that it is "curtains for our way of life" because the price being paid, or extorted, from the planet is too high. During my first meeting with her, she told me that while the information I was reporting from Iraq was brutal and difficult to hear, that kind of truth-telling was "like oxygen" for those who had been so long deprived of the truth.

Meeting her when I did, and having my heart broken open by that first intensive, could very well have saved my life. My experience showed me that if I had not evolved beyond my own war trauma, I, too, could well have become a negative statistic. If for me it was indeed "evolve or die," how can it not be thus as a species when we fathom the true gravity of crisis we call modern life?

WITNESSING CLIMATE LOSS

The natural progression of my journalism work took me from the front lines of the occupation of Iraq to the front lines of human-caused climate disruption. I had been researching and writing feature stories about climate disruption for six years before beginning the field research for my book *The End of Ice: Bearing Witness and Finding Meaning in the Path of Climate Disruption*. Much of my research was gleaned from monthly climate dispatches I had been writing for Truthout, the news website where I worked full-time. Each dispatch was essentially a collection of scientific studies and extreme weather events tied to climate disruption over the previous thirty days. Pulling all of them together in one place was always overwhelming to write as well as to read.

But I was angry again. I was writing these dispatches hoping they would wake people up to the crisis upon us, to the fact that we were already off the cliff and needed to begin adapting to our new world. And it was that energy I was taking into my book, thinking the writing would be something along the lines of 75 percent climate dispatch and 25 percent personal stories and nature writing.

But Gaia had other ideas.

When I began going into the field and writing the chapters—from the Amazon, the Great Barrier Reef, Denali in Alaska, and other magical places around the planet that I was so deeply fortunate to get to visit for the book—the script flipped. My heart was broken open by both the magnificent beauty and power in each place my book took me, as well as how quickly it was all being lost.

Standing on bare ground in Alaska once covered by two hundred feet of ice from the Byron Glacier where I used to go climbing felt like a gut punch. Snorkeling atop the Great Barrier Reef bleached white and dying from overheated ocean waters, I found my mask filling up with my tears. Each field trip broke my heart open with awe and sadness time and time again. And each time I was reminded of Joanna's teachings, that a broken heart can hold the entire universe.

Surrendering fully into this process, the book wrote itself. I felt like little more than a typist for Gaia as the feelings and words flowed out of me, as I bowed to and held in reverence our magnificent planet. With each passing day it became clearer to me that my work was truly in service to the planet, each chapter an homage to her. And along the way, she brought in Native American elders, which literally changed the ending of the book I had prepared. It was due to my training with Joanna that I knew what was happening and allowed myself to be Gaia's instrument.

"We have a longing for coming home to the sacredness of our belonging to the living body of Earth and the joy of serving that at every step," Joanna told me once during an interview. "I make it sound easy, but we can't do it alone. Just hearing the news of what is happening each day on the planet, I can't handle all of it alone. I'm not supposed to. Even looking at it requires we reach out to each other and take each other's arm and I can tell you how

I feel, and you will listen. The very steps we need to take bring us the relief and reward of the whole point of it, which is our collective nature, our nonseparateness, because this is the only thing that can save us."[1]

While on tour for *The End of Ice*, I've become encouraged by the deep responses from people as I've spoken from the heart about the devastating impacts of climate disruption across the planet and its people. No matter how difficult life on Earth becomes, we will only be able to withstand these times by sharing ourselves with one another. If nothing else, we can bear witness together and not suffer in isolation as the dominant culture prefers. In being a "we," humans can live as the deeply interconnected consciousness of Earth that we already are, just as Joanna has taught all of her life.

NOTES

1. Dahr Jamail, "On Staying Sane in a Suicidal Culture," Truthout, June 3, 2014.

WE ALMOST DIDN'T MAKE IT

Beverly Naidus

THE PIERCING ON-AND-OFF WAIL of the siren penetrated the walls of our elementary school classroom. Over the panic-inducing din came the harried voice of our teacher. We had time to head home to our family shelters. My ten-year-old mind wrapped around the impossibility of surviving for very long in our basement, but I anxiously made my way home.

Next week the blast of the siren was incessant; this drill meant that the missiles had already been launched. The teacher had us line up in the hallway. She told us to sit down, face the wall, and put our heads in our laps. The fears that erupted from those drills led me to read John Hersey's *Hiroshima*. A decade later, mushroom clouds began to appear in my nightmares.

Making art transformed my angst. I went to graduate school and started constructing worlds that resembled those nightmares—a white, barren landscape, cleansed of all living material, memories of what had once been on the surface blinking on a small screen, and the bright white flash of the bomb, over and over again. Haunting, dissonant sounds filled the space; voices speaking in hushed despairing and cynical tones: "It didn't feel like we had much time left—the world's gonna end someday, ya'know." "We never bothered reading the news." "Who believes that crap anyway?" After a minute or two of this challenging back-and-forth, a radio announcer interrupts, shouting, "THIS IS NOT A TEST; you are advised to proceed . . ." Then a teacher's robotic voice says, "Children line up, face the wall, sit still and put your heads down."

Visitors at the first exhibition came up to me wanting to share long-held memories about the terror they had felt during the Cuban missile crisis. Others shared fears that they would not live past thirty because World War III was around the corner. Hearing these stories gave me some odd comfort; I was not alone in my worries.

In another version of the piece, a few years later, I found messages from the audience hidden in the installation: "You hit the nail on the head. I wish more people were talking about these things." "I've been stewing with all of this, thinking I was alone." I was interviewed by a local television station, and the reporter questioned me earnestly, "Why are you so worried about nuclear war?" I told him that what worried me was that most people were not concerned.

I joined with other activist artists to do street art and protests, and eventually joined two million others in the center of Manhattan marching against nuclear weapons. But even that did not feel like enough. I was discouraged.

Thankfully I was invited to be a resident artist at Blue Mountain Center in the Adirondack Mountains of New York. As soon as I smelled the mountain air on that September day I arrived, I began to feel better. I hadn't been out of the city in years. I settled in quickly; all I wanted to do was soak up the autumn landscape and retreat from my worries about nuclear war. In my room, above my bed, I discovered a powerful ink drawing of a tree by the German political artist George Grosz. If Grosz, whose work often focused on the evil during the Weimar Republic, could draw such a life-affirming tree, I wanted to dive into drawing that kind of beauty as well.

A few days later, while resting on a rowboat on the lake, black fighter jets strafed the area only two hundred yards above me. Their roar was deafening! I was terrified. I soon learned that a nearby strategic air command base sent their jets on practice missions above our retreat center on a regular basis. I sought comfort in the retreat center's library, and as I pulled on a book from an upper shelf, another book literally fell down on my head. As soon as I read the title, *Despair and Personal Power in the Nuclear Age*, I knew it was no accident. I read the book eagerly, amazed to discover a series of exercises (and a community) addressing issues so close to my heart. I wrote to Joanna seeking guidance. I wanted to figure out how to move from my despair and cynicism into action. She wrote back and suggested that I work with two of her Interhelp colleagues who were leading a despair work workshop.

Meeting a cohort of peers that was deep in the work of antinuclear consciousness raising was transformative. Sitting in small groups and expressing long-held feelings of grief, pounding pillows in rage, and holding each other in gratitude broke open my heart.

When I rebuilt my antinuclear installation at the New Museum in Manhattan, I made a last survivor's shack out of scavenged wood and placed a wooden box next to the entrance. Visitors who were moved to, could leave their own nightmares and dreams for the future and drop them in the box. The audio track was revised to include the last lines: "We didn't realize that we had a choice." "You don't give up, do you?"

On the night of a blizzard, over a hundred people made their way through the subways and snow-padded streets to the museum. I tried to channel the Interhelp crew as we broke open the box, reading as many of the dreams and nightmares as we could manage. Activists, artists, and others spoke powerful truths. We cried and we ranted. It was 1984; Reagan was making jokes about bombing Moscow.

Thanks to the encouragement of Joanna's cohorts and their affirmation of my long-held angst, I was able to carry my installation, *THIS IS NOT A TEST*, to seven exhibitions across the country, creating talking circles and workshops to help others move from angst to activism. I finally put the work to bed in 1991 with a quote from Helen Caldicott scrawled across the wall of the exhibition space: "Not one of the 62,000 nuclear weapons has been dismantled since the Berlin Wall came down. There is more danger of a nuclear war today than ever. War is obsolete."

When I met Joanna in person a few years later at a workshop at the Ojai Foundation, it was a revelation. Her capacity for compassion and gratitude in the heart of the deep, dark mess of the world was truly heartening. I had begun to experience enhanced versions of cognitive dissonance about the state of the world, and I needed her medicine.

I had moved across the country to step into my role as a teacher of art for social change at a state university. Southern Californian life offered a complicated despair, and I was finding it hard to see around the contradictions. People were trying to live the good life while nuclear power plants sat on fault lines, caches of nuclear weapons lay ready for multiple ground zeroes, toxic waste was increasing in the ocean and on land, and the violence of racism percolated everywhere. On top of what I was witnessing, I had begun to take in the toxicity of it all. Breathing the smog and the pesticide spray was damaging my immune system. I was embodying what Joanna would call "the Great Unraveling" of our world. Making art about it wasn't enough.

After *Thinking Like a Mountain: Toward a Council of All Beings* was published, Joanna came to town to offer workshops specifically dealing with environmental collapse and how to stay strong in the midst of it. As I tried to feel the experiences of mycelia or humpback whales, I occasionally felt my East Coast skepticism interrupting. But an inner knowing loved speaking for various creatures and living forms, so I let the work teach me how to open to my pain and gratitude in new ways. A few months after working with Joanna, when I met my life partner, Bob, I learned that he had also trained with her. Both our faces lit up at this knowledge. We teased Joanna years later that she was partly responsible for our marriage.

Bob's studies connected me to the Institute for Social Ecology in Vermont, where I was invited to be an artist-in-residence. My understanding of ecocide began to expand exponentially to include deeper thinking about systems of oppression such as patriarchy and white supremacy. Though some people had challenges merging the points of view from deep and social ecology, I found that weaving them together through my art was the only way to move forward. Joanna's discussion of the Great Turning was totally harmonious with the "reconstructive visions" advocated by my social ecology peers. Even before encountering these ideas I had intuitively begun a project that would take me and my audiences into deep time.

The Nightmare Quilt featured fifty-four nightmarish images of the future on one side: "The streets were empty. No one dared go out." "Everyone became a scapegoat." "New forms of torture were invented." On the opposite side were fifty-four positive dreams for the future: "Intentional communities flourished." "Education and health care were free." "Racism became obsolete." Visitors were invited to write down their own nightmare or dream and place it under the quilt. Some people hesitated, but after they lifted the quilt, they discovered the dreams on the other side. They could ask for help to see the whole dream side—

the message being that we don't get those dreams unless we work collectively.

Soon after the quilt was exhibited for the first time, I was invited to a retreat for activist artists led by Thich Nhat Hanh. His dharma talks and our meditations together taught me new ways to inhabit the present moment with intention. My work with him over the next few years and the support of loving sanghas informed by his mindfulness teachings only reinforced what I'd begun to learn from Joanna. Seeing the beauty in the present moment gave me the courage to feel my pain, grief, and rage, to find solidarity with others, and move into action.

Many other audience-participatory projects followed, all with the goal of encouraging people to tell their stories, share their feelings in community, and step into their activism. But eventually my disabling environmental illness made it clear that we needed to relocate. A psychic healer told me that my antenna for the world's pain was too finely tuned, and I needed to pull it back in. I gave up tenure and took a leap of faith with my partner and infant son.

We moved three thousand miles to find our new rural village home. While slowly healing my body, I created a new art project on the computer, *CANARY NOTES: The Personal Politics of Environmental Illness.* "Canaries" filled the clinics I went to, so their portraits and their painful stories became digital images in the project. The last component of the project, *The Healing Deities,* which featured digital paintings of healing buddhas and bodhisattvas, was influenced by my work with both Joanna and Thich Nhat Hanh, as well as my four-year-old son's comment, "Why are you always painting sick people?" Once that series was done, I began to truly heal.

This experience of self-remediation has deeply informed the art projects that have emerged since I moved back to the West

Coast to teach at the University of Washington–Tacoma. I renewed my connection with Joanna when she spoke at the Puget Sound Zen Center on Vashon Island. I gave Joanna a print of my first *Healing Buddha* and told her about my challenging but powerful journey to wellness, and she spoke about her own struggles with health and her desire to slow down.

As my focus on remediation in the wider world began to grow, I studied permaculture design and developed an eco-art project, *Eden Reframed*, to demonstrate how to heal toxic soil with plants and mushrooms and create community through a "story hive." I created a series of sculptural works, *Curtain Call: Portable Altars for Grief and Gratitude*, that explored the devastating feelings many of us have about extinction and gave people a space to process them.

At a recent training for people who facilitate the Work That Reconnects, I was invited to share a mini version of my workshop, "We Almost Didn't Make It." I asked participants to imagine themselves as ancestors by thinking of something precious to them that might not exist in 150 years. They were invited to draw a representation of that precious thing with a partner, morphing their precious things together in one image. Then I asked them to write down on their drawing a commitment to an action that might help future generations thrive, not just survive. Joanna participated enthusiastically in this workshop and her praise once again affirmed my direction.

A few months later I created the installation to accompany the workshops. Visitors entered the gallery space, navigating their way through a gauntlet of hand-sewn plastic curtains. Words were scrawled across them: "monsters in power with fingers on buttons," "hurricanes, one after another," "gun massacres, again and again and again," naming many of the challenges we experience in our current world.

Once people emerged from the trauma curtains, they saw a bright red sign that said, "We almost didn't make it, but you did not give up and we are alive in your future. What choices you make, and what actions you take, may make it possible for us to not only exist but thrive."

At one end of the space, there was a work table where people could create objects representing their precious things. Into those objects they inserted commitments to actions. Fifteen doormats that said things such as "TOO TIRED," "OVERWHELMED," "WHEN WILL THIS NIGHTMARE BE OVER?" and "WE SHOULD JUST GO EXTINCT" surrounded a "portal of possibilities," a large white disk on the floor. After wiping their feet on the doormats to remove energy that might hinder action, visitors could place their artifacts into the portal.

The experience of watching and talking to visitors who came to the exhibits offered the opportunity to learn how people were moving through daily crises. They were eager to step into deep time and imagine themselves as ancestors. They were willing to speak about their grief and recognize that it was a collective issue. The courage to just step through the door and share feelings needed acknowledgment.

In this very chaotic time, I try to sit with the words I heard from Joanna and hold my despair with compassion. "We as a planet people are sick in our souls. We need pain to alert us to what needs attention." I take comfort in the fact that many people around the world are provoking others to wake up, and others are taking on the vision of healing traumas and building the world we want.

"YOU, DARKNESS"—MEETING THE OTHER IN RILKE

Anita Barrows

IN THE SPRING OF 1991, I WENT to a retreat at Mount Madonna on the mid-California coast. The teacher was Thich Nhat Hanh. The retreat was directed at people working in the "helping professions" and was conducted in silence except for nightly dharma talks. Throughout the week I often caught the eye of a very vibrant-looking woman with a gaze of tenderness and intensity, but I had no idea who she was. Then, one night toward the end, Thich Nhat Hanh introduced her as Joanna Macy and told us she would speak of her recent experience in Novozybkov, just outside Chernobyl, where the tragic nuclear accident had occurred five years earlier.

As she spoke that evening of the people whose forests had been contaminated by radioactivity, the people whose lives and whose children's lives, and their descendants for generations to come, would never be the same, Joanna wept. She spoke of the work she and her husband, Fran, had done with these people, the groups they had led there. By the end of the talk I knew that I needed to know this person, to study with her. I knew that this was the reason I had come to the retreat.

When I returned home, I looked up her schedule and saw that she would be offering a weekend workshop in San Francisco that June—in fact, on the weekend my younger daughter, Viva, was going to turn seven. I negotiated with Viva to have her birthday party a week early, and I've thanked her for her willingness ever since! On the Saturday afternoon of the workshop, Joanna led a ritual that would literally change my life—the Despair Ritual—in which we moved in a circle and named our grief and anguish for the world.

I remember speaking about how long it takes to gestate and nurture and teach a child, and how quickly a child could be murdered in war or on a street of our cities. I remember the weeping and keening in the center of the circle as we released grief long unspoken. When the workshop was over, I wrote a letter I would send to everyone I knew, telling them what I had experienced and how deeply it had moved me. I decided to send the letter to Joanna as well, just so she would know the effect her work had on me as one of the participants. Within a few days she had invited me for tea.

We discovered a mutual love of poetry. We discovered that each of us spoke and read other languages, with an appreciation for the poetic expression of other cultures. On long walks together and at the dinner table, our conversation ranged widely. I consulted Joanna about my own poems and found her to be my most perceptive editor.

When Joanna had a bout of pneumonia in 1993, she called me to see whether I could come up and read some poetry to her. I quickly threw into my backpack a random selection of books, including Stephen Mitchell's translation of Rilke. Joanna and I sat on her bed, afternoon sunlight pouring into the room, as I read Mitchell's translation of the "Eighth Duino Elegy." Since both of us knew German, we looked at the original, comparing it to the translation, quibbling with Mitchell's English at moments. Shortly afterward I visited again, and Joanna told me about a poem of Rilke's in *The Book of Hours* that she had always wanted to translate. Joanna had an original volume in Gothic script that she had carried all over the world. She wanted to give the poem to her activist friends who couldn't read German. Her first attempts at translation became stiff and forced in English when she tried to reproduce the rhyming patterns. She had asked Mitchell to translate it, but he had declined.

She took out her beautiful worn copy of *Das stundenbuch*, and we took turns reading stanza after stanza. "We could translate that together," I said. I suggested we follow Denise Levertov's example, recognizing that since World War I, some frame of the world order that had been held as "orderly" had been broken and had given way to ambiguity and lack of closure. The closed, resolved feeling of perfect end rhymes would not be true to this sense of everything as relative, of formerly held truths now stood on their heads.

"You are not surprised at the force of the storm— / you have seen it growing . . ." Rilke's work, which each of us had cherished individually for years, yielded new and powerful meanings when we began to consider it—and then to render it—together. Soon we had translated several poems; soon after that—miraculously!—we had a contract to translate *Das stundenbuch*, eventually published as *Rilke's Book of Hours*.

Our process in translation evolved from the beginning in an entirely dialogic way, and it has remained so. People frequently ask us, "Which one of you knows German? Which one of you made this into poetry?" And our answer is that every word, every bit of punctuation, every line break, every footnote—*all* of it—has been done by both of us *out loud* together. There is no "my part/her part."

It goes like this: We sit down in Joanna's living room after, perhaps, having a meal or a cup of tea together, talking about our work, our families, our latest adventures, the political outrages of the moment. We may sit side by side or facing each other. Each of us has the German text in hand and a legal pad or a notebook and a pen or pencil. (I prefer pen; Joanna, pencil.) First we read the poem together to see how it feels as a whole. Then one of us will read the first line or so in the German (*Du Dunkelheit, aus der ich stamme*), and before long each of us is speaking possible translations: "You, darkness, from which I come . . ." "Hmm, that's good, but do you think 'from which I am born' sounds stronger?" "It does! But how about 'of whom I am born'?" We keep going like that, back and forth, with various possibilities, writing and crossing out and rewriting, in amazing synergy, becoming bolder and more imaginative than either of us could have been alone. (Why, we have wondered, would anyone want to translate alone?) Because we are working together *aloud*, we get to hear the sound of our translation; so that, though we have chosen not to rhyme, we are highly attentive to the musicality of our work.

What has guided us through twenty-six years of this collaboration is our love for each other, our tremendous respect for Rilke, and the ways in which we have found Rilke expressing thoughts we have both held as central. Understanding these truths in another language, as a bridge to other histories, to other cultures, to other ways of experiencing the world, has shown us another dimension of the Deep Ecology work. Language reveals our human stories of place and time, and translation allows us access to stories apart from our own.

When we reached the end of the third poem of *The Book of Pilgrimage*, for instance, we sensed that Rilke had stated—and we had found English language for—something each of us had felt since our earliest days: a truth about human grief and suffering and the solacing, transformative presence of the natural world.

> Always there are some awake
> who turn, turn and do not find you.

Don't you hear them blindly treading the dark?
Don't you hear them crying out
as they go farther and farther down?
Surely you hear them weep, for they are weeping.

I seek you, because they are passing
right by my door. Whom should I turn to
if not the one whose darkness
is darker than night, the only one
who keeps vigil with no candle
and is not afraid—
the deep one, whose being I trust,
for it breaks through the earth into trees,
and rises,
when I bow my head,
faint as a fragrance
from the soil.[1]

The intimacy inherent in the act of translation—to enter into another's mind, another's heart, to find revealed the meanings there; and then—oh, incredibly!—to restate them in words that have resonances in one's own life and soul, and in one's own culture—is an extraordinary thing to share with another person. I consider it one of the greatest blessings of my life to have shared this with Joanna.

NOTES

1. Anita Barrows and Joanna Macy, trans., *Rilke's Book of Hours: Love Poems to God* (New York: Riverhead Books, 1996), 101.

BREAKING THE SILENCE IN GERMANY

Gunter and Barbara Hamburger

IN 1979, NATO WANTED TO DEPLOY American nuclear intermediate-range missiles, such as Pershing II, and cruise missiles in West Germany (the former BRD, or *Bundesrepublik Deutschland*), very close to the Iron Curtain. In response to this threat, we joined a small nonviolent action group in the town of Lübeck as part of the German Peace Movement. Four years later, I (Gunter) had the opportunity to serve as a delegate to the National Peace Congress, a gathering of activists in the psychosocial professions from all over West Germany opposed to the NATO plans. The main speaker was psychotherapist Dr. Horst-Eberhard Richter, founder of the German section of the International Physicians for the Prevention of Nuclear War (IPPNW) and a leading figure in the German Peace Movement.

At this galvanizing conference I noticed a workshop called "Despair and Empowerment Work." I had no idea what it meant—I was a political activist! However, something attracted me, and the experience was like a flash of enlightenment—it changed my life completely. The basis for the workshop was a small brochure titled *Despairwork* by Joanna Macy, which had been translated into German by Bea Fröhlich, a close friend and psychologist from Hamburg. I immediately thought the members of our peace group should become familiar with despair work. From this moment on, I knew deep inside how important it is to bring cognitive, emotional,

spiritual, and practical action approaches together and not to separate them from one another.

In 1986, some psychologists from this same peace group
translated Joanna's book *Despair and Personal Power in the Nuclear
Age* under the German title *Mut in der bedrohung: Psychologische frie-
densarbeit im atomzeitalter.* I met Joanna that year as she made her
first workshop tour in Germany. The influence of her work spread
like wildfire among political activists, social workers, and psychologists. In a three-day workshop in Hamburg, Joanna began with
these strong words: "What we do is a high-intensity workout."
For the first time, we were learning about general systems theory,
about "power over" and "power with," about patriarchal worldviews, about the relevance of being vulnerable and compassionate
in creating strength to act. We were impressed by the Council of
All Beings, developed with John Seed and others that same year
in Australia. At the end of the workshop, Joanna's closing message was this: "The heart that breaks open can contain the whole
universe."

On my way home from the session, I was watching the clouds
and suddenly I saw a shape of an eagle with wings opened wide.
I stopped and got out of the car, having this strong feeling: *Yes, I
can be unafraid while knowing that I can deeply trust that I will be held.*
Joanna's last words to me in Hamburg were, "You are on the right
path," and I knew a new challenge was waiting for me.

CHERNOBYL WAKE-UP

A year later, in 1987, I traveled from northern Germany to Lake
Constance to join Joanna's first eight-day intensive in Tüfingen,
a small village. We were particularly alert to the impact of Chernobyl radiation in this area, as Bavaria was fairly contaminated.

This was an intense self-awareness training, different from all the other social therapist trainings in my studies. It is still very precious to me, and I keep it close in my heart. Whenever I meet participants from this training, it is like coming home to my deep ecology family. There were eleven women and four men, all of us learning to "become mature," in the sense of "not to withdraw from pain but to face it and stand with it." Joanna explained what it means to live in a time of "positive disintegration." We were urging each other to take responsibility for our actions and to see ourselves as a part of an open living system and a self-organizing network—similar to what John Seed had pointed out as a change in his identification: "I am that part of the rainforest recently emerged into thinking."

It was here that Joanna mentioned the term *deep ecology* for the first time. The most important emotional content in this intensive was the explosion of the nuclear power plant in Chernobyl one year before, on April 26, 1986. Its radioactive contamination had impacts for everyone in Germany and affected some of our food products, especially in the forests of southern Germany. Thirty years later, the German consumer office still issues warnings to avoid venison and some mushrooms from the forests, as parts of the forest soils are still contaminated with Cesium-137.

I (Barbara) remember vividly a dreadful scene after the Chernobyl disaster. It was a rainy day and our nine-year-old son, Florian, had returned from school in his wet rain slicker, crying "I am polluted!" From that day on, our two sons never played outside in their sandbox. It was the end of childhood for them. Two years later in 1989, I finally met Joanna at our home in preparation for a workshop near Gorleben. Our ten- and eleven-year-old sons were around while we talked about the danger of nuclear power and the contamination by plutonium. After listening to our words, our son

Christian painted a picture as a present to Joanna, showing Mother Earth held by two open protective hands. You can still find this picture on her kitchen wall in Berkeley.

The next day we drove to the seminar house near Gorleben. At that time, Gorleben was planned to be the first disposal site for nuclear waste in Germany. Until now, the resistance of a large population has stopped the decision, but still there is no solution in sight. One woman taught us the Elm Dance, and from then on, the dance became an integral part of our work. Most significant to us was Joanna's introduction of the Nuclear Guardianship Project (NGP). As part of the training, we all walked together like pilgrims, singing and dancing, to the fence of the planned disposal site in Gorleben. Some of our friends translated the NGP materials into German and founded the German Fire Group. After the Fukushima disaster on March 11, 2011, we extended the Nuclear Guardianship Project and began calling it Guardians of the Poison Fire.[1]

DEEP ECOLOGY AND INTERBEING

At the same time, from 1989 to 1990, I (Barbara) was finishing my thesis in psychology, *Mit der bedrohung leben* (*Living with the Hidden Danger*), at the University of Hamburg. I held two interviews with Joanna, one at our home and one during the first big Deep Ecology conference in Kronberg. We talked about "Self," our relationships with all life phenomena, and about the relationship between Deep Ecology and Gestalt therapy. Joanna took issue with Fritz Perls's famous Gestalt prayer: "You are you, and I am I, and if by chance we find each other, it's beautiful. If not, it can't be helped." She felt that from a Deep Ecology perspective, this should be radically reinterpreted:

You are you and I am me, and together you can become more you and I can become more me! Because in the systems theory perspective of Deep Ecology, we deeply affect each other simply by coming into interaction, we mutually create each other. Therefore, as I interact with you—my "Joannaness" becomes more defined, thanks to you. You help me become more who I am, you challenge me. We have enriched each other or helped each other to arrange ourselves differently because of our interaction."[2]

The 1990 Deep Ecology conference in Kronberg was titled "Our Life as Gaia," and more than seventy people participated. Just one year earlier, the Berlin Wall had fallen, and the two Germanys were united. During the conference we celebrated the first anniversary of this reunification on October 3, 1990. Some political activists from the formerly separated East Germany (the DDR, or *Deutsche Demokratische Republik*) were there, and I interviewed Irena from East Berlin, one of the founders of the famous Neues Forum, a civil movement in the DDR. I remember how insecure the women from the former DDR felt. They went so far as to think that "even here in the group we are surrounded by spies surveilling us and noting what we say." She spoke of how family members and close friends had betrayed her political activities to the Stasi, the secret police, the most repressive of any Soviet satellite country.

The participants from East Germany had very different expectations about reunification, born of their rejection of Western capitalism for their own culture. They wished that reunification could help bring together the "good" parts of both systems. Unfortunately that didn't happen. Our leadership team debated long into the night how best to proceed. The next morning, as participants gathered in the big hall, Joanna felt intuitively that it was impossible to continue with her planned program.

Out of this strong energy field was born the first Truth Mandala, one of the most intense and powerful rituals in the Work That Reconnects. All of us experienced how precious it was to speak our individual truths without fear and without being condemned. It was like breathing fresh oxygen, a gift of the present moment. The ritual emerged as part of a breakthrough process between the participants to a new way of dealing with one another with all of our differences.

The Truth Mandala, as well as other exercises, helped to unlock years of emotional blockades due to the silence of our parents' generation, who lived and suffered under the terror of the Nazi regime or were even soldiers or members of the Nazi Party. This was key for understanding our parents' situation and served as a starting point for reconciliation with our ancestors. For many of our parents and grandparents, it was desirable to be part of a bigger, powerful, and more meaningful system as promised by Hitler and his Nazi ideology. They didn't realize that living in a closed system that only existed by building walls and creating enemies from outside would be self-destructive. For us, as their descendants involved in Deep Ecology work, we also had the longing to be part of a larger system serving life. We found that systems theory was very helpful for us to see the contrasting impacts of a closed system such as the Nazi regime and an open system that encompasses all life forms in the web of life.

A NEW NGO AND THE HOLON TRAINING

In 1992, we established the German Society for Applied Deep Ecology (GATOE) in Munich, supported by the Schweisfurth Foundation for sustainable agriculture. When the founder Karl Ludwig Schweisfurth met Joanna and learned of her Deep Ecology work, he was very impressed and decided to support her work. With the help of the foundation, the GATOE took up the intention to further Deep Ecology work in Germany. This included publishing books such as the anthology *Tiefenoekologie* and sponsoring deep ecology conferences for academics and activists. The goal was to create continuing education in deep ecology in all aspects of the work—cognitive, emotional, spiritual, and practical elements.

Under the umbrella of the GATOE, a group of experienced deep ecology colleagues supported by Joanna worked intensely for two years to put together a curriculum we called "Holon Training." I (Gunter) was one of five trainers to launch the first Holon Training in 1994 with thirty participants engaged over a period of two years. We adapted the design based on our experience in the first round and incorporated the shifting social, political, and environmental issues as they affected the work. The second Holon Training in 1998–99 was launched with a big conference with Joanna at Hotel Schloss Beuggen close to Basel above the Rhine. The training includes the spiral of the Work That Reconnects and supplementary aspects to further what we call "rediscovering our ecological self." There are four key elements of the training: (1) an evolutionary journey from the beginning of our history as planet Earth 4.6 billion years ago, in the form of a three-hour bodywork exercise developed by Gunter; (2) an eleven-day rite of passage in the deep mountains of the Swiss Alps; (3) the Nuclear Guardianship Project role play with PowerPoint presentation; and (4) shadow work, grief work, and reconciliation adapted from our hospice work.[3]

Our special approach to the rites of passage is based on what we learned from Meredith Little and Steven Foster in the School of Lost Borders and also in our hospice and bereavement work in the Yukon, Canada, with First Nations people, especially women, who as children had been abused in boarding schools. It is a deep healing process called "Healing Lodge Vision." For the two of us, it was very clear that hospice work and Deep Ecology work represent sensible complements to each other. Therefore, we used elements of hospice work and the Work That Reconnects in both fields of work.

I (Barbara) managed a hospice group and together we developed an educational program for hospice volunteers using exercises from the Work That Reconnects, and offered the Elm Dance in each group. Likewise, we drew on exercises from the hospice work in the Holon Training, noting how feelings of grief and steps in the grieving process are very similar on an individual and on the collective level. Despair work especially has been very useful. Together we are mourning collective and irretrievable losses, from extinction of species to overshoot of Earth's carrying capacity and breakdown of social processes. We have always viewed our task as supporting a new perspective of death as an integral part of natural life.

THE WORK GOES ON

The Deep Ecology work continued in Germany, with major international conferences in 2008, 2010, and 2013, highlighted by visits from Joanna. More than two hundred people came from foreign countries to strengthen our worldwide networking. Intense facilitator trainings followed the last two conferences in 2010 and 2013. The meeting in 2013 was held at a beautiful place called Helfensteine near Kassel, close to a place of worship and a magnetic ley, or *dragon*, line. An engaged film team accompanied us during this conference, producing seven DVDs titled *Deep Ecology: Basic Principles for Inner and Outer Transformation*. Those DVDs are available in both English and German.[4]

Across this time, the Holon Training passed through different stages of transformation and is ongoing. In 2016, after twenty-four years, the GATOE was turned into an open source network called the "Deep Ecology Network." The Holon Institute, founded in 1999 and run by the two of us, had begun as a regional office of the GA-TOE and is now an independent member of the network.

In 2017, we once again met up with Joanna in Aspiran in southern France. A close friend had invited some colleagues to stay with her for a few days. Together we enjoyed beautiful hot summer days, surrounded by the thick and cooling natural stone walls of the house. We cooked delicious meals of freshly caught fish and drank dark red wine, offered by Joanna across our deep conversations.

We had just finished the German translation of the latest edition of *Coming Back to Life, Für das leben! Ohne warum* (*Coming Back to Life: Encouragement of a Spiritual-Ecological Revolution*). This book is so valuable for the work that needs to be done—so many strong exercises and teachings! We were particularly happy to have the book preprint with us, and we handed it to Joanna on behalf of her German publisher, Junfermann. She was very glad about it, and at the end of her blessings for the book, she wrote, "My gratitude for the work you now hold in your hands is beyond measure. May you find benefit in the experiences and understandings it offers." After over thirty years of working together, as we said goodbye, Joanna was waving one last time wistfully. Would we ever meet again?

The Work That Reconnects—or as we call it in Germany, Deep Ecology—is like a bright bouquet of flowers influencing many initiatives and organizations. You can find it in the eco-village movement, in community-building processes, in the transition town movement. You can find it in schools or classes in universities, in hospice work and rites-of-passage work, or in different therapy groups. In all these arenas, one finds Joanna's books in use, filled with important teaching materials and suggestions for study-action groups. Thousands of people all over Germany and Europe have now been influenced by the precious gift of these teachings.

NOTES

1. See https://www.holoninstitut.de/bilderpool/seiteninhalte_12146.pdf (in German).
2. Barbara Hamburger-Langer, *"Mit der bedrohung leben"* (diss., University of Hamburg, 1991), 166.
3. It is described as a one-and-a-half-year-long training in the first issue of the *Deep Times Journal* (Spring 2016): 3, https://issuu.com/dharma seeds/docs/wtr_journal_spr16_final1pg/5.
4. Joanna Macy, *Tiefenoekologie: der grosse Grundlagen Workshop für den inneren und aeusseren Wandel* (*Deep Ecology: Basic Principles for Inner and Outer Transformation*), Helfensteine 2013. To order, see www.neue -weltsicht.de.

ECOLOGICAL AND SOCIAL JUSTICE HEALING

Jeanine Canty

I FIRST ENCOUNTERED THE WORK of Joanna Macy during the mid-1990s. I was living in Arizona, completing a teacher education program while working full-time. I was particularly drawn to multicultural education. The school was dedicated to ecological issues and, in part, social justice issues, and required us to look at these within every subject matter. I decided to look into the field of ecopsychology and ended up taking a course with Laura Sewall.[1] One day Laura came to class quite excited from a workshop she did with Joanna Macy. She popped an audiotape into an old-school boom box and had us do some of the Work That Reconnects exercises. The school was very experiential, so it was not too hard to get our class to participate.

At the time, I remember thinking that this was something really different. Hearing Macy on the recording while moving my body and engaging my peers felt quite enlivening. During this and a follow-up course with Sewall, my awakening to and readiness to address the ecological crisis exploded. For me, this awakening was intensified by my understanding of racism and systems of oppression responsible for injustices to both peoples and the planet. Macy's work, and particularly her writing with Molly Young Brown in *Coming Back to Life*, intrigued me—not only her exercises but also her pointed teachings on why people choose not to look at the ecological crisis.[2]

The field of ecopsychology looks specifically at the disconnection people have from the rest of the natural world. There is a heavy emphasis on Western culture and corporate globalization–based societies. Ecopsychologists recognize that our disconnection from the natural world has resulted in both the ecological crisis and our collective human suffering. The field is closely related to the deep ecology movement that centers around the intrinsic value and rights of nature. Joanna Macy is often identified with the unfolding deep ecology movement because of her Work That Reconnects, particularly the Council of All Beings exercise co-created with John Seed, Pat Fleming, and deep ecology founder Arne Naess. An important concept emphasized in both ecopsychology and deep ecology, as well as by Macy is the *ecological self*. The term indicates a process of maturation where a person extends their identity from an ego-centered self to a social self, and finally to a more metaphysical or ecological self that connects with aspects of both the seen and unseen natural world. Macy calls this process the "greening of the self" through widening circles of interrelatedness.[3]

My concurrent studies of ecopsychology and multicultural education led me to design and complete a graduate degree in cultural ecopsychology. Toward the end of my studies, I taught my first residential college course in multicultural education. The experience was quite difficult for me. As a woman of color, I found myself teaching a group of nondiverse students, many of whom were not interested in the course topic. The chair of the program, who also served as my liaison for the class, was not supportive and felt the course focus should debate whether multicultural education was of value or not. At one point in the semester, one student raised her hand and asked, "If African Americans are so unhappy in this country, why don't they go back to Africa?" It would be an understatement to say that I was dismayed, frustrated, and pained from the entire experience.

A dear colleague[4] came to my support by introducing me to the work of Milton Bennett and his developmental model of *intercultural sensitivity*, which is essentially a framework that explains the process adults go through in their awareness about race and culture.[5] I have described this model as it outlines how one shifts through several stages of development. As I wrote in an article in 2014, "Bennett's training model moves from stages of denial where one has had no exposure to cultural differences to the final two stages of adaptation and integration in which the self is first able to emotionally relate with one diverse worldview until finally one can integrate multiple, diverse worldviews into one's self-identity to such an extent that the original self-identity or worldview is transformed—the self is flexible and exposure to differences no longer results in conflict to one's worldview."[6]

This model of awareness enabled me to let go of what I perceived as ignorance and hostility around issues of race and instead allowed me to see a bigger process of adult development around these issues. Many people have little to no exposure to issues of culture and race, and they inhabit worldviews that deny and minimize the relevance of diversity and larger systems of oppression. This was a major turning point for me in that I now saw someone holding such a small perspective as *oppressed*, regardless of their apparent privilege, because their inability to look at these issues not only fostered the conditions that perpetuated the suffering of others but also their own suffering.

This recognition of the denial and diminishment of issues of social justice reminded me of the profound teachings I had read from Joanna Macy and Molly Young Brown surrounding the causes and consequences for denying and repressing our ecological crisis. Macy's work continually emphasizes the apathy people employ in order to not address the deep pain we feel for the suffering of the world. As I have written elsewhere, "The reasons why one shuts down one's feelings include: not wanting to experience despair, guilt, and the gloomy reality of the crisis; not wanting to seem anti-American, causing others distress, and seeming irrational, emotional, and weak; or simply associating these feelings with personal problems rather than the state of the world."[7] Putting this list together with Bennett's developmental model, it became clear to me that these causes and consequences for not looking at the ecological crisis translated seamlessly to issues of racism and other social injustices. Our pain for the world cannot be parceled out into separate issues. We often view them as singular, yet they are deeply connected, and the process we go through to avoid them as well as to authentically accept them are quite similar.

During this same period, I was also able to connect the deep ecology concept of the ecological self to that of the *multicultural self*. Environmental justice activist and author Carl Anthony introduces the multicultural self as the need to learn the stories of diverse peoples in order to decenter whiteness and the Western dominant paradigm.[8] Anthony defines the multicultural self as "the capacity for empathy with many people and cultures, and also with our capacity for empathy with living creatures."[9] The parallels of these concepts are extremely important for our ability to expand the limited ego identities so dominant in our society, to ones that hold the widest perspectives. This is at the heart of compassionate action.

Viewing our collective suffering through the lenses of individual and jointly held identity, as well as through psychology, ecological and social transformation, and compassion, led me to complete doctoral studies focused on transformative learning and the processes adults go through to change their worldviews. To me, this was a key aspect of the larger Work That Reconnects. During my doctoral program, I was delighted to meet Joanna Macy for the first time during a 2002 conference paying tribute to Thomas Berry at the California Institute of Integral Studies. My dear friend Drew Dellinger introduced me, and I was able to share a bit of how I had been using her work to address issues of social injustice. I could tell she was intrigued, and I was touched by her response.

Several years later I would have the pleasure of working more closely with her when I took a faculty position at Naropa University in Boulder, Colorado. Macy has a long history with our Buddhist-inspired institution, and I have been blessed to build a connection with her. Each occasion she comes to visit, she reaches out to spend some time with me and always wants to hear about my work. One thing I truly appreciate is her ability to sometimes step into the mess of getting things wrong about social injustice, particularly race, and to take the feedback and address it. The Work That Reconnects will always need to be open to making mistakes and learning from them. This is an essential aspect of reciprocity, action, and healing. As I have written in my book *Ecological and Social Healing: Multicultural Women's Voices*, "If we bring together the concepts of these various broken identities and capacities for expanding our worldviews, our sense of self, a person who holds both a multicultural and ecological self has immense power to see and act outside our dominant worldview that purports social and ecological oppression and instead to move toward a life affirming paradigm."[10]

There is still so much work that needs to be done in these areas. The ecological movement—including ecopsychology, deep ecology, and the Work That Reconnects—is still sorely lacking in centering around issues of social injustice. However, the framework for transforming this is clear and available through transforming worldviews, addressing our collective pain, and entering into authentic compassion with and for one another. The systems of oppression that we are embedded within work diligently to keep us separate. They are exploitative and create deep forms of mistrust and division that will not be healed instantly. The oppression of people and Earth go hand in hand. In order to radically reform and heal, we must come to this understanding and unite with diverse movements for reform. This is "a movement of movements."[11] It is no longer enough to identify with a single issue such as the rights of nature. We must join in a collective understanding that brings multiple identities together and unites us in shared, unstoppable power for positive change. This is the Work That Reconnects.

NOTES

1. Laura Sewall, *Sight and Sensibility: The Ecopsychology of Perception* (New York: Tarcher, 1999).

2. Joanna Macy and Molly Young Brown, *Coming Back to Life: Practices to Reconnect Our Lives, Our World* (Gabriola Island, BC: New Society Publishers, 1998).

3. Joanna Macy, *World as Lover, World as Self: Courage for Global Justice and Ecological Renewal* (Berkeley, CA: Parallax Press, 2007), 183–92.

4. With appreciation to Dr. Vicky Young, core faculty at Prescott College.

5. Milton J. Bennett, "Towards Ethnorelativism: A Developmental Model of Intercultural Sensitivity," in *Education for the Intercultural Experience*, ed. R. Michael Paige (Yarmouth, ME: Intercultural Press, 1993), 21–71.

6. Jeanine M. Canty, "Walking Between Worlds: Holding Multiple Worldviews as a Key for Ecological Transformation," *International Journal of Transpersonal Studies* 33, no. 1 (2014): 17.

7. Canty, "Walking Between Worlds," 19.

8. Carl Anthony, "Ecopsychology and the Deconstruction of Whiteness," in *Ecopsychology: Restoring the Earth, Healing the Mind*, ed. Theodore Roszak, Mary E. Gomes, and Allen D. Kanner (San Francisco, CA: Sierra Club Books, 1995), 263–78.

9. Jeanine M. Canty, et al., "Race, Environment, and Sustainability: Part One," *Sustainability: The Journal of Record* 4, no. 5 (2011): 240.

10. Jeanine M. Canty, "Seeing Clearly through Cracked Lenses," in *Ecological and Social Healing: Multicultural Women's Voices*, ed. Jeanine M. Canty (New York: Routledge, 2017), 35.

11. Brian Tokar, "Climate Justice and the Challenge of Local Solutions," in *Globalism and Localization: Emergent Approaches to Ecological and Social Crises*, ed. Jeanine Canty (New York: Routledge, 2019), 1–19.

RE-CONECTANDO IN THE WOUNDED LAND OF COLOMBIA

Helena ter Ellen

COLOMBIA, WHICH HAS NOW LIVED through more than fifty years of war, has a very special place in my heart. My story begins in 2002, when I joined the International Peace Brigades. For a year I accompanied an Afro-Colombian peace community in Cacarica in the mega biodiverse Chocó province. This unforgettable experience would bring me face to face with the real meaning of the words *courage* and *determination*. My admiration for the immense resilience displayed by communities and activists in this country only deepened on each of my frequent visits over the following years. Ever since I came across the Work That Reconnects (WTR) in 2008, I dreamed of offering it one day in Colombia, the land that had given me so much.

After some years as a WTR facilitator in Belgium, where I cofounded the association Terr'Eveille, I met up again with Joanna Macy in July 2013 at Hardwick in the United Kingdom. This encounter awoke in me the confidence and energy I needed to make my dream a reality. Joanna connected me to Felipe Medina, a young Colombian deeply committed to peace and aware of the Work That Reconnects. After five months of online preparation between Brussels and Bogotá, I arrived in Colombia in January 2014 for our first three workshops in his war-torn country.

For more than five decades, Colombia has lived through indescribable horrors, impacting more than eight million victims with continuing violence by paramilitaries, army, and guerrillas, accompanied by forced displacement of six million people. The country has also suffered environmental destruction due to mushrooming megaprojects, illegal mining, and coca crops. In 2012, a very rigorous peace process with the FARC guerrillas started in Havana, Cuba. After six years of negotiations, and a painful and surprising "no" vote referendum, a revised peace agreement between the state and the FARC was finally signed in November 2016. Since the signing of the peace accord, attacks against social and environmental leaders (including many women) have increased at an alarming rate, with more than four hundred killed since November 2016, and the numbers are rising.

It is well known that Colombia is fortunate to still harbor a great deal of *magía salvaje,* or "wild magic." The war paradoxically preserved a lot of Colombia's natural beauty, despite the increasing number of megaprojects and coca crops. Now many international investors and national companies see opportunities in what they believe will be a more stable political climate for exploiting Colombia's resources—legally or illegally. According to the biologist Alejandro Salazar and his co-authors, Colombia is the world's second most biodiverse country. Its terrain supports about 10 percent of all the planet's species, including hundreds of animals that are found nowhere else on Earth. They suggest that "the peace agreement is, of course, good for the country, but the end of the conflict may also create new threats to the natural environment. . . . The decisions made at this crucial moment in time will likely have ecological, climatic, and biogeochemical consequences with global implications."[1]

We felt that bringing the Work That Reconnects to grassroots spiritual leadership on the ground could help create resilience, renew alliances, and inspire creative visions. If and when the war finally comes to an end in Colombia, reconciliation may still take generations, unless the Great Mother brings them—and us all— back to our senses, helping us to come home.

OUR FIRST CIRCLES

In early 2014, Felipe and I presented the Work That Reconnects in two mini-workshops for a broad audience at *El Llamado de la Montaña* (The Call of the Mountain), a national ecological festival attended by hundreds of people from very different communities, including indigenous people. The vision of deep ecology under-pinning the Work That Reconnects resonates strongly with their native ancestral wisdom. After this first enthusiasm, we filled our circles with people from different classes, color, and walks of life, making sure our invites included at least half victims of conflict.

The first circle acted as "social acupuncture" for the wounded land. In the circle were five displaced Afro-Colombian women leaders, heirs of a tradition rich in wisdom, magic, and folklore; an environmental rapper-activist; two permaculturalists; a Jesuit priest, who five years later would become the president of the Truth Commission; and a business coach. This opened a space where privileged people could meet those from poor and still violent neighborhoods in Bogotá. Some of the Afro-Colombian women had hidden expression of their culturally robust wisdom, their elder voices locked within silent and wounded memories of their relationship to the land. During the Truth Mandala, a great vault of pain and anguish opened up from the stories of these women. Some were able to express their suffering in complete trust for the first time. All too often, those who have suffered from the war and its consequences (especially in the countryside) stay silent for fear of reprisals. Others, farther away from the conflict, don't speak about it, as if they were anaesthetized from the cruel realities of their own country. Afterward, these bright women put on their party dresses and shared music and stories from their land as we had never heard before.

The second circle included biologists, indigenous people, and upper-class activists of the Pachamama Alliance conscientizing around the rights of Mother Earth. This combination generated strong magic. Fernando is from the Nasa people of Cauca, well known for the peaceful resistance put up by their *guardia indígena*. Since October 2014, the Nasa had declared themselves in a process of "*liberación de la Madre Tierra*," a ritual act of recovering and occupying ancestral lands nonviolently. In the center of the Truth Mandala, with the stick of anger in his hands, he pledged that the Nasa will continue to defend Mother Earth (*Sa'th Tama Kiwe*) even if they have to sacrifice their lives. These are not empty words—on average, the Nasa lose one of their people every three days in the course of their nonviolent resistance. With him, we chanted, "*Por la tierra! Hasta cuando? Hasta siempre!*" (For the Earth! How long? Forever!)

The ritual enabled several people to open up and overcome their powerlessness, hearing Gaia not only crying but also dreaming in them. Monica, working with the indigenous peoples of Colombia's Amazonia, where whole communities are crushed by the steamroller of capitalism, was deeply touched by the isolation of traditional medicine men who are likely to die before their knowledge can be passed on. She wanted to create "lifelines" so indigenous youth and disoriented youth from the cities could meet and take up this life-bearing wisdom. One woman, a committed activist from the upper class, was upset by what we were doing: "We've all suffered in our lives at one time or another. Why not just go forward? What's the point of wallowing in pain?" A fair question here, where so much still needs to be rebuilt. But can a country that has experienced almost fifty years of war just turn the page without first reading it? In the afternoon we set up a role play between "perpetrators" and "victims" of the war in Colombia to continue opening up wounds and compassion and challenging our sense of identity.

During the evening harvest circle, a real awareness seemed to take root. It was as if the soft fire of compassion had burned through encrusted layers of fear and apathy, and we were standing naked in a circle, reflecting to one another and honoring our true nature. I spoke of my pilgrimages across Colombia, about the "law of silence" I so often encountered: *"A boca que no abre, tira no entra"* (a mouth kept shut doesn't take a bullet). This silence is understandable in a country where there is no safety for victims and almost total impunity for perpetrators. But we believe that "keeping quiet" will not help repair Colombia's torn social fabric. Perhaps when everyone seems so shut up in their own stories, anger, and pain, it takes "midwives" to come in from elsewhere and offer a path forward.

Under a mango tree, Felipe and I sealed an alliance: our shared adventure was only just beginning. I returned to Belgium, my heart filled with joy. The seeds of the Work That Reconnects had been well sown in the thirsty yet fertile soil of the land I love.

ROOTING THE WORK

A decisive factor for the rooting of the Work in Colombia is support from the well-known Jesuit peace worker Francisco de Roux, who participated in our first workshop in 2014. Thanks to his mediation, we receive funding from a British Catholic NGO that resonates strongly with Pope Francis's *Laudato Si* and feels that our approach is a beautiful implementation of his ecological encyclical. In the summer of 2015, the three of us carried out a special workshop for indigenous, Afro-Colombian, and peasant community leaders from the heavily disputed Cauca region. They share similar concerns regarding the use of land but experience significant difficulties in joining forces to resist foreign and extractive interests. Our intention is to revitalize their leadership and help them find common ground that could unite their efforts for the sake of the Earth.

An Afro-Colombian delegation from River Tapaje near Buenaventura represented the association *Sé quién soy* (I know who I am). Each night, Pachita, colorfully dressed as a queen from the woods, offered us some pearls of the day in poetic verse that she invented and sang on the spot, as they used to do in her traditional oral culture. Next to her in the circle was Nasa Elder Alcibiades, the spiritual leader and mayor of Toribio (the heartland of the Nasa), who spoke of the nonviolent resistance of their *guardia indígena*. Armed only with their "dignity sticks"—striped green for the love of the land and red for the blood that has been shed by the people—they have been able to safeguard their territory, displace armed parties, and maintain their communities.

Together we drew collective life maps as a powerful way to honor their ancestors, sharing the wisdom and deep wellsprings of solidarity in their culture and opening to the pain of the present times. "What is your relation to the land?" we asked Alcibiades. "We cannot speak of our relation to the land because we *are* the land. We are the land made human. They have tried to turn us into persons. But we have chosen to remain natural as part of the earth." When Priest Francisco spoke of the Catholic Church's feelings of superiority toward negros and indios for so many centuries and presented apologies in the name of the church, Luz Eida, of mixed Afro and Nasa origins, broke into tears. "All these years of feeling ashamed of even being seen!" she said.

After sharing our common bonds, marveling in our diversity, and speaking our common pain, we had the chance to see the present conflict in a new light. We decided to undertake a Forum Theater Play to deal with the interethnic tensions between these three parties—Afro-Columbian people, indigenous people, and farmers—fueled by political inequalities and a lingering ghost of an enemy figure hidden in the "Other." Shifting from fiction to reality, we landed after four hours in a collective recognition of our common responsibility toward the Earth. "I am released of all restrictive doctrines! I choose to join forces for the sake of Earth!" shouted Alcibiades at the end of the play.

We spent the last morning in one of the five-thousand-year-old archeological parks of San Agustin, a mystical place in a spectacular landscape. We could not have dreamed of a better setting for our ending ceremony, Ancestors Meeting the Future Beings. For people so proud of the strength and spirituality of their ancestors, it was a revelation: "But . . . WE are the future ANCESTORS! We are links of a chain, heirs of a story that will not be broken." We sang with Pachita in a huge celebration as it rained gently outside. Alcibiades, looking up into the sky above the lush green mountains, exclaimed, "In our culture, when it rains and the sun shines like this, it means that Earth has received and accepted all of our gifts."

ACCOMPANYING THE TRUTH COMMISSION

In 2018, as part of the peace agreement with the FARC, a Truth Commission was installed with a three-year mandate. Francisco de Roux was appointed president of this completely autonomous state institution. Its mandate can be summarized in three ethical challenges: (1) clarification of the truth, (2) recognition of the victims and of individual and collective responsibilities, and (3) promotion of co-existence. By then we had given twelve workshops, and we offered to accompany the Commission on its difficult mission. Our team had been enriched with several marvelous persons from the fields of theater, nature rituals, and peace education. A few months later our initiative, "Re-Connecting: Laboratories of Truth and Reconciliation in the Womb of Mother Earth," was born. If we are to work on truth and reconciliation, the truth of our deep connection with the earth should be acknowledged and honored. The earth is a victim of this war, as are the more than six million Colombians forcibly displaced from their lands. We believe that part of the healing of the wounded and divided Colombian people will be found in the reconnection with living nature. As far as we know, this is the first time that a version of the Work That Reconnects is being applied and sponsored on an official, institutional level by a nation-state.

Following the pilot project in 2018, *Re-Conectando* will offer workshops in the regions where the Commission is working. Our intention is to invite people from all sides of the conflict, both victims and those responsible, and especially those who are willing to give testimony during the hearings of the Commission. The idea is to prepare their "inner ground" through a profound and transformational process in safe and inspiring natural surroundings, where Mother Earth will be one of the main teachers.

ADAPTATION OF THE WORK

Thus far in our five-day workshops, the WTR spiral has been the guiding principle. But dealing with traumatized and intensely polarized people requires careful listening to sense what is appropriate in any given moment. First of all, these broken individuals need to be rewoven into the fabric of the community, mostly through the power of ritual. The gathering is more of an initiatory than an educational process. Ex-combatants feel received as newborn peace warriors, and longtime community leaders find new strength and blessings for their fierce stand for life. We take time to honor the suppressed ancestral wisdom of those present and also to value the beauty of the Christian faith (Colombia is still a very Catholic country), linking it with the need to take care of God's creation, as Pope Francis is calling us to do.

In the WTR spiral phase of *gratitude*, we organize a creative Market for the Care of Life, putting at the participants' disposal all kinds of material. This becomes a way for them to talk about their identity (no one knows "who is who" when starting the workshop) and share their dreams and battles. This first day we also include a guided tour on the intelligence of nature: What does it teach us about building peace? In what ways is nature selfless, generous, cooperative, and willing to sacrifice itself for a greater good? In the afternoon we send people out on individual medicine walks, where nature will mirror back the state of their inner landscapes. For some it is the first time they walk in nature without carrying a weapon.

In the spiral's second phase, *honoring our pain*, we (or the elders present) invite the Beings of the Three Times. This takes on special significance when so many have died in the war, especially those working for peace. To prepare us for the Truth Mandala, we offer a theater exercise, the Museum of the Unspeakable, where statues and frozen scenes represent the horrors of the war locked up in our bodies. As we "visit" the museum and project our own memories on the statues, we discover the many faces of suffering and begin to embrace the complexity of Colombia's history.

In the spiral's third phase, *seeing with new eyes,* we ask what is needed to build a new country where all of them can feel at home. We guide them through My Choices for This Life (an adaptation of the Bodhisattva exercise), using questions such as "In what kind of family did you grow up?" "In what way did the armed conflict affect your life?" These stir up many emotions, with many mothers having been raped, many fathers having been killed or kidnapped. This gives ex-combatants a chance to talk about their reasons for taking up arms. It is a powerful way to invite them to embrace their life conditions, to see the hidden gifts in their wounds and prepare for a peace walk in consciousness.

We organize a special Peace Walk where the group is linked together by only a fragile thread. They walk through the forest and wade through a river full of obstacles. We ask, "How do we sustain this fragile peace accord? Can we walk together despite our differences, respecting our own and others' sense of timing and needs?" We invite them to think of what prevents us from working wholeheartedly for peace and for the earth, and we ask them to pick up three stones that represent those obstacles. They carry them to the riverside and immerse them in the crystal clear water, in this way making the obstacles conscious and realizing that they are the only ones who can let them go. They recognize that their power can come from a much deeper wellspring of wisdom and compassion. A dive into the water becomes a moment of reconnection with the flow of life, a rebirthing. On the other side of the river we are welcomed with singing, drumming, and smudging in the new village, in the new Colombia.

I often think with such gratitude of Joanna's prophetic words, that the Work That Reconnects helps us create a "rough weather network," a resilient solidarity network that we can rely on when the storm breaks. We are convinced that this work has even more meaning in countries such as Colombia and others where armed conflicts have devastated the landscape, both external and internal. The aim is both to prepare for the uncertain future we all face on our vulnerable Earth, and at the same time to heal the wounds of war, visible and invisible—wounds on which this work can shed light and begin to heal.

NOTES

1. See Alejandro Salazar et al., "The Ecology of Peace: Preparing Colombia for New Political and Planetary Environments," *Frontiers in Ecology and the Environment* 16, no. 9 (September 2018).

Joanna Macy and Australian rainforest activist John Seed
teaching at Findhorn, Scotland, 1989 (photo by Pat Fleming).

PART THREE

THE INTERPLAY
OF REALITY

Core to Joanna Macy's philosophy and teaching is her understanding of what she calls "mutual causality." In her original doctoral research, she studied the early Buddhist texts in depth and compared the key principle of *pratityasamutpada* with systems thinking concepts. Also known as "dependent co-arising" or "interbeing," *pratityasamutpada* refers to the infinite web of causes and conditions that reflect a creative and emergent view of reality. Joanna describes her first experience of this powerful truth as a cascade of images and thought forms, "shifting patterns of breathtaking elegance" linking everything she had ever learned and experienced.

At root is the Buddhist insight that the ground of being is fluid and relational, not to be captured by the idea of a permanent and separate self. From systems theory Joanna highlights the self-organizing nature of the universe and the role of feedback in shaping life patterns. These are more than just ideas for the work; they are the foundations for ethical action in an ever-changing world. The Tibetan Buddhist teacher Elizabeth Mattis Namgyel invites us to be "citizens of the great nature of infinite contingency." The Buddhist scholar Christopher Queen highlights direct investigation into the nature of reality, the playing out or "interplay" of myriad dynamics. For Joanna, the call is to trust the interconnectedness and respond with compassion, seeing that one's own well-being is linked to the well-being of others.

Here in the heart of the human predicament, we see that everything we do matters, that nothing is outside the web of causality, that we are inherently empowered to be active agents in the web. In this way we can use the work to address the challenges of racial injustice and marginalization and the deep conditioning of white consciousness. Writers in this section take up the radical nature of positive disintegration, decolonization, decomposition. How do we care for death, allow things to die, let go of what no longer serves?

In this vibrant space of insight awareness, the work of healing and releasing is infinite. Experiments fail, beliefs unravel, worlds fall apart. And yet the universe continues to offer ways forward, teaching us who we are and what is most needed in our time. The stories offered here are spoken strongly from the heart, with clear reporting of challenges in progress. They suggest the need for deep listening to hear the widest possibilities for the "natural play of creativity."

In her teaching, Joanna evokes two radiant metaphors of systems thinking—the flame and the tree, both growing and changing constantly. The tree is a system of roots and branches, embedded in earth and sky, reflecting the seasons of weather, flowering, and decay. Sherry Ellms likens Joanna to such a tree, a "mother" aspen at the center of a great grove, bound together with so many other trees by time, reciprocity, and the elements of Earth.

—STEPHANIE KAZA

THE BLESSING

Joanna Macy

IN EARLY FALL OF 1974, His Holiness the Sixteenth Karmapa arrived in the United States for his first-ever visit. This was a powerful moment for Tibetan Buddhism in America. Revered as the embodiment of the ancient wisdom of the Kagyu lineage, the Karmapa's office was the oldest in Tibet. This historic visit had been arranged by Freda Bedi, or Mummy, as the Tibetans called her. Mummy was spending her later years in service to the Karmapa as his right hand in Rumtek, his monastery in Sikkim. At his request, she became a fully empowered nun of the highest ordination, a status quite unusual at the time. Having persuaded His Holiness of the utmost importance of this trip to America, she had come to the US the previous spring to inspire the preparations. At that time, she stayed with us in Syracuse, where I was pursuing a doctorate at the university. During her visit one unforgettable afternoon in my study, she officiated as I took refuge in the Triple Gem: the Buddha, Dharma, and Sangha.

That fall, eager to see His Holiness again now that his lineage had become my own, I drove with Fran to attend his first teachings in America. On that sunny September afternoon, throngs of well-dressed people drifted about the grounds of the Long Island estate of the Karmapa's host, waiting for the reception hall to open. A monk appeared at my side, inviting us to meet with His Holiness in his private quarters. There on a chaise lounge sat the Karmapa, flanked by Mummy and Chögyam Trungpa Rinpoche. By this time Trungpa was already a notorious and gifted teacher of the Vajrayana in the West. After fleeing Tibet, Trungpa had lived with Mummy's family as a teenager while she groomed him to bring the Buddha Dharma to the West. Here in his monk's robes, Trungpa was soberly and attentively serving as interpreter. His Holiness, in contrast, from the waist up, was clad in only an undershirt. His laughing eyes, to say nothing of his attire, seemed to mock the formal protocols with which he surrounded himself. Again I felt the warmth of contact as I had when we first met in Delhi eight years earlier.

He gently questioned me. Yes, I answered, I was studying now; I had decided for this lifetime to take the scholar's path. I hoped to make a fresh translation of a *Perfection of Wisdom* scripture that I loved. "Since that is the case," I heard myself saying, "I would appreciate it very much if Your Holiness would bless my head." Taking his smiling silence for consent, I drew near and leaned my head over his lap, expecting him to waft his hands above it in a generalized benediction. Instead, I felt my head grasped in both his hands like a football. Over and around me rolled his deep-chested rumble, which I later assumed was a blessing of Manjushri, the celestial bodhisattva of wisdom. With the strength and warmth of his hands, the vigor of the chant, and whatever else—my own astonishment—it was like having my head in an electric socket. For long moments I felt a strong charge going through me. That is all—except that I barely slept for the next three weeks.

When I returned to Syracuse, where I was in my third year of graduate studies, the days were normal, but each night was a torrent of revelation. After an hour of sleep, I would snap awake, my eyes open, my mind stretched wide like the large end of a funnel. For a while I would just lie there as Fran slumbered beside me, images and thought forms cascading through my mind and body. Soon I'd be sitting upright in full attention as shifting patterns of breathtaking elegance interlinked all that I had ever learned and experienced—from Jesus to Descartes to the Buddha Dharma—was displayed in an intricate dance.

Though I laughed and wept, it was the mind more than the heart that ignited with knowing. Two visual themes predominated. One was tree, with its branching limbs and roots. The other was nerve cell in a neural net, with its slender dendrites and synaptic connections. In their continual self-transformations there was not one stable point, nothing to hang on to. Though the laws that governed this interplay of forms, bringing forth worlds and dissolving them, were clear to me then, all that I now recall are the images. And that I felt no fear—just wonder and a kind of exultation.

It was during these sleepless weeks that I stopped by an early session of a graduate seminar on general systems theory. Although it was offered by the religion department, I couldn't imagine it would interest me. Yet almost immediately I saw that this systems view of reality fit the patterns that I had been seeing all those wakeful nights since the Karmapa's blessing. Clearly I had no choice but to enroll.

Indian summer that year was unseasonably warm. After school we'd drive out to our lake cabin, have a swim and supper, then the children and I—Peggy in seventh grade and Jack in tenth—would sit around the table with our homework. For me, homework was my first readings in systems thinking. Our introductory book by Ervin Laszlo described flows of energy, matter, and information—flows that interacted in coherent patterns, patterns that gave rise to galaxies, cells, minds. The first night or two I stopped every few pages and went outside. Walking back and forth on the bluff over the lake I could see the whole sky. I looked up at the stars and hugged myself and wept to know that my world was so coherent, so alive, and so real.

I had known this excitement once before. It was when I encountered the Buddha Dharma. Back then, with the Tibetans, I saw the Dharma as a luminous way of being, a selfless ground for serenity and compassion. Later, studying the scriptures, I discovered this way of being grew from a very distinctive understanding of reality—that the ground of being is fluid and empty of everything but relationships. Now, here came systems theory with concepts and empirical data, showing how these relationships interweave to make a world. This understanding completed the foundation for my doctoral research that would ground my life's work of decades to come. In the long intense hours, weeks, and months of crafting my dissertation, the charge I first felt in the Karmapa's blessing never left me.

THE CARP IN THE CASTLE MOAT

Joanna Macy

IN EARLY 1985, I WAS OFFERING workshops across Australia to activists resisting nuclear testing, uranium mining, and the logging of their last old-growth forests. They found that the Despair and Empowerment work freed them from burnout and kindled their love for one another. Communities around the world were welcoming these workshops, and meeting the forest activist John Seed was a milestone for me and the work. After his first workshop, John challenged me: "How can we adapt despair and empowerment work to free us from the notion that we humans are the crown of creation?" That challenge increased both my awareness of the damage we humans had done to ourselves and our world and my appreciation for the gifts we would harvest by enlarging our identification with all life.

We had been out all morning, walking in the green-lit stillness of the primeval rainforest, with only birdcalls and water splashes breaking the silence. Now we were squatting on the bank of a pond a short distance from the vine-covered bus that served as John's office for his rainforest activism around the Pacific Rim. Three years before we met, John's life had been seized by a larger purpose when he found himself defending the Nightcap Range, a vestige of the great primordial rainforests of Gondwanaland, Australia's mother continent.

As he described the confrontation, I could hear the screaming chainsaws, the crashing of trees as they fell, the police shouting on their megaphones at the protestors defending the trees. John and his crew were fighting for time. It was a holding action, waiting for an injunction to stop the logging. In the midst of the conflict, he and his mates stood there with nothing but their bodies between the loggers and the trees. He suddenly had an experience of knowing deeply and clearly who he really was. "I felt rooted in all life, in the primordial cradle of existence."

John's story riveted my attention. Given the pace of industrial deforestation, it was clear that even if activists won every battle they waged, it would hardly make a dent. John saw this with total realism, yet he kept on giving his life to this work. "How do you deal with despair?" I asked him. And he said, "That week of the protest I had a realization of who I really was. It wasn't John Seed protecting the rainforest; the rainforest was protecting herself through the humanity she had cradled into life." Oh, of course! If we could feel the earth acting through us, if we could experience being held by a power greater than our own, it would change everything. We would feel graced.

The story was fresh in my mind as we sat by the pond in the forest, and John was challenging me once more to take the group work deeper. "How do we break free of our anthropocentrism?" he asked again. I remembered a book our family had enjoyed together when our kids were young. *The Once and Future King* by T. H. White was a retelling of the legend of King Arthur. At the hands of the wizard Merlin, Arthur received a most unusual education. Knowing that great responsibilities were in store for the boy, the wizard changed him for periods of time into various creatures—a falcon, an ant, a badger, a wild goose, a carp in the castle moat. As we read each of Arthur's adventures in learning, they stretched our minds and enlarged our perceptions and perspectives beyond what we were accustomed to as humans.

Now, with John, I realized we were talking about the *ecological self*, a term we both knew from the Norwegian philosopher Arne Naess and the deep ecology movement he had launched. I had thought the term a helpful secular analogy for the Buddha's teaching of dependent co-arising. The discovery of the term *deep ecology* excited me when I encountered it, striking me as relevant to the work I was using. But here, talking with John, I soon realized he took the human-centeredness of our culture more seriously than I had. What would it take, we wondered, what kind of group work could move us beyond our narrow human self-interest?

We stripped and dove into the pond, shaking off the noon heat. John's question turned in my mind as I swam down into the murky depths. Plunging into this other world, I became the carp in the castle moat, and Arthur's story became mine.

As we emerged from the pond and dressed, the seed of an idea was taking shape in my mind. Rainforest, Merlin, carp came to me and gave me an answer—a Council of All Beings. In this council, people would step aside from their human identities and speak on behalf of other life forms. It would be a simply structured ritual, both playful and solemn, engaging our imagination and proceeding in stages, widening our understanding and deepening our commitment to life. Back and forth we riffed with mounting enthusiasm for this new form. I decided to give it a test run to see if such a ritual could actually work. "I'll do it in the weeklong training near Sydney," I said, referring to the final workshop before my departure for the States, "but you've got to promise to be there."

It turned out to be easier than I expected. I simply invited the forty participants to let themselves be chosen by another life form. With cardboard, markers, paste, mud, and leaves, we made masks for our new identities. In slow procession, we followed the drum and didgeridoo to a wide gorge below a waterfall. Gathering in a circle on flat boulders, surrounded by water, trees, sun, and stone, each person called forth their being to the council.

Soon John and I found ourselves leading councils around the world, inspiring others to do the same. With the help of our colleague Pat Fleming and including a key chapter by Arne Naess, we published *Thinking Like a Mountain: Toward a Council of All Beings*. For us and people around the world, the ritual has opened up dimensions of perception and motivation that John and I, that day beside the pond, could not have imagined.

EVERYTHING LEANS

The Creativity of Dependent Arising

Elizabeth Mattis Namgyel

I FOUND MY WAY INTO Joanna Macy's world in 2011 through reading her doctoral thesis, *Mutual Causality in Buddhism and General Systems Theory.*[1] There are no words to express the delight I felt when I recognized that she had brought to life a topic that has haunted me (in the most spectacular way!) for my entire adult life: the Buddha's insight into the natural principle of *pratityasamutpada*, most commonly translated from Sanskrit as "dependent arising" or "interdependence."

I received the transmission of pratityasamutpada from my teacher, Dzigar Kongtrul Rinpoche, when I was in my early twenties. His studies were grounded not only in the spoken words of the Buddha but also in the commentaries of renowned Indian spiritual geniuses such as Nagarjuna, Shantideva, Chandrakirti, Shantarakshita, and many others. The way my teacher passed these teachings on to me completely shook my world, but to encounter a contemporary Western woman who brought to this topic such authenticity and brilliance, and who could articulate its timeless relevance to the human condition, engendered in me a newfound confidence to deepen my studies and write a book on the topic, *The Logic of Faith.*[2] What I found in Macy is quite rare, even within the realm of contemporary Buddhist scholarship.

It surprised me to learn that Joanna Macy, whom I had always known for her tireless commitment to environmental activism, was also a student of Buddhist wisdom, which has a unique and radical vision of social change. On the path of the bodhisattva, one embodies the responsibility that comes from recognizing oneself as part of a greater interdependent whole. Through the understanding that one's own well-being is inextricably linked to the well-being of others, and that spiritual maturation does not happen in a vacuum, one makes a fierce commitment to awaken the heart through altruistic responsiveness. Inwardly, one does the work that liberates one's entire being from the burdens that come from clinging to the myth of a singular, separate self.

But the commitment to cultivate altruism is only part of the equation. In exploring contingency, one begins to discover something about the nature of reality—that life doesn't lend itself to being known in a determinate way. Why? Because, well . . . "it all depends." This deceptively simple insight poses a significant challenge for the mind that searches for ultimate truths and confronts our tendency to want to fix things. How do we live in a world that bursts from the seams of our ideals? The insight into dependent arising interrupts any and all manifestations of fundamentalism, rigidly held principles, or expectations we might cling to, including those that are core to even our noblest endeavors.

As I got acquainted with Joanna Macy, I became deeply curious as to how she reconciled her activism with this insight into the nature of pratityasamutpada. Before long, we met in Boulder, Colorado, and it was like reuniting with a kindred spirit and finding a mentor at the same time. Since then, we have met several times to discuss our most cherished topic: pratityasamutpada. During our dialogues I have been continuously touched by the fierceness of her curiosity, the depth of her understanding, and her passion to live in the heart of this challenging and gorgeous conundrum.

PRATITYASAMUTPADA

The teachings of pratityasamutpada emerged when the Buddha, at the dawn of his awakening, had an insight into the nature of reality. In fact, you might say it was the essential insight that lay at the heart of everything he taught. He expressed his discovery in a curious and powerful way, saying:

> This being, that becomes;
> from the arising of this, that arises;
> this not being, that becomes not;
> from the cessation of this, that ceases.[3]

The Buddha further elucidated this statement by describing two bundles of reeds leaning up against each other, illustrating that each bundle stood by virtue of its dependence upon the other: if one bundle were to fall, the other would fall as well. What was he pointing to? That *nothing* exists outside the nature of contingent relationships: that *everything leans.*

You can find many translations of *pratityasamutpada,* the most common being "interdependence," "dependent arising," and "dependent origination," but there are others. The activist and Buddhist teacher Thich Nhat Hanh translates *pratityasamutpada* as "interbeing." Herbert Günther, the German philosopher and early translator of Sanskrit and Tibetan to English, used the term *open-dimensionality* to indicate that things find definition, meaning, and function *only* in dependence upon their contexts. Joanna Macy translates *pratityasamutpada* as "mutual causality," which she describes as "a reciprocal dynamic at play."

In the simplest terms, pratityasamutpada refers to the nature of relationship. Cause and effect is one way of talking about the nature of pratityasamutpada. If we pay attention, we will see how we impact our environment, and do what we must to live our lives in a more compassionate way. However, the Buddha took the teachings on pratityasamutpada even further—in fact, as far as they could go—into the nature of "things" themselves.

NATURAL CREATIVITY

It is easy to miss the subtle implications of pratityasamutpada. Macy describes it as "a jewel, [often] taken as either too obvious to be interesting (everything has a cause) . . . or too arcane to be relevant to real life."[4] Her words echo those of the Buddha himself, when he cautioned us not to underestimate the subtle and transformative power of this insight. The Buddha's teachings on pratityasamutpada describe the natural play of creativity itself. He wanted us to see for ourselves how the world of appearances and possibilities—either conscious or material, animate or inanimate, coarse or subtle—arises, expresses itself, and falls away due to the play of contingency. That everything leans has deep implications.

The inquiry into the nature of things is a formal practice in the Buddhist Mahayana tradition. These queries guide us through a series of specific investigations that poise the mind for a direct glimpse into the nature of pratityasamutpada. The teachings present three challenges: they ask us to search for something that exists as a singular whole (that is not made of parts), for something that doesn't change, and for anything that exists outside the nature of conditioned reality. In short, we are looking for something that exists *in*dependently versus *inter*dependently. Can we find such a thing?

For a moment, try to imagine yourself as existing outside the nature of causes and conditions, as an independent entity. How would you perceive the world around you? How would you feel pain and pleasure? How would you communicate? You might even ask yourself how you could move, because movement requires a multiplicity of interrelated parts searching for balance in the field of gravity.

Our ability to know is also only possible *because* everything leans! Try for a moment to locate exactly where you end and your world begins. Can you separate your awareness from the world you experience? Probably not. And yet you also can't say that you are one and the same as the world you perceive. Could it be that what we call "experience" is simply a playful exchange between our subjective awareness and the dynamic play of the world we encounter? Again, mutual causality at work.

These investigations into the nature of pratityasamutpada give us a lot of information about who we are. We often search for a sense of intrinsic identity. But when we search for a singular, permanent, or independent self, we might find that who we are resists absolute definition. For instance, if we are parents, we are only parents in relationship to our children—in relationship to *our* parents we are children; when standing in line at the grocery store we are customers; at the dentist we are patients. Yet again we find that things find meaning, function, and characteristics *only* in dependence upon their respective contexts.

This practice of "looking and not finding" an independent, self-defining "I" is often misconstrued as an attempt to diminish the suffering of a particular identity group, or as an unconscious strategy used to "spiritually bypass" something we don't want to face in the name of "transcendence." But in searching for an autonomous, self-defining identity, we are not undermining the power of relationship and all the joy and suffering that comes along with it. *Au contraire.* We are taking up the responsibility of knowing ourselves as part of this intricate and sensitive system in which everything we do matters, while reminding ourselves that we are not limited to the labels we assign ourselves.

The point here is that nothing exists outside the nature of pratityasamutpada, which is not a thing but rather a process. Macy emphasizes that everything arises in reciprocal interaction, reflecting not a thing or essence, but an orderly process, just how things work. This way of understanding creation stands in stark contrast to our conventional linear view of causation or evolution, in which one thing begets another thing. Yes, we all understand that, in an unexamined way, an apple seed begets an apple tree. Who would argue with that? But if we look at things in a more nuanced way, we find that the nature of the seed itself is made of parts and relies upon a universe of other conditions—most of which we will never see—in order to sprout.

It is because nothing stands on its own that life will always have an element of mystery, and it is right to be in awe of it. That we can't pin down the entirety of the causes and conditions that brought us to this very moment does not indicate a flaw in our ability to discern. Rather, it is a testament to the fact that life doesn't lend itself to being known in a determinate way. As Macy explains, "From the viewpoint of mutual causality the impossibility of arriving at ultimate definitions and formulations of reality does not represent a defeat for the inquiring mind. It is only final assertions that are suspect, not the process of knowing itself."[5] It must be acknowledged that this can unsettle the mind that wants to know. But we can remedy that with a bit of wonder and curiosity, which will poise our mind to engage the world *in accord* with its nature.

CITIZENSHIP

We have been looking at pratityasamutpada as the ground of reality, but you may be asking, "Well, what does this have to do with me?" This question shifts the conversation away from merely looking at the nature of reality toward how we might navigate our lives realistically. This is a practical matter that has to do with agency. It forces us to ask, "What kind of choices do I have in a world in which everything leans? How does this inform my spiritual path and activism?"

We all identify ourselves as a member of a family, perhaps a community, or a citizen of a nation. But in the most essential way, we are citizens of the great nature of infinite contingency. This means that we are not in total command, nor can we ever bring this dynamic expression we call the world to a static state of peaceful equilibrium. When I say we can't fix the world, I don't mean to imply that the world is necessarily broken. The world is anything and everything we can imagine and experience it to be—and more—which makes it too rambunctious for the likes of our ideals, as noble as they may be. It's all very humbling, isn't it?

Fortunately, on the path of the bodhisattva, awe and humility are highly valued as practical and crucial elements for clear seeing. Humility protects us from our tendencies toward fundamentalism. We are probably familiar with our tendencies toward rightness, even regarding our noblest aspirations. Yes, it is possible to become a fundamentalist vegetarian or activist, even a fundamentalist bodhisattva! However, in a world that doesn't lend itself to being known in a determinate way, absolute rightness is not possible.

Ironically, it is only when we can bear *not* shutting down

relating to any object—be it "the world," an altruistic cause, or another person—in a determinate way, our ability to read patterns increases. Through openness and curiosity we can receive vital information that we may otherwise overlook in being so *right*, and we can make informed choices that bring our actions together with our intentions. We may even come to recognize that the greatest respect we can have for anyone (or any thing) is to *not* assume we know who they are. In these moments of grace, as Macy describes it, we are "released into action."

LIVING IN THE HEART OF THE PREDICAMENT

If you think about it, pratityasamutpada provides the perfect setting for awakening. On one hand, things are not random; there are limits. If the causes and conditions for something to occur are present, it will occur; otherwise, no matter how desperately we try, we will never make it manifest. At the same time, things are not predetermined. We have tremendous efficacy and choice within this responsive system, which is why we have to pay attention. "Interdependence sets the limits and provides the scope for our conscious participation in reality," says Macy.[6]

If you think about it, it is truly amazing how living beings find their way amid the nature of infinite contingencies. In observing seed and fruit, humans have sustained themselves through agriculture; we have built civic infrastructure so that we can live together in communities; we have devised languages to communicate; we see the transformative power of kindness; we observe the destructive power of hatred. And yes, we often lose our way, too, which is why we need to refine our understanding of who we are in relationship to the world we live in. As Macy notes, "The world itself has a role to play in our liberation. Its very pressures, pains, risks can wake us up, release us from the bonds of ego, and guide us home to our vast true nature."[7]

We need the world to teach us who we are—not in an ontological sense but rather, as Macy says, "to guide us home to our vast true nature." Because, like everything else, we are not limited to the labels we assign ourselves. We are not big, nor are we small; we are not all-important, nor are we insignificant. So why get bloated about our achievements or collapse into complacency? We are citizens of the great nature of infinite contingency and everything we do matters.

Understanding our true identity gives us a pathway out of our habitual limited ways of responding to suffering—trying to fix our world, getting overwhelmed when we recognize we can't, or falling into a state of indifference so that we no longer have to feel the world around us. In exhausting these possibilities, we may see there is an alternative: we can live in the heart of the human condition. To step up to this meaningful and demanding task requires we embrace the work of a bodhisattva and its unique view of evolution.

We ordinarily think of evolution as things progressing in a linear way. We may invent a new vaccine, rocket to the moon, or even save many lives. But there will always be aging, sickness, death, loss, and injustice. The commitment to live in the heart of the human predicament—to burn with love in this unfixable world—provides us with a resting place that is compassionate and realistic. You might frame it as a healing approach versus a fixing approach.

I see Joanna Macy living this kind of life. We are desperate for such examples in our world! I have no doubt that the Buddha would have been quite delighted to know Joanna Macy, a true bodhisattva of the twenty-first century.

NOTES

1. Joanna Macy, *Mutual Causality in Buddhism and General Systems Theory: The Dharma of Natural Systems* (Albany: State University of New York Press, 1991).

2. Elizabeth Mattis Namgyel, *The Logic of Faith: A Buddhist Approach to Finding Certainty Beyond Belief and Doubt* (Boulder: Shambhala, 2018).

3. Quoted in Macy, *Mutual Causality*, 53.

4. Joanna Macy, cover commentary for *The Logic of Faith.*

5. Macy, *Mutual Causality*, 130.

6. Macy, *Mutual Causality*, preface, xiii.

7. Joanna Macy, *World as Lover, World as Self: Courage for Global Justice and Ecological Renewal* (Berkeley, CA: Parallax Press, 1991), 23.

THE DHARMA OF NATURAL SYSTEMS

Christopher Queen

AMONG HER MANY ACHIEVEMENTS, Joanna Macy is a leading philosopher of socially engaged Buddhism. Her focus on the correspondence of ancient Buddhist teachings and modern systems theory, which she calls "the dharma of natural systems," has never strayed from her deep commitment to respond to the suffering of others and to heal the world and its creatures. Her integration of philosophy and science with morality, service, and activism is a special mark of the Work That Reconnects.

From the earliest times, the Buddha's followers have interpreted his teachings in complex philosophies of mind and morality, approaching questions of being, knowing, and acting through logic and argumentation. Readers of these works have often been fellow monastics and scholars who benefited from elite training in classical languages. Yet most Buddhists over the centuries have lived their lives far from the study and debate halls of monasteries and universities. Their experience has been marked not only by sickness, old age, and death but also by instances of social suffering—poverty, injustice, tyranny, and environmental destruction. Traditional Buddhists have tended to focus on individual suffering and its relief—the teachings of the Four Noble Truths and the moral virtues and perfections. Mahayana Buddhists speak of the infinite compassion to save all beings, and modern Buddhist thinkers have included the findings of modern science in their reflections. Yet few have related these studies to the challenge of social suffering and social action as Joanna Macy has.

The key to understanding Macy's unique place as a philosopher of Buddhist engagement is her mastery of the principles of general systems theory. These principles are both maps to understand the structure of the world and powerful guides to transform it. Founded by the Austrian biologist Ludwig von Bertalanffy in the 1930s and extended by the cybernetic and information sciences of the 1940s and 1950s, general systems theory holds that living natural systems—from single-cell organisms to plants, animals, humans, societies, and ecosystems—are open to their environments, changing and being changed by internal and external conditions, and hosting reciprocal flows of matter, energy, and information.[1]

Changes in natural systems are guided by two types of feedback. *Negative feedback* stabilizes the internal patterns of the system, as when we shiver or sweat to maintain our body temperature. This is also called *adaptation, self-regulation*, and *cybernetics 1*. When conditions become more extreme, *positive feedback* prompts new patterns of organization, such as wearing protective clothing or, over long periods of time, evolving new physical characteristics or behaviors. This is also called *emergence, self-organization, evolution*, and *cybernetics 2*. These systems principles are supplemented by the principles of *integration* (the evolving system seen as a whole) and *nestedness* (the system's interface with its own subsystems and the larger systems of which it is a part). These four systems principles—adaptation, emergence, integration, and nestedness—may be identified at all levels of the natural and social worlds, and they provide a new paradigm for analyzing the relations and behaviors of systems large and small.[2]

After years as an activist and teacher in the US and abroad, Macy encountered the principles of general systems theory during her doctoral studies at Syracuse University in the 1970s. The writings of Ervin Laszlo, the Hungarian systems philosopher who became one of Macy's dissertation advisors, influenced her earliest publication on the congruence between systems thought and Buddhist teachings. Her article "Systems Philosophy as a Hermeneutic for Buddhist Teachings" was published in the journal *Philosophy East and West* in 1976.[3] Modestly calling her insights "rudimentary" and "exploratory," Macy analyzed the traditional Buddhist meditation techniques of *satipaṭṭhana, vipassana, shamatha,* and *parinamana* through the application of Laszlo's cybernetic systems paradigm. This bold and original comparison of systems thinking to Buddhist thought ultimately formed the foundation of Macy's approach to social engagement as a teacher and activist.

I discovered Joanna Macy's pathbreaking work during my own research as a doctoral student in the 1980s. When her article on systems theory and Buddhist meditation appeared in a computer search, I could hardly believe my eyes. She was doing what no one else had attempted: linking ancient spiritual teachings with modern science in ways that supported social analysis and activism. Soon I was reading her doctoral dissertation, "Mutual Causality in Early Buddhist Teachings and General Systems Theory," as well as *Dharma and Development,* her book on socially engaged Buddhism in Sri Lanka; attending her workshop for social activists at a local Zen center; and reconsidering my own assumptions about the study of religion in a time of rapid social change. This led me to write my own dissertation on the topic of systems theory in religious studies and to apply Macy's insights to my fieldwork among the Dalit ("oppressed" or "untouchable") converts to Buddhism in India.[4] Again, I discovered that Macy had trod these paths, having visited the new Buddhists in the 1970s. So it was that Joanna became an early pathfinder for my own development as an engaged Buddhist scholar and practitioner.[5]

Macy argues that modern systems theory and early Buddhist teachings are distinctive in strikingly similar ways. They are *empirical*—rooted in observation, not speculation. For the meditator, learning takes place by watching the mind and body; for the scientist, by watching phenomena in nature and in the lab. The teachings are *operational*—asking how, not why or what. The Buddha stressed that the past and future may not be known, only the ways in which we act in the present; for the scientist, the variables in an experiment are measured in real time, not in memory or anticipation.

The principles of systems theory and the Buddhist dharma are *process-oriented*—rooted in universal change, not the appearance of permanence. For the Buddha, impermanence was a fundamental mark of reality; for systems thought, the cybernetics of adaptation and emergence are the dual faces of natural systems. And most importantly for Macy, both systems principles and Buddhist teachings are *nonlinear*. Causes and effects are mutually conditioned, interdependent, reflexive, holistic, and organismic. In Buddhism, mutual causality lies at the heart of the Buddha's awakening, while in systems science, feedback loops connect natural systems with their internal subsystems and their external metasystems.

In her philosophy and practice of engaged Buddhism, Macy shows how systems philosophy recapitulates traditional Buddhist ideas. These include direct investigation (the Buddha famously said, *ehi passiko*, "Come and see"); the nature of phenomena as impermanent (*anicca*) and compounded (*anatta*); and the master teaching of dependent origination (*pratityasamutpada*), which Macy calls "mutual causality." This is the heart of the Buddha's enlightenment and the lynchpin of his social philosophy. No other philosophies, Macy has argued, at the time of the Buddha or in modern times, have arrived at just these interrelated principles and applied them to problems of cognition, embodiment, decision-making, morality, and social action.

Macy's dissertation, published in 1991, zeroes in on the concept of mutual causality. Drawing on early Buddhist texts and systems literature, Macy spells out the parallels in their analysis of classical philosophical problems: the self as process (nature of mind), the interdependence of knower and known (epistemology), the interdependence of body and mind (dualism/nondualism), the interdependence of doer and deed (free will/determinism), and the ethics of mutual causality (social action).[6] In each case, she shows that the one-way cause-and-effect analysis of classical philosophy and science fails to account for the deep interaction and interdependence of natural systems. In the co-arising of self and society, for example, Macy describes how individuals shape and are shaped by biological and social networks, and how "they form larger self-sustaining patterns, which in turn relate to build yet more inclusive and more varied forms." She illustrates her analysis with the Buddha's satirical story in the *Aganna Sutta* of the origins of society, in which the selfishness of competing food thieves results first in the rise of social mayhem and the Hindu caste system, but ultimately in the egalitarian social contract of the Buddhist sanghas and their symbiotic relationship with the state.[7]

In 1983, Macy published two works that illustrate her commitment to apply systems theory to the challenges of social crisis and transformation. *Dharma and Development: Religion as Resource in the Sarvodaya Self-Help Movement* is Macy's account of her fieldwork in Sri Lanka in 1979–80 among one of the best-known Buddhist liberation movements. Although she did not explicitly apply systems analysis to the village development work of A. T. Ariyaratne and his teams, she invited the systems philosopher Ervin Laszlo, then serving as the director of programs for the United Nations Institute for Training and Research, to write the foreword. The Sarvodaya Shramadana movement may best be understood, according to Laszlo, "in terms of the dynamics of complex open systems." When "economic, environmental, and social stresses—producing poverty and starvation, conflict and alienation, and sapping the will to live—threaten to destroy the balance of collective human systems that are normally self-stabilizing," the system is disrupted. If the system is to survive, the normal adaptation of self-stabilization devolves into "a period of indeterminacy," which, with good fortune, leads to self-organization and the emergence of a new social order based on new understandings and initiatives. These changes, Macy shows, are guided by the creative application of Buddhist teachings.[8]

In *Despair and Personal Power in the Nuclear Age*, Macy turns to a survey of general systems theory as a map for social activism.[9] Here she summarizes the theories of Bertalanffy and Laszlo, the anthropologist Gregory Bateson, the cybernetician Norbert Wiener, the political scientist Karl Deutsch, and others. In response to the impending collapse of planetary systems at every level, Macy writes that modern science, in perhaps its greatest achievement, "has broken through to a fresh discovery of this relatedness of all life phenomena." Instead of dissecting nature into ever smaller pieces, biologists

> began to look at wholes instead of parts, at processes instead of substances. What they discovered was that wholes—be they cells, bodies, ecosystems, and even the planet itself—are not just a heap of disjunct parts, but dynamic, intricately organized and

balanced systems, interrelated and interdependent in every movement, every function, every exchange of energy. They saw that each element is part of a vaster pattern, a pattern that connects and evolves by discernible principles. *The discernment of these principles is what is known as general systems theory.*[10]

In these pages, Macy sets aside the formalities of academic argumentation for a rhetoric of urgency and empowerment. She invites readers and students passing through the darkness of social despair to "re-member our collective body" and recover the capacity of open living systems for exploratory self-organization. Echoing her early upbringing in Christian spirituality, Macy advises leaders to "trust the interconnectedness of open systems. Let the knowledge of that web guide and sustain your work—like grace."[11]

In *World as Lover, World as Self,* published in the same year as her dissertation, Macy addresses the audiences of activists, meditators, academics, and concerned citizens she has attracted by her workshops and incisive writings. Once again, she devotes early chapters to the parallels between Buddhist and systems principles, and then goes on to apply them to threats to social, political, economic, and environmental justice around the world.[12] She reprises her work in Asia, celebrating the resilience of Buddhist communities under stress in Tibet, India, and Sri Lanka. She places her systems analysis and field investigations alongside the emerging bodies of thought known as deep ecology; the ritual of identification and engagement called the Council of All Beings; and the teachings of Arne Naess, Thomas Berry, Thich Nhat Hanh, and many others. These connections have only deepened in Macy's publications, workshops, and her online presence.

In these works, gazing fearlessly into the future, amid the existential threats and spiritual pain of our time, exercising her abiding impulse to link theory and practice, the ancient and the modern, and contingent patterns with abiding principles, Joanna Macy strives to make philosophers and activists of us all.[13]

NOTES

1. Ludwig von Bertalanffy, *General System Theory: Foundations, Development, Applications* (New York: George Braziller, 1968).

2. Ervin Laszlo, *System, Structure, and Experience: Toward a Scientific Theory of Mind* (New York: Gordon and Breach, 1969); *Introduction to Systems Philosophy* (New York: Gordon and Breach, 1972).

3. Joanna Rogers Macy, "Systems Philosophy as a Hermeneutic for Buddhist Teachings," *Philosophy East and West* 26, no. 1 (1976): 21–32.

4. Christopher Queen, "Systems Theory in Religious Studies: A Methodological Critique" (PhD diss., Boston University, 1986).

5. Seven years prior to my first trip to meet the Ambedkar Buddhists in India in 1987, Macy had already written on the movement with Eleanor Zelliot, "Tradition and Innovation in Contemporary Indian Buddhism," in A. K. Narain, *Studies in History of Buddhism* (papers presented at the International Conference on the History of Buddhism at the University of Wisconsin–Madison, 1976) (Delhi: B. R. Publishing, 1980), 133–51.

6. Joanna Macy, *Mutual Causality in Buddhism and General Systems Theory: The Dharma of Natural Systems* (Albany: State University of New York Press, 1991).

7. Macy, *Mutual Causality*, 183–91.

8. Joanna Macy, *Dharma and Development: Religion as Resource in the Sarvodaya Self-Help Movement* (West Hartford, CT: Kumarian Press, 1983), 7–8 passim.

9. The first edition was followed by significantly expanded revisions in 1998 with co-author Molly Young Brown under the new title of *Coming Back to Life: Practices to Reconnect Our Lives, Our World*, and in 2014 with Molly Brown as *Coming Back to Life: The Updated Guide to The Work That Reconnects*, both from New Society Publishers.

10. Joanna Macy, *Despair and Personal Power in the Nuclear Age* (Philadelphia: New Society Publishers, 1983), 24–25 (emphasis added).

11. Macy, *Despair and Personal Power*, 28, 78.

12. Joanna Macy, *World as Lover, World as Self* (Berkeley, CA: Parallax Press, 1991).

13. For the continuing relevance of Macy's systems analysis for Buddhist ethics today, see Christopher Queen, "The Ethics of Engaged Buddhism in the West," in *The Oxford Handbook of Buddhist Ethics*, ed. Daniel Cozort and James Mark Shields (Oxford: Oxford University Press, 2018), 522–25.

DECOMPOSING THE EGO

Wendy Johnson

I BEGAN TO PRACTICE ZEN MEDITATION when I was twenty-four years old and have continued to this day, almost fifty years later. My roots are in old Zen—long feeder roots fanning down into bottomless ground. My true home is a boundless field, alive with decay and far beyond form and emptiness. I did not take up Zen practice for spiritual solace or to pacify my mind. I was not looking for an escape from the challenges borne of grieving and loving a broken-open world that I knew I was made of. I was called instead to enter the core of this world and to follow its pulse, beating in my own throat.

In 1973, I moved to the coast of Northern California to immerse in a program of intensive residential Zen training at the San Francisco Zen Center. This began with two years of monastic training at Tassajara Zen Mountain Center, located in the remote Ventana Wilderness of central California. For the next twenty-five years I lived and trained at Green Gulch Farm Zen Center, at the edge of the Pacific Ocean, not far from the iconic redwood forest of Muir Woods National Monument.

At Green Gulch Farm, my primary practice was training in meditation and working in regenerative agriculture and restoration ecology. I met and married my Zen farmer husband at Green Gulch, our two children were born and raised there, and together my husband and I shared an uncommon love for building hot compost piles. Along with other pioneer Zen colleagues we cultivated a thriving seven-acre year-round organic farm that continues to grow and prosper to this day.

Traditionally, when practitioners come together in community to study the Buddha Way they are identified as *sorin*, or "forest thicket." This Japanese word refers to a gathering place of refuge where many distinct plant species grow together in close proximity. In a forest thicket of this nature, diverse root systems intertwine, enlivening common ground. From my earliest years of Zen training, I cherished the forest-thicket model of practice. Sometimes after a long day of planting rainbow chard and hoeing butter lettuce in the organic fields of Green Gulch Farm, I would escape three miles north to take refuge in the redwood sanctuary of Muir Woods. There, by the root system of seven-hundred-year-old arboreal giants, the invisible fungal network of the old-growth forest thicket pulled me into its mycelial matrix.

Grounded in the deep ecology of the living earth, I began to study Buddhism in earnest with the peacemaker and Vietnamese Zen teacher Thich Nhat Hanh, whom I first met following a Buddhist Peace Fellowship (BPF) retreat at Tassajara in 1983. Around the same time, I began to train with Buddhist scholar, author, and BPF board member Joanna Macy. In these early years of study, Thich Nhat Hanh and Joanna both emphasized the primary teaching of *interbeing*, or the expanded awareness that radiates out from keen mindfulness practice. Once interconnectedness is recognized, corresponding action arises. In this way, engaged meditation and the practice of deep ecology share a common commitment to the well-being of the living world.

Although I am grateful for rigorous Zen training, my years of observing randy decomposition have left me somewhat wary of domesticated teaching. Unknowing, undoing, and unraveling generate unlikely possibility. They unsettle settledness. Some years ago, Joanna presented the vital work of the psychiatrist Kazimierz Dabrowski, who studied positive disintegration in his clients. Dabrowski observed that when human codes and established organizing principles are no longer valid, then only disintegration may allow for a more adaptive and resilient sense of interbeing to emerge from calamity. This is one way that living systems adapt and evolve. When old forms become dysfunctional, the system enters a form of limbo, sorting out new directions and processes.

I find the truth of positive disintegration alive in every compost pile; it is the engine of decay. From functional food stocks to disintegrating stems and leaves, the living system takes new shape. Positive disintegration also fuels the mycological network of the forest thicket. Even in times of unprecedented destruction from mass extinction, severe habitat loss and human-driven climate disruption, interlacing mosaics of mycelium are repairing damaged networks. These membranes reweave the fabric of a disintegrating forest tapestry, creating new soil from woody debris and cycling nutrients through the food chains of forest ecosystems around the earth.

Over the years, those of us training with Joanna have developed a repertoire of rituals and practices to enliven the primary teachings we are investigating together in community. One ritual that has been particularly valuable for me in the context of gardening and restoration work is the Dance to Dismember the Ego. This playful and potent process is rooted in the traditional Tibetan lama dances that Joanna witnessed at the Buddhist refugee community of Tashi Jong in northwestern India. Every spring this monastic community honors its Buddhist lineage with three days of ceremonial sound, masked dancing, and tantric ritual. In the center of their community the monks create a formal Mandala of Mind, a sacred space for the dances to unfold.

Joanna's favorite ritual during this annual event was the Dance to Dismember the Ego. In the inner cortex of the Mandala of Mind, a small clay ego effigy sits alone, encased in a three-sided box representing the prison of greed, hatred, and delusion. Around this paltry little ego figure, the monks of Tashi Jong dance and offer prayers and rituals to release the stranglehold of self-centeredness. The Dance to Dismember Ego closes with monks dressed as elegant stags reaching down into the shrine of ego to toss the tiny separate-self fetish high into the air before devouring it outright. Ego consumed, the stags leap with unhindered delight.

In the 1980s, Green Gulch Zen Center, where I was head gardener, hosted a number of Days of Mindfulness organized by the Buddhist Peace Fellowship. One particular day, Joanna offered a Sunday morning dharma talk on the greening of the self. After lunch we met in the peace garden for a surprise ritual. Earlier that dawn I had filled a wheelbarrow of raw ochre clay gouged from a wet seep at the base of the coastal headlands. As participants arrived in the garden for the ritual, each person was given a little board with a mound of moist clay on it. Joanna introduced the ritual by telling the story of the lama dances at Tashi Jong. Then we spent time in meditative silence fashioning our own representations of clay ego figures. After an hour or so we reconvened to introduce our manifestations of separate self to the group.

We were both portentous and revealing in our presentations, and also strangely vulnerable:

Behold! The tiny self of monkey mind with paws covering eyes, ears and mouth just to be sure to see no evil, hear no evil, and speak no evil.

Ta-da! Here is modest little ego mouse, hiding under the dharma table and scarfing up crumbs from the great wisdom feast.

All hail! Meet Saint Ego-less-ness herself! Notice her subtle halo shining with good intention.

After each introduction, we bowed in unison to the ego being introduced. Someone even called out, "Long live the separate self!" With great reverence, each ego figure was placed on a central table to dry in the sunny wind.

Later in the day we closed our ritual with a celebratory circumambulation of the table of separate self. *"Gate, gate, paragate, parasamgate, Bodhi Svaha!"* we chanted. Then we ceremoniously smashed the little dry egos to smithereens and gathered the clay dust into a miniature Mount Sumeru mound where we offered sticks of incense and final closing prayers to end our day of mindfulness.

At sundown I returned to the empty garden by myself. I swept the fragments of dismembered ego into a wheelbarrow and rolled it down to our newest hot compost pile brooding at the dark edge of the field. The throne of decomposition was laid open, covered with a fresh robe of golden oat straw and hungry for material offerings. With just enough veneration, I spread ego ash on the compost pile, covering all trace of separate self with sweet drifts of blond straw layered with dank, microbially rich redwood duff gathered from the heart of the forest thicket.

Radical disorder is the master key to the kin-dom of decay. Into this palace of organisms, decomposing organic matter dissolves life, generating a wealth of manifestation at every level and scale. When the new compost pile was finished, it was full night in the garden. I closed my eyes for a moment, swaying to the distant sound of ceremonial skull drum and long tantric horns. In the blessed dark the new compost pile shimmered with the eerie light of positive disintegration. Forest litter danced cheek to cheek with dismembered ego, while all beings in the ten directions marked rhythm and kept time in the vast Mandala of Mind.

RADICAL DISORDER

From that ceremonial day forward, my practice has been inoculated with the yeasty culture of decomposition. And although I am grateful to have trained with some of the boldest Buddhist teachers of our time, my true master is microbial decay. As a reverend of rot, I have worked for decades alongside fellow Zen farm apprentices practicing dharma and ecology. Since 1998 I have taught and studied aerobic decomposition with thousands of avid middle-school students and their teachers at the Edible Schoolyard Project in North Berkeley, California. Most recently I have taught in our local community college system, training young indigenous leaders from the urban intertribal community in the principles and practices of establishing an agricultural and composting system for their traditional Native Foodways garden project.

Recently I had the privilege of working at Upaya Zen Center in northern New Mexico, helping to train fifty dedicated chaplain candidates in a two-year program of engaged ministry. My role was to provide a one-day immersion in the field of ecological chaplaincy for candidates training in contemplative end-of-life care, prison ministry, frontline environmental service, and programs of active peacemaking in refugee camps at the edge of war zones.

We spent the morning practicing meditation and investigating applied ecology and the braided teachings of interbeing, dependent co-origination, and positive disintegration. The team of chaplains seemed to have an insatiable appetite for immersion in living systems that are inherently messy and nonlinear. Comfortable with turbulence and ever-changing relationships, this dynamic cohort of chaplains was hungry for dismemberment of any separate self.

In our afternoon session we met in the compost yard at the gateway to Upaya Zen Center. There, professional chaplains, steeped in the practice of sitting contemplatively at the bedside of expiring hospice patients, tore apart a towering mound of fecund, steaming hot compost to investigate in intimate detail the dominant world of death and decay. Having heard my retelling of Joanna's account of the tantric Dance to Dismember the Ego, some chaplains sat in the cool afternoon shade of the southwestern garden, fashioning clay figurines to offer to the fire of the compost pile. Others sang and chanted in raucous abandon, praying and dancing with decomposition. Not a single chaplain turned away from the blunt truth of positive disintegration moldering in our midst.

At the end of our day of deep ecology, we gathered in a *sorin* circle of chaplains to bear witness to our newly turned compost pile. Positive disintegration fueled every layer. I imagined all the ingredients in this fresh mandala of mind decomposing over time into mature, humus-rich compost where no two molecules of humus are ever alike. Our tiny figurines full of inflated ego would soon come apart to testify as freshly alive compost. Radical disorder calls forth the path of unraveling, of brokenness, of full release. Here in this smoldering pile of debris, decomposition is the radical source of new life.

RITES OF PASSAGE

brontë velez[*]

TEN-DAY WORK THAT RECONNECTS INTENSIVE |
SUMMER 2017 | OCCUPIED POMO TERRITORY

here come summer running cross the meadow for us - thick in they fire, relentless in they gravity - roaring they crimson throat chorused by laughter, talm bout, *oh, so y'all came here for an intensive huh?!*

and sure enough, here sixty of us went, all sorts of ages, colors, classes, languages, cosmologies, and traumas, running to find home in other homes, tryna meet where love begins in us, singing an emphatic *yes!* longing to grow, to be stretched, to be reflected back to, to be held, to be found, to be witnessed, to resurrect, to belong ---

oooh child . . . but i learned bout being flippant, ambitious, & unspecific in our prayers for liberation - you best come correct during this apocalypse - these times intend *to uncover* and *reveal* - you gotta ask *how* you want the truth to be revealed in you, cuz you know creator likes to play games! and when we long for clarity, we'll for sure be encountered by ourselves - *encounter* at its root

[*] this here written in the grammar of blackness—ancestral practices in fracturing, contracting, collapsing, and reclaiming time. this here a draft, *draft* from *draught*, also giving life to *draw*, as in *to pull*, as in to *draw water from the well*, as in *to draw in a deep breath.* future beings: please feel free to challenge/ decompose/inoculate/pray over/use other languages/dance/sing this/add your wisdom/forgive us —

means to *meet the adversary* - the great turning demands us to turn all the way inward *first* - ain't nothing we gon do out there that we ain't first done in here ---

so summer and the thousands of ancestors we all brought with us go, *y'all sure?! you know we coming with the heat right? we pulling up with the sun in tow - y'all ready to be exposed? them doug firs and redwoods ain't gon protect you from this revelation!*

and here we go still talm bout, *yes!* talm bout some big ol' prayer to do *the work that reconnects* - when we don't really know a thing about what that's really gon require of us. done incarnated during a time of such profound separation with a prayer of profound relationship - yet, we so incredibly far away from one another - so incredibly far away from source - so many inheritances we gotta reckon with - especially reckoning with the impacts of the experiments of white supremacy, patriarchy, capitalism - those oppressions that feel like the never-ending kind - kind that ain't got no death cycle in them, kind that find themselves sewn into the atmosphere, kind that make every breath scarce, kind where every inhale feels like a confirmation that there ain't never gon be enough and that you ain't never gon be enough ---

and we ain't know it but we didn't come to do no work that reconnects. nope. they took on they own life. they became fugitive. unhinged themselves in the night from being owned by a doctrine - let alone a leader. the work that reconnects decided they was gon be done through us. decided to take us through a glimpse of the initiation that's really gon be required for climate justice. the great turning ain't some far off isolated event, the world ain't gonna one day unravel - for indigenous folks, for people of color, for the marginalized, for those most impacted by the violences of colonialism, US imperialism & war, for our more-than-human kin this been going on since time immemorial - since the womb of time was mined open by hungry ghosts, since black folks were kidnapped and made into currency, since english was stuffed into our mouths to replace the languages that once echoed mirror - the prayers that let home know we saw them . . . this shit been going on. whose apocalypse is coming? whose bodies will be used again to curtail accountability?

the intensive was *in-tense*, without a doubt - bout as reflective of this moment in time as it gets - each morning finding ourselves grieving - the rapid deforestation of the Amazon to the rage of Philando Castile's murderer being acquitted[1] - it's all the same violence - Alice Walker's words echoed around us, *but, in truth, Earth itself has become the nigger of the world* - but it be hard to see one another when traumatized behavior and supremacist ideology[2] come into confrontation in the same room - both unhealed, both needing to be supported but requiring an ecosystem of spaces in order to hold the complexity - elders socialized as white folks conflating discomfort with unsafety - not feeling seen or heard, not feeling honored, feeling silenced - and then folks of color and youth feeling unseen, unheard, dishonored, silenced when talk of environmental justice lacked an anti-oppressive framework - and you know we can't just skip over racial justice. environmental justice is racial justice. ain't one without the other - they are bound up in each other and must co-liberate together. but there we was confused for sure - needed each other but kept missing each other - bet the earth was feeling the same way! didn't think to call upon their wisdom to speak through us - the council of all beings longed to be welcomed into the room to interrupt what we thought we knew ---

taut between the urgency of a world inflamed, the grief of mass extinction, the oceans prepared to swallow us whole and then the truth on how we got here, how climate change is a product of white supremacy, colonialism, indigenous genocide, slavery, patriarchy, capitalism - inseparable from these truths - and how ain't none of this going nowhere no time soon unless we instigate cycles of death into their rhythm, unless we acknowledge these violences and our complicity, unless we grapple with and humble ourselves before our inheritances, unless we stare into the face of what we must be accountable to, unless we listen to what is really being asked of us, unless we trust ourselves, unless we dream.

but folks ain't wanna let go, ain't wanna let the work unravel us, some thought it was supposed to just bring us back together and that Joanna was the one to do it - to save us - what a daunting thing to ask of one womxn! all the practices in the world and we still couldn't find our way! death be scary when we don't wanna face it.

Joanna be saying, *there's no such thing as private salvation* - so spirit heard that and tried reminding us we gotta ecologize our liberation and our leadership to make god public, gotta go through the death and mythos of ego and martyrdom - the season of saviors has come to its close. we gotta fold back into the wisdom of the circle - gotta root our listening - pedestalizing those who came here to be vessels, not omniscient beings, will always disappoint us. to herald someone as god is actually a practice in dehumanizing them - doesn't afford them the room to grow, to breathe, to make mistakes, to be real. whether we wanted to or not, we were made visible in a collective initiation and rupture towards releasing the work to become something else.

RITES OF PASSAGE

i don't know how i ended up in my 23rd migration around the sun posted up at Canticle Farm working for Joanna Macy - little blk girl from Atlanta tryna make guns into shovels, tryna plant trees, tryna hold ceremony, tryna disrupt environmental racism, tryna instigate pause, tryna heal my relationship with the earth, tryna love myself, tryna make spaces for black people to mourn, rest, grieve. not surprised that on that journey of black liberation and spiritual ecology, i ended up living in a *community of initiation* rooted in the work that reconnects practice and started supporting Joanna and Anne Symens-Bucher as the coordinator for what was being called Joanna's last ten-day intensive.

what a gift those months were! what an honor to sit with Joanna each Tuesday, tears welling up in my eyes as i transcribed her voice through emails while she proclaimed poetry - what a privilege to learn alongside such an incredible teacher.

i ain't know what i was getting myself into! i thought i was moving back to Atlanta to join a dance company, then i found myself at this intensive - what a vortex! what a reflective microcosm of where we are right now - what a difficult, hilarious gift from spirit. if only we could have found the dance of humor in us then - remember falling asleep hearthed by horsetail in the forest - coyotes singing us to sleep asking us to listen and be gentle on ourselves.

what an intimate, miraculous and significant moment to be able to bear witness to what happened during and after the intensive. and the truth of how painful it is when our child starts speaking back to us, starts telling us bout ourselves, starts deciding their own path. the rage when other folks tell you how you need to raise your child. the work was going through a rite of passage and dying was a part of that process. i trust that what transpired that summer, though in many ways disheartening and disorienting, was divine - it felt like the ultimate gift when a body of work asks to utilize its very prayer within its own practice - that it speaks to the strength of the work - and the big prayer that it is to practice reconnecting to one another in spite of living within an atmosphere crowded by unfathomable inequity and separation.

the future beings are asking us to get real intimate, buoyant, and joyous with our relationship to collapse, to deformation, to death. to be willing to surrender to mystery. how can we relax into death as a security? how can we care for death? how can we trust death as the one thing we know for sure happens to everything? decolonization will require decomposition, it's gon require mushrooms, it's gon require us to be in our dignity, it's gon require us to revel.

i find myself surrendering to this study in revelations as an apprentice to death in a practice called Lead to Life.[3] this practice comes deep in contact with the ecology of death work that must happen at this moment - both seeding rhythms of death into states of oppression while also supporting the grief that letting go demands of us.

as wake workers[4] attending to and interrupting the impacts of police brutality, white supremacy, ecological devastation, & environmental racism, we are also interested in interrupting what Stephen Best and Saidiya Hartman describe as the "ongoing production of [black] lives lived in intimate relation to premature death (whether, civil, social or literal.)"[5] in environments impacted by persistent-traumatic stress, systems of oppression arrest our possibility to grieve and honor those we have lost to violence - we find ourselves in the wake of violence *fighting* for freedom - in resistance, in protest - this prevents us from being able to gather to practice and embody that freedom - there are rarely spaces where we can come to grieve, to heal, to restore, to repair, to reconnect, to be. our gatherings, teach-ins and rituals are rooted in healing justice as the work that will reconnect us - suturing folks of color's proximity to healing modalities, closing nature-connection gaps, grief-tending and opening the room and reparations for radical imagination anchored by rest. our alchemy ceremonies bring us into a quality of deep time that allow us to attend the horrors and traumas left unacknowledged and unattended that remain present while also dreaming us into black futures where all beings are free from suffering.

a beloved friend and teacher Jiordi Rosales asked us of this practice, how will you know when it's time to stop doing Lead to Life ceremonies? which in that question i hear, *when will you know Lead to Life must be laid to rest so another life can come through*? i offer this question to this work - what if decolonizing the work that reconnects simply means it must meet its own death? what happens when we let the work move through us? what happens when we surrender?

if the medicine we need is relationship, what if we surrendered to relationship with our trauma, with our inheritances, with our ancestors, with our bullshit, with our fears so that we could begin to make possible relationship with one another? what happens when we *be* with our inheritances, when we bow to them, when we thank them, when we bear witness to them, when we eulogize them, and then when we send them on their way?

THE SNAKES OFFER US PROPHECY

we halfway through the intensive and find ourselves inside a day with so much missing one another, and two groups of folks separately encounter snakes making love - a group of us come across two kingsnakes on the path, our bodies tense up at the eroticism, our breath drops down us in real low like an anchor's passing through our center - we're stunned by bearing witness to their bodies coiling around one another, black and white disappearing into each other - you cain't tell who is who - and they ain't got no interest in us at all, givin us absolutely no attention - they just continue to wind their bodies around one another as they cross the path (or the path humans made cross they home!) - what it was to witness snakes, moving their bodies with the earth together to move forward, surrendered, one long muscle ---

oh, the snakes, the ancient shape of them wound together as medicine song - we were humbled - their bodies born bowing - in reverence - crawling - listening closely to the earth - shedding continuously - growing again - the way they teach us about dancing into the pleasure of our entanglements, of being bound up with one another in our journey towards liberation, of being willing to surrender, of being willing to let love make us ---

NOTES

1. Philando Castile was an unarmed black man who was killed by officer Jeronimo Yanez in Falcon Heights, Minnesota, in front of his girlfriend, Diamond Reynolds, and her four-year-old daughter, Dae'Anna Reynolds, who were also present in the car.

2. Sarah Schulman, *Conflict Is Not Abuse: Overstating Harm, Community Responsibility, and the Duty of Repair* (Vancouver, BC: Arsenal Pulp Press, 2016).

3. Lead to Life is a collective that transforms weapons into shovels and holds ceremonial tree plantings at sites impacted by violence and sacred sites.

4. *wake*, as in the hauntology of blackness, described by black feminist scholar Christina Sharpe, *In the Wake: On Blackness and Being* (Durham, NC: Duke University Press, 2016).

5. Stephen Best and Saidiya Hartman, "Fugitive Justice," *Representations* 92, no. 1 (Fall 2005): 1–15.

CANTICLE FARM—
EMERGING LIKE A RIVER

Anne Symens-Bucher

JOANNA'S HANDS MOVE TO THEIR own music as she describes emergent properties: "When hydrogen dances with oxygen, who could imagine that water would emerge?" This revelation never ceases to delight her. I am once again enthralled, furiously taking notes in hopes that I, too, will be able to share the beauty of living systems theory when I offer the Work That Reconnects workshops. Joanna calls these lectures "Systems I," "Systems II," and "Systems III"; to get all three, one usually needs to participate in a ten-day intensive. At a certain point, I decided to put the notebooks away and let the learning sink in by osmosis. I realize now that the way I think has changed because of those specific lectures, and that my shift in perception has played a dramatic role in laying a foundation for "the way of Canticle Farm."

It was 1984 when I first discovered Joanna Macy and her workshop, "Despair and Personal Power in the Nuclear Age." I was a young activist involved in a nonviolent campaign to end nuclear weapons testing at the Nevada Test Site. A member of the first generation born into the nuclear age, I was always aware on some level of this fact and in despair about living in a world with nuclear weapons. My faith, which was formed in a progressive Franciscan parish and family, had taken me first to the New York Catholic Worker house where I lived with Dorothy Day, to creating a Catholic Worker house in Oakland, and then to the Nevada Test Site.

189

I had meaning, purpose, and community, but my grief, fear, and anger about the nuclear threat had yet to find validation or a place for expression. I believed I was "too emotional and too intense."

At the workshop, through the power of Joanna's experiential practices, I named my deep emotions as a normal and healthy response to the insanity of nuclear weapons. I understood that my ability to suffer with a suffering world was evidence of my humanity, my sanity, and my compassion. In an Open Sentences exercise I heard myself say something I had not consciously acknowledged: I was longing to be a mother yet in deep grief about bringing children into a nuclear world. I sobbed as I spoke these words. In the expression of my grief, I found a well of determination to continue my activism for peace and nuclear disarmament.

Eighteen years and five children later, I would invite Joanna and Fran to bring the Work That Reconnects to the Nevada Test Site; and in the fall of that year, I attended my first ten-day intensive. In 2005, we met for lunch because Joanna was interested to hear about a recent Hiroshima commemorative event I helped organize. I offhandedly mentioned that my twenty-five-year tenure with the Franciscan Justice, Peace, and Integrity of Creation Office had come to an end. Five minutes later, in an intuitive and spontaneous move I have now experienced from her many times over, Joanna invited me to come work as her personal assistant. In saying yes to this amazing and surprising invitation, I knew I was in for an experience I could not begin to imagine, and one that would once again change my life.

Back in 1982, I had moved out of the Oakland Catholic Worker house to take a break, regroup, and create another community. I relocated a few blocks away to a "mother-in-law" unit on land that even in its neglect was an oasis in an urban landscape. There were two lots and four houses, all in various stages of disrepair. From the first time I walked onto this property at 36th Avenue in East Oakland, I saw the potential for community. When people ask, "When did Canticle Farm begin?" my answer is, "It depends." W. H. Auden says, "We are lived by powers we pretend to understand." Thus there are several ways to tell the story, and it has not been a linear process, nor one I pretend to understand.

The story begins with the legacy of colonization and its particular impact on the Huichin village of the Chochenyo Ohlone people. Our presence and efforts to heal are done on their ancestral land. We seek both forgiveness from these indigenous ancestors and their blessing for the work we now do. We humbly undertake this task in response to the legacy of colonialism from which some of us continue to benefit and some of us continue to suffer. As we wrestle with how to repent and repair, the Work That Reconnects reminds us to locate the effort in relationships.

Another way to tell the story of Canticle Farm is to speak of the Mystery and my own faltering attempts over many years to discern and begin what "was mine to do" on 36th Avenue. Over time, I initiated many conversations; it was first with Terry Symens that the vision of what could be an intentional community based in the values of both Franciscan and Catholic Worker spirituality seriously took hold. Our vision of intentional community led to our marrying on the Feast of St. Francis, October 4, 1986. The vision was nurtured as each of our five children was born, all of them bringing gifts and learnings that shaped and strengthened us for the work ahead. We learned skills such as nonviolent communication, permaculture, natural building, and facilitation of restorative justice circles as we deepened in our spirituality, fought and forgave, fell and stood up again. The vision waxed and waned over the years, some of which left me feeling despair that the community we longed for would ever fully manifest.

When I started working as Joanna's assistant, the vision of living in an intentional community was still stirring in me. I was deeply disturbed by the growing evidence of global warming and found it nearly impossible to discuss with Terry what I was learning every time I worked with Joanna, reading and responding to emails that were full of dire revelations about climate change. I had never believed there could be anything more terrifying than nuclear war, but now there was another equally frightening source of planetary devastation. In August 2009, Terry and I attended a ten-day intensive together. Five days in, he turned to me and said, "Okay, I get it. What are we going to do?" In that moment, an idea emerged: What if we invited young activists to come live in our front house on 36th Avenue? I spoke to Joanna about the idea; she agreed to offer a course in living systems, and we would offer a place to live. Two months later, I met four young people at the first intergenerational Work That Reconnects intensive. Each of them approached me individually and asked if there were any opportunities to deepen in study with Joanna. Incredibly, all four moved to 36th Avenue two months later. By August 2010, our front house had become a kind of hostel for young climate activists.

In early 2011, as I was pondering how to acquire the adjoining lot with its two houses, one of them was vacated, paving the way for Pancho Ramos-Stierle and Adelaja Simon to join our fledgling community. Their move-in date coincided with the Fukushima Daiichi nuclear disaster. I was in such anguish that all I could think to do was hold a Truth Mandala. I encouraged our newest community members to attend. One of them asked me if I was inviting them to a special welcoming ritual. I realized that in fact a Truth Mandala was a very appropriate way to initiate people into the spirituality of Canticle Farm.

As our community formed, Joanna's influence and the people I met in my travels with her continued to shape and sculpt our vision. I brought people from Canticle Farm into the Work That Reconnects, specifically inviting them to participate in ten-day intensives. I also met people at these intensives, most notably Bernadette Miller, who would join the community and shape its early formation. A beautiful synergy was emerging between Joanna, Canticle Farm, and me.

In February 2012, the original vision once again expanded when we purchased a house on Harrington Avenue that backed up to our 36th Avenue lots. All I knew was the house "wanted to be in service," and I needed to raise the money for its purchase. I was grateful for Joanna's teaching that you do not have to have everything figured out before you take action. Solutions and plans emerge as systems self-organize. I clung to that wisdom as I was repeatedly asked, "What is the plan for this house?" As the poet David Whyte writes, "What you can plan is too small for you to live,"[1] and that is most certainly true when I think of what has emerged in this house we fondly call "Sister Water." Today it is home to four men who were all serving life sentences when I first saw the For Sale sign in December 2011.

The "plan" for Canticle Farm was continuing to reveal itself. We had five houses: "Sister Water," dedicated to supporting men paroled from life sentences; "Casa de Paz," dedicated to integral nonviolence; and "Sister Moon & Stars," dedicated to hosting events, including WTR workshops facilitated by Joanna and me. The other two houses continued to support my family and other community members. As we struggled with what strategies would best embody our shared values, it was with relief that I recalled Joanna saying, "Diversity is a characteristic of a healthy living system." Each house was invited to embody its charism and purpose as fully as possible, and we did not all have to be the same. I thought of the Systems II lecture on the four properties of living systems and could see that each house was simultaneously a "whole" and a "part" of the larger system that was Canticle Farm. I could feel the synergy from which emergent properties were generated. Franciscan spirituality, the Work That Reconnects, integral nonviolence, nonviolent communication, restorative justice, reparations, relational economy, the Catholic Worker movement, urban permaculture, initiation rites, and "soul work"—all these different streams of thought and practice were feeding and forming Canticle Farm. They were dancing together like Joanna's two hands, and something wholly unpredictable was emerging, like a river formed by many streams.

In September 2012, Joanna and I initiated the first of three cohorts offering facilitator training in the Work That Reconnects for people of color. Canticle Farm hosted these six-month courses between 2012 and 2015, and by the last cohort, the primary leadership for the training was assumed by Canticle Farm resident Adelaja Simon. These courses began the still-in-process journey of examining how the Work That Reconnects could both serve diverse communities and reveal structures of racism and other patterns of injustice. By 2015, my own inquiries to address racism led to a yearlong immersion experience for fifteen black people and fifteen white people titled "The Work That Reconnects: Exploring White Privilege, Structural Racism, and Black Oppression." As the year came to a close, we found ourselves *honoring our pain* for the world, the stage of the spiral we had inhabited for most of the year.

One of my learnings from this experience was that we did not have sufficient relationship with one another to tackle racism. At the conclusion of the 2016 ten-day intensive, and with the foundation of relationships that had been forged, a diverse group of us continued to meet monthly at Canticle Farm for a year to deepen in the Work while looking at all forms of systemic injustice. These various experiences left me seeing some ways in which the Work

That Reconnects could address racial injustice; they also left me broken open by the pain of my own racism and humbled to the core as I began to name it in the workshops I facilitated. I continue to live into the question of how to address racial injustice with the Work that Reconnects, which I see can offer a way of healing together while not looking away from the pain, and a way of remembering that we are not separate. This task of healing requires time to build trust, tools such as restorative justice, and truth-telling that is rooted in nonviolence. I have come to believe it is best done in long-term relationships. As a direct result of these years and experiences in both the Work That Reconnects community and in an increasingly racially diverse Canticle community, another priority for the mission of our intentional community is now working to heal across the differences of race, gender, class, and age.

As we humbly continue to embrace this path, we are grateful for the spiral of the Work That Reconnects and how it facilitates our processes—even a wedding. In the fall of 2018, Joanna created a spiral ritual and officiated at the marriage of Catalina Mahecha and Simon Salinas, our dear friends from Colombia who wanted to be married at Canticle Farm. We use a ritual form of the spiral in our weekly meetings and liturgies. The spiral holds and guides us individually and collectively. We remember to come from *gratitude*, the first stage of the spiral, before moving to explore the inevitable pain that comes from living together. The spiral is the background of our lives.

We are currently a community of twenty-four people, with six houses all named for stanzas from Francis's thirteenth-century song, the "Canticle of Creation." "Sister Moon & Stars" is now hosting young activists, harkening back to how we originally formed. "Casa de Paz" has become "Mother Earth," home to gardeners and healers. "Brother Sun," "Brother Wind," and "Brother Fire" are inhabited by community members contributing in a variety of ways. "Sister Water" is home to men paroled from life sentences and dedicated to restorative justice. "Sister Death," located on the land, is a place of ritual and prayer. We have a restorative circles' room where we go to work out our conflicts, and we have a Moon Tent for ceremony and rest.

When Francis, facing his own "unraveling," wrote the "Canticle of Creation," he chose to put his attention on gratitude and sing a song of interdependence, a song of gratitude and praise for all creation. Inspired by Francis and Joanna, we too choose to put our attention on gratitude in this time of the Great Unraveling and Great Turning. They both remind us that gratitude does not depend on external circumstances. Canticle Farm is an intentional community inspired by, influenced by, informed by, and immersed in the Work That Reconnects. We are singing in the Great Turning: one heart, one home, one block at a time. Here the three aspects of the Great Turning—holding actions, Gaian structures, and shifts in consciousness—dance together in an emergent experiment. As we do the "work" to "reconnect" these seemingly distinct aspects of our activism, it becomes hard to distinguish them from one another because we act from all three simultaneously. As they reweave together, a new form of activism emerges—one that is experimenting at the intersection of faith-based, social justice–based, and Earth-based nonviolence.

NOTES

1. David Whyte, "What to Remember When Waking," *The House of Belonging* (Langley, WA: Many Rivers Press, 1997).

POWER AND PRIVILEGE
IN INDRA'S NET

Tova Green

WHEN I WAS SEVENTEEN I HAD a conversation with my father that changed the course of my life. It was December 1957, and I had just finished my first quarter at Antioch College in Yellow Springs, Ohio. I took a Greyhound bus back to New York City, and my father met me at the terminal. As we were walking across town to catch the subway to the Bronx, I spotted a storefront with the sign SANE, for a sane nuclear policy, recognizing the name from conversations on campus. I pointed it out to my father and wanted to go inside. My father froze, would not enter, and told me not to go in. "What difference can one person make anyway?" he said.

His question has reverberated in my life ever since. It led me to participate in a voter registration campaign in Greensboro, North Carolina, and in the March on Washington in August 1963. These experiences sparked an awareness of racial injustice in the United States that has been a lifelong concern for me, a white-racialized lesbian raised in a secular Jewish family.

Eventually my father's question led me to attend a weekend workshop in 1982 with Joanna Macy titled "Despair and Empowerment in the Nuclear Age." Joanna's clarity, passion, and ability to create a space in which a large group of strangers could feel safe enough to express grief, rage, fear, and love for a world in danger were, and continue to be, inspiring to me. Joanna's resonant voice, skillful choice of words, and body language expressed her own grief, anger, tenderness, and a sense of her integrity. She "walked her talk."

Joanna wove Buddhist teachings together with an array of experiential exercises to enable us to move through painful emotions, allowing our truths to strengthen rather than paralyze us. We were then able to envision how we could participate in the healing of our world and emerge with action steps that would bring us closer to our vision.

That weekend motivated me to train with Joanna to learn how to lead despair and empowerment workshops. She was a role model and mentor for me as I followed in her footsteps to lead workshops and trainings in Australia, Japan, the Netherlands, and Canada. I asked several friends who had attended the workshop to join me in forming an activist support group.[1] I also became a member of a women's civil disobedience affinity group and, with many others, climbed the fence of a nuclear arsenal in upstate New York and got arrested. I began to see that one person, together with others, *can* make a difference in their community, country, and beyond.

INDRA'S NET

Joanna's presentation of Indra's net and the neural network—a way of viewing the power that comes from our interconnectedness—is a perspective that has resonated throughout my life. The Buddhist teaching metaphor of Indra's net, with its multifaceted jewels at every node of the infinite net, shows how each of our lives reflects and is reflected by all others. The neural network illustrates how the openness of communication between neurons contributes to the flow of energy and power, and the possibility for positive change. These images express the Buddhist teaching of mutual causality, which Joanna studied extensively in her doctoral work.

Mutual causality teaches that the self is neither enduring nor separate; it arises in relationship. We are shaped and conditioned by when and where we were born, our families, education, friendships, communities, and the institutions of our society. We are also shaped by our own thoughts and actions. What we think, do, and say not only affects others but also influences who we become. The karmic effects of the past can be modified by our actions in the present. Joanna writes, "In the flow of decisions and deeds, choices can be made that open broader vistas to perceive and know, wider opportunities to love and act."[2]

When we understand the teaching of dependent co-arising, we see a shift from a hierarchical, top-down expression of power to one in which individuals are empowered. Joanna highlights "the political implications of this view, in terms of the free flow of information and the welcoming of diversity."[3]

In part influenced by my contact with Joanna, I have made several key decisions that opened broader vistas in my life—moving to the San Francisco Bay Area in 1990, becoming involved with the Buddhist Peace Fellowship, and engaging in the practice of Zen Buddhism. Buddhist practice has deepened my lifelong engagement in social justice issues, especially after meeting Joanna in 1982.

DEEP LISTENING

Listening deeply to the concerns of others, including concerns of those with whom we disagree, is another core teaching of Joanna's that has been relevant in my work for racial justice. Her workshops include exercises that encourage open communication and curiosity, and that develop the ability to bear witness to others' pain. "The effect of a deed upon a person . . . depends on the person's character as shaped by other deeds," writes Joanna. "Previous behavior molds the subject by shaping habits and inclinations, patterns affecting perception, thought, and feeling. . . . The Buddha repeatedly emphasized that the effects of the past can be modified by present action."[4]

Deep listening has helped me understand the struggles of people of color who feel marginalized at San Francisco Zen Center (SFZC) and other Buddhist centers. For me, a longtime resident and senior student at SFZC, this happens both through conversations with other Zen students and through absorbing the dharma talks and writings of Buddhist teachers of color. These voices include Mushim Ikeda, Ruth King, Rhonda Magee, Zenju Earthlyn Manuel, Spring Washam, angel Kyodo williams, and Larry Yang. Through their writing and teaching they address the pain of feeling marginalized and suggest practices that address racism in our sanghas on the personal, interpersonal, cultural, and institutional levels.

RECOGNIZING THE WALLS WE ERECT

Joanna writes that "the walls we erect to block our perception of the needs of others wall us in also, stifling our capacities to comprehend and adapt."[5] These walls, which arise from our conditioning, may be experienced as fixed views or firmly held beliefs about ourselves and others, including stereotypes. We may develop aversions toward individuals or groups of people who are different from ourselves. We may only speak with people whose views (or skin color) are similar to our own, or we may only listen to media that reflects our thinking, thus reinforcing these walls. Stereotypes, when combined with political and economic power, can affect the culture, laws, and institutions of communities, organizations, and local and national government. In the US, white people have shaped many of these organizations and institutions, leading to what some have called "white supremacist culture."

This view of the conditioned and ever-changing nature of the self is one of the underpinnings of work on white conditioning and unconscious bias.[6] When those of us who are white recognize our unearned and unconscious privilege and bias, we come to understand that we are deeply conditioned by our environment, our families, and our history. We cannot change the past, though we can change how we relate to the past in the present, for the benefit of those who will live on after we are gone.

INSTITUTIONS, LIKE PEOPLE, CAN CHANGE

Joanna writes, "As co-creators of our world, we cannot extricate ourselves to claim a vision of its workings that is aloof from our own participation in it."[7] Our views shape our institutions, and just as people can change, so institutions can change. In looking at systemic racism in our society, it is easy to see how our institutions have been shaped by the racist view that white people are superior to people of color. Even though the Declaration of Independence states that all men are created equal, that was not intended by its framers to be true for men of color, nor for women or transgender people. Despite the Voting Rights Act of 1964 and the laws outlawing school segregation, many African Americans today are still denied the right to vote, and schools in many cities are still de facto segregated.

Over the course of the last sixty years, Buddhism in the United States has been influenced by many significant streams of cultural thought, including psychology, feminism, ecology, and social activism. Conversations in many Buddhist sanghas are now addressing and embracing current issues in diversity, inclusion, equity, and accessibility related to the gender spectrum, physical ability, and race. When we look at convert Buddhist centers in the United States today, most are led by white teachers in predominately white sanghas. This has become a cause of concern in the last three decades. The Buddhist Peace Fellowship (BPF) and SFZC are two of the many convert Buddhist organizations that have been examining racism in some depth.

At the time I encountered BPF, their mission was "to bring a Buddhist perspective to the peace movement and to bring the peace movement to the Buddhist community." I resonated strongly with this intention and served as a board member and later joined the staff. The multidimensional work of BPF included a focus on racial justice, spurred by an awareness of the difficulties encountered by people of color as they tried to participate in Western Buddhist sanghas. This was particularly acute as BPF engaged in working with prisoners, most of whom were people of color. Many BPF staff and members contributed to discussions that led to the publication of *Making the Invisible Visible: Healing Racism in our Buddhist Communities.*[8]

In this publication, Hilda Gutiérrez Baldoquin wrote about her first ten years at SFZC. When she first started practicing there, she began to ask the question, "Why is everybody white?" She was invited to join the board of directors and was involved in many diversity initiatives at SFZC as early as 1993. By the time I became a resident of City Center in 1999, some of these changes had faded away. There have been many sporadic efforts to address racism at SFZC in the last twenty years, leading to an increasing awareness among SFZC's board and leadership of the need to embed a Diversity, Equity, Inclusion, and Accessibility (DEIA) focus in every aspect of our Zen training and organizational structure. I am learning, though, that in a culture of white supremacy, the gains made by an institution at a given moment cannot be taken for granted and must be reinforced.

I have come to see that unconscious bias and privilege among those of us in leadership roles at SFZC may make it difficult to understand the perspectives of students of color and create the conditions that enable them to flourish. It is essential for those of us who are white to see ourselves not as separate individuals who may be "good white people" but as part of a white supremacist culture that shapes many of our policies and decisions. SFZC is one of many Zen centers and other Buddhist centers across the United States that are waking up to the vital importance of addressing racial inequities in our communities. At the 2018 Soto Zen Buddhist Association conference, diversity and equity were themes running through the four-day gathering, beginning with a keynote address by Dr. Ann Gleig.[9] The conference also included a panel of speakers, break-out groups, and TED-style talks on the topic. I learned that there is both *resistance* to thinking that this issue is vital for Zen centers to address as well as *recognition* that it is necessary to do so, especially in the current political climate.

Thus, as Joanna notes, "in the flow of decisions and deeds, choices can be made that open broader vistas to perceive and know, wider opportunities to love and act."[10] This is true on both the individual and institutional levels. I can see how this truth, which I first heard from Joanna in 1982, has broadened my view and made me more effective as an agent of change in my community, coming from a place of love. She has indeed shown me, in so many ways, that *together* we can make a difference.

NOTES

1. See Tova Green and Peter Woodrow with Fran Peavey, *Insight and Action: How to Discover and Support a Life of Integrity and Commitment to Change* (Gabriola Island, BC: New Society Publishers, 1994).

2. Joanna Macy, *Mutual Causality in Buddhism and General Systems Theory* (Albany: State University of New York Press, 1991), 177.

3. Macy, *Mutual Causality*, xiv.

4. Macy, *Mutual Causality*, 170–71.

5. Macy, *Mutual Causality*, 203.

6. See Ruth King, *Mindful of Race: Transforming Racism from the Inside Out* (Louisville, CO: Sounds True, 2018), and Larry Yang, *Awakening Together: The Spiritual Practice of Inclusivity and Community* (Somerville, MA: Wisdom Publications, 2017).

7. Macy, *Mutual Causality*, 196.

8. A publication prepared for the Buddhist Teachers in the West conference in Woodacre, California, June 2000.

9. Ann Gleig is associate professor of religion and cultural studies at the University of Central Florida. Her book is *American Dharma: Buddhism after Modernity* (New Haven, CT: Yale University Press, 2019).

10. Macy, *Mutual Causality*, 177.

TRANSFORM YOURSELF, TRANSFORM THE WORLD

Sherry Ellms

IN FALL 2018, AS I SAT AT NAROPA'S convocation, a ceremonial tradition that formally opens the academic year, I heard our provost, Dr. Janet Cramer, evoke Joanna Macy's teaching of the Great Turning, which she saw as an inspiration for how we personally and as an institution of higher learning could proceed into our new year and the future.

"Many of us here are students of Joanna Macy," said Provost Cramer. "She declares that this is an incredible time to be alive, a great privilege. In other words, you are here at this time in this place, with these people, experiencing all that is, for a reason. . . . There is a great mystery and magic in that . . . a glimpse of a new thing. It may feel like an individual experience, but there is a collective energy that moves us through the spiral of *gratitude, honoring the pain, seeing with new eyes,* and *going forth* . . . and this ultimately is about hope."

As I listened to the provost, I reflected on how our institutional and personal stories have influenced each other over the years to culminate in this present moment, and I considered how resonant Joanna's teachings are with Naropa's motto, "Transform yourself, transform the world." As Joanna would say, we are a mutual co-arising of insight and activity. The relationship between Naropa and Joanna has been and continues to be an evolution of learning, inspiring connection and expanding awareness.

EARLY DAYS

Along with Gregory Bateson and other systems thinkers on the cutting edge of shifting cultural consciousness, Joanna was drawn to a new educational experiment called the Naropa Institute in the summers of 1977 and 1978. Naropa Institute (now Naropa University) was a magnet for the counterculture, drawing college students, scholars, artists, dancers, scientists, poets, and therapists, including luminaries such as Allen Ginsberg, Anne Waldman, Herbert Günther, Gary Snyder, and Ram Dass. It was a place where Buddhist sensibilities and Western thought encountered each other in fruitful dialogue. Naropa's founder, Chögyam Trungpa, wanted to establish a new academic model that would embrace the world's wisdom traditions. Even more boldly, he wanted to create an "enlightened society . . . based on the premise that there is basic human wisdom that can help solve the world's problems."[1] These were years of great social upheaval, marked by opposition to the Vietnam War, the resignation of Richard Nixon, and the questioning of outmoded cultural and educational institutions.

For over a decade, Joanna had been hearing about Trungpa from her mentor, Freda Bedi. She finally met him in the early 1970s at his retreat center in Vermont, the Tail of the Tiger. While she was not interested in Trungpa as her personal teacher or in his Buddhist community, which she found to be very hierarchical, his teachings were singularly important to her, especially his book *Meditation in Action.*[2] That book provided a clear rationale for Buddhist engagement that provoked lively discussion about whether activism was an escape from facing your own problems.

The relationship between dharma and activism was, and still is, a ripe line of inquiry at Naropa. From the very early days, the campus and students were strongly impacted by the presence of the Rocky Flats Plant ten miles south of Boulder, Colorado. This once-secret nuclear weapons plant was responsible for making all the plutonium triggers for the US nuclear bomb arsenal. The plant was in operation from 1952 to 1989, generating and storing extremely hazardous radioactive waste on-site. During this time there were two major accidents, multiple fires, and contamination of nearby creeks and reservoirs due to leaking drums of plutonium waste and use of unlined trenches.

Allen Ginsberg and Anne Waldman, faculty in Naropa's School of Disembodied Poetics, joined others in nonviolent action to spread awareness about the nuclear plant and the need to shut it down. Students gathered regularly at Rocky Flats, where Allen played his harmonium as people sat on the railroad tracks blocking the exit of radioactive waste from the plant. They helped pressure the owner corporation, Rockwell International, who eventually pled guilty to multiple violations of environmental laws.

Around this same time, Joanna's deepening commitment to address global nuclear contamination led her to develop the concept of nuclear guardianship. Francis Harwood, Naropa faculty and board trustee, collaborated with Joanna in the late 1980s to create a nuclear guardianship slide show as part of the emerging Nuclear Guardianship Project. The images drew on themes of pilgrimage and sacred space, envisioning a way for trained guardians to monitor and protect the legacy of the "poison fire."

Cleanup of the highly contaminated site went on for over a decade. Though the area was by no means free of radioactivity, the cleanup was declared "completed" in 2005. Part of it was even officially designated a US National Wildlife Refuge, with areas set aside for public recreation. The buildings were taken down and the first six feet of earth were "cleaned" of contamination, but below six feet, all radioactive materials were left on-site. The history of the plant is almost invisible now, its lethal legacy out of public sight. There is limited data about the actual safety of the place for any living beings—human or otherwise. This new threat has generated a second wave of guardianship action.

In 2011, Naropa joined the Rocky Flats Nuclear Guardianship Project to cosponsor a semester-long "teach-in" that included specialists on airborne radiation, wildlife biologists, legal experts, former employees affected by the contamination, and photographic displays. Participants considered whether the former plant site should be closed to the public or become a research facility to study remediation of plutonium and other radioactive materials. The semester culminated with a weekend program with Joanna, introducing the "Nuclear Guardianship Ethic."

Anne Waldman recalls the early days of nuclear activism at Rocky Flats and Joanna's influence on Naropa. "She was part of those of us who were asking . . . the tantalizing questions of who we are, what energies of consciousness might we draw on, and what our life actions, our path should be. . . . [She was] one who still held the horrors of Hiroshima and Nagasaki in her heart and could answer the famous question, 'Can there be anything after Atrocity? . . .' Her powerful multimillennial ethos of the Guardianship Project . . . brought her back to Boulder and Naropa."[3]

Naropa University established the Joanna Macy Center in 2011, and it now cosponsors initiatives with Rocky Flats Nuclear Guardianship Project to bring awareness to this serious issue and to advocate for public safety and closure of the site.

JOANNA'S INFLUENCE AT NAROPA (2011–19)

The collaborative dance between Naropa and Joanna began with her teaching several weekend public seminars and quickly

evolved to her specific involvement with the master's degree program in Environmental Leadership (now called Resilient Leadership). Joanna became a visiting instructor in the program, whose
purpose was to bring the contemplative mind to social and ecological transformation. Her weekend teachings were part of the
required curriculum for our master's students, who experienced
the Work That Reconnects with different topics and focus each
year. Many students found this to be a highlight of the program.
One student said, "I reconnected with my original motivation to
do environmental work. Her concept of deep time allowed me to
go to the origins of sustainability, in terms of intergenerational
equity—providing for the needs of the future generations, guided
by our ancestors."[4]

In 2011, Naropa University honored Joanna as the Frederick
P. Lenz Distinguished Lecturer in American Buddhism. In receiving this award, she spoke not only of her appreciation of the award
but also that it brought her to Naropa once again. She called on us
to "imagine an institution of higher learning in this critical time in
history when we are not sure we are going to make it; imagine an
institution that is based on contemplative education . . . [where] we
can befriend our experience and find our own authority the way
the Buddha taught that we can."

In addition, she offered teachings to the broader Boulder
community. The Boulder Shambhala Center filled to capacity as
she gave a "transmission" of the twelve-century-old Shambhala
prophecy that she received from Choegyal Rinpoche of the Tashi
Jong monastery in India in the 1980s. Her presence and talk were
electrifying. The prophecy speaks of Shambhala warriors who
are to meet in times of great danger and employ the weapons of
wisdom and compassion. Joanna called for those of us who are
alive today to meet our responsibility to be awake and engaged.

Earlier in the 1960s, while meditating in a cave in Bhutan, Naropa's founder, Trungpa Rinpoche, had written a text called the "Sadhana of Mahamudra," where he spoke of declining social structures and extreme difficult conditions that lay ahead and would require spiritual warriorship not based on aggression. This text is traditionally practiced twice a month in Shambhala Buddhist centers and also at Naropa. Both he and Joanna asserted that darkness must be met with light, and aggression must be met with love. Joanna was not aware of Trungpa's experience, nor was Trungpa aware that Joanna had received such a transmission.

In 2014, Naropa invited Joanna to be the keynote speaker for its fortieth anniversary event, an international Radical Compassion Symposium. President Chuck Lief lauded Joanna: "She has had an incredible impact on Naropa and Naropa students and faculty over the years in her visits here . . . providing a profound underpinning to the Environmental Leadership and Environmental Studies programs and beyond to a number of our other programs." He also spoke of Christopher Hormel, a member of Naropa's board of trustees, who became a student of Joanna's and who then demonstrated his dedication to her work by donating seed money to start the Joanna Macy Center at Naropa in 2015. Both Joanna and Naropa were thrilled. Joanna explained, "It is a wonder to me, a marvel, a great piece of news at this stage in my life, bringing certain key streams of my life's work to the rainbow of Naropa's interests and strengths—a place that can carry on and add to this work and change it long after I am gone. This is great news for an eighty-five-year-old."

The mission of the Joanna Macy Center at Naropa is "to advance the vision and legacy of Dr. Joanna Macy's work in order to empower present and future generations in building a more resilient world that works for all." The three areas of emphasis for the Center are: (1) advancing the root teachings of the Work That Reconnects, (2) promoting research on the confluence of Buddhist teachings and general systems theory, and (3) supporting her vision of nuclear guardianship. These apply to all three pillars of Naropa's mission: contemplative education, diversity and inclusive community, and environmental sustainability.

Today Joanna's work has become part of the curriculum and culture of Naropa. At the undergraduate level, entering students use her book *Active Hope* as a framing for a required class. The physical geography course for environmental studies majors includes Gaia theory, the new cosmology, the Truth Mandala, and the three dimensions of actions necessary for protecting the earth. Students in the master's program in Resilient Leadership take a first semester course called "Inner Work for Resilient Leaders," where they are introduced to systems theory and the spiral of the Work That Reconnects. The framing of the Work That Reconnects allows students from various spiritual traditions and scientific and artistic backgrounds to encounter a contemplative, nonviolent approach to working with environmental and societal issues.

The second semester takes the graduate students more deeply into mindfulness meditation, loving kindness, compassion practices, nonviolent communication, and the sacred quality of the natural world. The framing of the three dimensions of the Great Turning (holding actions, life-sustaining systems and practices, and shifts in consciousness)[5] expands the definition of "activism" and diminishes the tendency to glorify or devalue any single way of engaging with environmental and social issues. All these practices are contained within the spiral and culminate with students "going forth" from a place of compassion and an understanding of their inherent interconnectedness to the social inequities endemic to this country. They see that ecological and social justice are inseparable.

Faculty have used many of the exercises from *Coming Back to Life* in the classroom. Open Sentences is frequently used as a structure that allows students in pairs to be spontaneous in their thoughts and to be heard with deep receptivity. The Bodhisattva Check-In, or Owning My Life, is a practice from the archetype of a bodhisattva, who vows to put others before themselves and work toward the liberation of all beings who are suffering. This gives students the opportunity to embody the perspective of the urgency of what is needed for now and future generations. Adaptations of many of the exercises in *Coming Back to Life* have been used in our bachelor of arts core classes as well as in our visual arts, religious studies, ecopsychology, environmental studies, theater arts, resilient leadership, and counseling programs. Outside of the classroom we have offered the Truth Mandala, a ritual that allows participants to express in a safe environment their strong emotions of anger, fear, grief, and discouragement, as well as joy and inspiration. This has been hosted by Student Affairs and the Diversity and Inclusion Office and has proven to be an effective way to relate to intense campus situations as well as the continuing barrage of difficult information about the environment, climate change, and social injustice.

BEYOND NAROPA: TAKING THE WORK OUT

The Joanna Macy Center is currently developing a "Living into the Work That Reconnects" program as a way of furthering Joanna's legacy. The purpose of the program is to provide resources and training for people who want to apply the Work That Reconnects in their work environments and in the world. Increased demands and requests for more exposure to her work continue to pour in. Although Joanna no longer travels to teach at Naropa, she is fully engaged in this process and is creating podcasts and webinars that will guide and inspire the hands-on programming we do on campus. The Center's intention is to make her teachings as accessible as possible and to demonstrate the inseparability of ecological awareness and social justice. This includes exploring the impact of the culture of whiteness as it has evolved in the United States.

When I think of Joanna's relationship to Naropa, the image of an aspen grove comes to mind. Similar to how aspens grow, Joanna is a "mother" at the center of a network of underlying roots that are binding, interconnected, and embedded in the earth. One grove of aspen trees can be connected for miles. We do not know how her work will grow, but given the legacy of her teachings so far, the challenges we face, and the principle of emergent co-arising that is central to her life's study and practice, we can trust her influence will continue to evolve and spread.

NOTES

1. Chögyam Trungpa, *Shambhala: The Sacred Path of the Warrior* (Boston: Shambhala Publications, 1998), 25.

2. Chögyam Trungpa, *Meditation in Action* (Boston: Shambhala Publications, 1991).

3. Anne Waldman, personal communication, email message to author December 5, 2018.

4. From an integration paper assignment in my course, Innerwork for Environmental Leaders, Spring 2017.

5. Joanna Macy and Chris Johnstone, *Active Hope: How to Face the Mess We're in without Going Crazy* (Novato, CA: New World Library, 2010), 28–32.

Joanna and Fran Macy on the coast, circa 1990s.

PART FOUR

DEEP TIME

Deep time is as old as the universe, as old as human consciousness, as old as our collective memories can imagine. Buddhists speak of karmic time, the long unfolding and repercussions of actions over millennia. Biologists speak of evolutionary time, the development of species, behaviors, ecosystems. Geologists know geological time, the great workings of wind and ice, lava flows, eruptions, and tectonic plate movement. For Joanna, deep time arises from gazing fiercely at the implications of nuclear waste—a legacy for countless generations to come.

In her opening stories, Joanna describes how the vision of nuclear guardianship came to her at a women's protest camp in the UK. For people of the future to know what dangers had been left to them, she saw the need for monitors who could guard the knowledge of nuclear radiation and guard the memory of the horrors of nuclear war. These revelations arose out of a call to understand and fully appreciate how the past and future are alive in every one of us today—genetically, environmentally, and karmically. Truly reinhabiting time means taking a long view of time, of feeling the very ground of our being as planted in time. This is perhaps more challenging now, when digital reality and the pace of change seem to accelerate by the moment, faster than at any other time in history. How many of the world's cultures can still rely on wisdom elders for a sense of continuity across past and future?

The work of "being time" is medicine for countering human-centric worldviews and patterns of domination and exploitation that override long-view wisdom. Joanna's powerful deep time exercises are some of the most transformative in her whole work. They draw strongly on the human capacity to imagine into the past and future and to see how actions today reflect choices of the past and potentials for the future. In Russia and Japan, two countries beset by terrible nuclear contamination, the work in deep time is restorative and hopeful. The legacies of Chernobyl and Fukushima will be playing out for a very, very long time, affecting living beings of all sizes and life spans in unforeseeable ways.

The writing in this section is sobering and often difficult to fully take in. How do people live with disasters that continue to shape their lives and communities, soils and waters? How do we find a path of responsible care for long-lived nuclear and chemical materials in the midst of grief and loss at their widespread impacts? It can seem as if nothing can be done to mitigate this horrific legacy. And yet the work in deep time is energizing and highly motivating, as it affirms our deep connection to Earth itself as ground for action. As Daniel Ellsberg suggests, we are invited to participate in a miracle, to consider, in deep-time terms, that "nothing is impossible."

—STEPHANIE KAZA

PILGRIMAGE TO GREENHAM COMMON

Joanna Macy

IN THE SPRING OF 1983, after a run of Despair and Empowerment workshops in Great Britain, I took off for a week on my own. With a rented car and a map, I drove out to visit some of the peace camps I had heard about. They had sprung up around the bases where the United States had been deploying planes, missiles, and nuclear warheads to be launched against the Soviet Union. This escalation of the Cold War, with its thundering presence of military convoys and low-flying training maneuvers, alarmed the citizenry, igniting a resurgent peace movement and new forms of protest. Instead of turning out for a day's rally and returning to the comforts of home when it was over, people of all ages and walks of life just headed off to one of the bases and settled in near the gates to block its traffic and interact with its personnel. It mattered to me greatly that people were capable of disrupting their lives for the sake of distant others they would never know.

Sometimes a camp started out as a peace walk of many days and miles. I had heard how the camp at Greenham had begun. A group of women, along with infants and toddlers they couldn't leave behind, set out from Cardiff in Wales and headed to the Royal Air Force base in Oxfordshire to implore the base commander to stop hosting America's first-strike weapons. Meetings were held at towns along the way, and their numbers swelled. When they finally arrived at the base, the commander was too busy to meet with them, so they spent the night by the main gate to wait until he was free to talk. However, the commander wasn't available the next day, nor the day after that, by which time the women had settled in along some hundred meters of the barbed wire fence. The Greenham Common peace camp, eventually to become thousands strong over weekends, had become a reality . . . and a beacon to activists around the world.

Making my way from camp to camp—Porton Down, Molesworth, Upper Heyford—I was haunted by a sense of déjà vu. Names such as Canterbury and Santiago de Compostela surfaced in my mind. I thought of the paths that lead the pilgrims to the great monasteries that kept the flame of learning alive after the breakdown of the Roman Empire during the long Dark Ages. They, too, had been training grounds in nonviolent community devoted to an austere and long-term task for the sake of those who came after. Over millennia pilgrimage has been in our bones.

I had tasted this in Sri Lanka just three years before. With a friend from the Sarvodaya movement, I, too, had gone on pilgrimage from one ancient temple to another. These were the oldest temples, established 2,300 years ago when a royal brother and sister came from India to bring the teachings of Gautama the Buddha. What I remember most is how we all sang together along the way, especially on the scary roads. We took a bus to manage the steep hills, and also to carry the cooking pots for those marvelous meals, stopping by a riverbank or paddy field. At night we would stay in the temples. I remember how I almost learned to sleep on the marble floor of the vihara with just a cotton sari as my mattress, and how happy we were. Being a pilgrim taught me that one's devotion can make a place holy.

By happenstance, my visit to Greenham Common was on the day the police or bailiffs were attempting to evict the women.

In a steady rain the bailiffs were dragging the women still sitting in the entry road. I watched as the uniformed and booted men trod on hands and breasts, set fire to tents and gear. I watched a child's gas-soaked doll explode into flames. Standing there in shock, I could hear the women, calling to each other over the heads of the men assaulting them. They were singing high, lovely calls, as if helping one another remember, and there was an unhurried patience to their resistance. It felt as if they would just keep on and never think about quitting, as if their steady commitment could outlast the killing power of the radioactive warheads they were blocking.

"How much longer do you count on staying?" I asked a punk-haired woman rocking her baby as we hunched under my umbrella. She had been an office worker in London. With her free hand she fingered the wet strands of her spiky hairdo. My question puzzled her. "Well, I can't rightly say, I don't know how long it will take." "Take for what?" I asked. "To close the base. I'll stay till then, of course." It took thirteen more years.

I took her and her baby in my car as I drove out for food for the women. When we returned with supplies, the bailiffs were gone, the rain had lifted, and the women were starting to make supper. The vision came as I was squatting by a cooking fire, too exhausted to speak. Through the smoke from the damp wood fire, and beyond the women's bodies and their pots, I saw in the middle distance cooling towers of a nuclear station. And moving around them, I saw human silhouettes.

The vision brought a sense of relief, because I immediately understood it to be a guardian site. Of course! For life to go on, this is what would have to happen around our nuclear installations. These peace camps had modeled a possibility from the future: that even after disarmament, even after the last reactor closed, something like a citizens' presence would be needed to care for the containment of the radioactivity. For every element of the nuclear fuel chain—from uranium mines to the warheads—would remain both contaminated and contaminating for many millennia to come.

As I found my way to an inn and a dry bed, I already knew that this vision and its message would never leave me. The ancestors whom I sensed had been accompanying me would help me grow my own kind of perseverance and devotion.

THE PRESENCE OF THE FUTURE BEINGS

Joanna Macy

ON THE FRONT DOOR, BEFORE our monthly meeting, I stuck a sign reading "CHERNOBYL TIME LAB: November 11, 2088." I put on one of Fran's tapes of Russian liturgical chanting as the others arrived. "Welcome!" I said, ushering them in. "Our work here at the Time Lab of this guardian site centers on cultivating the capacity to journey back through time. This is important because the decisions made by people in the late twentieth and early twenty-first centuries on how to deal with the poison fire have such long-term consequences. We must help them make the right choices. So, you have been selected to go back in time to a group on the West Coast of California that has come to our attention. They are meeting exactly one hundred years ago today to try to understand, with their limited consciousness, the ways their authorities are containing the poison fire. Therefore, we will go back to enter their body-minds as they proceed with their study, so that they will not become disheartened."

The vision from Greenham Common had stayed with me. I had come to imagine it as a glimpse of a guardian site of the future, where nuclear waste containers and irradiated structures could be monitored and repaired, and where our planet's wisdom traditions could provide contexts of meaning and disciplines of vigilance. Over the intervening five years I had looked at current practices to see if this made any sense.

Now, choosing to engage our moral imagination as well as our native intelligence, I had organized a study-action group. The Fire Group, as we came to call it, included a fine diversity of folks—an anthropologist, a nuclear engineer, a dancer, a potter, a writer, an astrophysicist, an environmental lawyer. After awhile, my husband, Fran, joined us, too, bringing his clear mind and his enjoyment of group learning. What he absorbed with the Fire Group was foundational for the Center for Safe Energy, a nonprofit he soon organized to catalyze and support environmental groups throughout the former Soviet Union. This work brought Fran the Nuclear-Free Future Award, which he was thrilled to share with the great Russian scientist Alexey Yablokov.

On this November day, 1988, it was my turn to take the teaching role, and the topic was current US containment practices for radioactive materials. The information I'd outlined on sheets of newsprint was fairly technical; it was also so horrific that I worried about my colleagues' ability to sustain their attention and motivation. We needed some help.

"Our research reveals," I continued, "that in time travel, an essential factor is intention: a strong, unwavering belief in the purposes the heart has chosen. If our intention is clear, we can travel back a century to embody ourselves in this very group. Now, if you are ready . . . this will take about thirty seconds."

I turned up the basso-profundo chanting. Then switching it off, I proceeded with the day's topic. In the course of the session, no comments were made about its unusual introduction; everyone was too focused on the material itself. But each of us, I think, sensed a heightened caring, like an internal presence that wanted us to understand the poison fire and not underestimate our own intelligence.

What we learned so far in our study-action group confirmed what I had discovered in the years since Greenham Common: government and industry were so preoccupied with putting nuclear waste out of sight and out of mind that they ignored the inevitability of leakage. No container lasts as long as its radioactive contents, because of embrittlement and cracking caused by the radiation. Even buried deep underground, the poisons leak and travel, for rock layers shift, fissures open, waters trickle into streams, wells, rivers. The managers and policy makers I interviewed chose to count on some future technical solution and saw no need to inform the generations to come or to develop a system of long-term care.

I racked my brain about whom to ask for guidance, but the only answer that came up was the future beings themselves, those who would have to live with our radioactive legacy. There was, of course, the problem of their not being born yet. But one renowned radiation scientist didn't see future generations as out of reach. I could never forget the words of Sister Rosalie Bertell: "Every being who will ever live on Earth is here now. Where? In our gonads and our ovaries, and in our DNA."

Since we wanted to develop an understanding of what future generations will need and want to know about our radioactive legacy, we found the best way to hear from them was to have them speak through us in role plays and ritual. That's how, for example, we heard the name *poison fire*. These role plays soon became Deep Time exercises, beloved around the world. They enlarge the temporal context of our lives. They expand our experience of responsibility and agency beyond our personal life spans. As we discover how natural and rewarding it feels to act on behalf of future generations, we recapture the potent ancestral motivations that bequeathed us cathedrals and intricate irrigation systems.

Working for the sake of future lives we will never know, we develop the spiritual strength exalted in the Bhagavad Gita and evoked by Gandhi—to act without attachment to the fruit of one's actions.

Thanks to our study group on nuclear waste, which lasted four years, the beings of the future and their claim on life became so real to me that I began to sense their presence, and to imagine them by my ear—and that if I turned my head fast enough, I could glimpse them over my shoulder. After Fran died, my preoccupation with time deepened. From winter solstice 2010 through spring equinox 2011, I undertook a home retreat. I had felt the presence of the future beings and wanted to open myself, with as little interruption as possible, for communication and insight. I spent many hours in contemplation and reading philosophical and scientific studies relating to the experience of time—Merleau-Ponty, Eihei Dōgen, the *Avatamsaka Sutra*. I was strict in honoring my solitude, allowing only a few thinking partners in my inquiry.

On March 11, 2011, near the end of the retreat, the triple disaster at Fukushima Daiichi unfolded, in one inescapable horror after another. The world I emerged into was changed forever. I instantly sensed the suffering this would bring for generations to come.

Since every release of radioactivity has an unstoppable, irreversible, and immediate effect on all those impacted by it, thereby bringing the future ones into the present, it is plausible to me that the future generations want to lend us courage for what we do to keep the world livable for them. The sense of their presence comes to me like grace and works upon my life. I imagine the future ones asking us, "What did you do with the poison fire? Did you hide it out of laziness and shame? Did you abandon it where we who come after you cannot understand or find the source of the contamination that eats our bones, stunts our minds? Did you ever think of caring for the poison fire? Did it ever occur to you to share with us the knowledge of what it is and how to guard it?"

BEING TIME AND DEEP TIME

Taigen Dan Leighton

JOANNA MACY'S WORK ON DEEP TIME and on beings of the future echoes and amplifies traditional Mahayana Buddhist teachings on temporality. These teachings include the subtle Chinese Huayan Buddhist holographic array of the ten times as well as the writings of the Japanese Zen pioneer Eihei Dōgen (1200–53), especially his renowned essay *Uji* (Being Time). In the more than thirty years since I met Joanna as a graduate student at the California Institute of Integral Studies, I have spoken regularly with her about her work for future beings in relation to Buddhist teachings on temporality. Joanna's courage and insight in facing the threat to time itself from the abiding peril of nuclear weapons and nuclear waste, and now from climate breakdown, has deeply resonated with my own concerns and inquiries into the quality of temporality. She has been an important inspiration and mentor for my Buddhist studies work and social activism.

ANCESTORS OF THE PAST AND FUTURE, AND VAST TIME

In 1994, I filled in for Joanna when she was invited to a Global Future Generations conference in Kyoto, and delivered my paper "Meeting Our Ancestors of the Future."[1] I had worked with Joanna in her Nuclear Guardianship Project in Berkeley, and then presented her views of nuclear waste issues when I lived in Kyoto from 1990 through 1992. When we connect with and appreciate our ancestors, whether from spiritual, artistic, or social action traditions, we enrich our sense of time and see our purpose in time. As Joanna later wrote in *Coming Back to Life*, "To make the transition to a life-sustaining society, we must retrieve that ancestral capacity—in other words, act like ancestors. We need to attune to longer ecological rhythms and nourish a strong, felt connection with past and future generations."[2] Such ancestors are not only in the past and acting in the present. When we engage beings of the future, we can venerate our as yet unknown future ancestors who are looking back to support us.

Having a wide, inclusive view of vast time scales deepens our appreciation of this present time. Such a range of time is expressed by Dōgen's twelfth-century Chinese predecessor, Chan Master Hongzhi (1091–1157). He wrote, "This is the time and place to leap beyond the ten thousand emotional entanglements of innumerable eons. One contemplation of ten thousand years finally goes beyond all the transitory, and you emerge with spontaneity."[3] When we awaken from denial of the vast depths of time with willingness to contemplate the whole ten thousand years, then finally we can dynamically and freely inhabit and exert our present being time.

MULTIDIMENSIONAL INTERCONNECTED TIME

Joanna's work on general systems theory connects with the Huayan school of Buddhism in China, which centers its teaching on the *Flower Ornament* or *Avatamsaka Sutra*. With its rich depiction of the multidimensional quality of time, this sutra weaves a psychedelic web of similes to expound the interconnectedness of all particular phenomena with the whole universe. Its vision is far-reaching and comprehensive, from the macroscopic to the microscopic. Throughout many universes and dimensions, there is not a single place or time lacking buddhas and bodhisattvas. Joanna celebrates the Huayan teachings in the closing chapters of her masterpiece *World as Lover, World as Self*.[4]

The Huayan teaching of universal Buddha nature and interconnectedness describes how we do not exist in isolation. Rather, all beings are intimately interrelated in our effects on one another. We are the product of our genetic and cultural inheritance and of innumerable other unknowable conditions that bring us to our present state. One famous *Flower Ornament* depiction of this reality is the net of Indra, the Indian creator deity. In this metaphor, the universe is described as a vast net, and at each junction where the meshes meet, sits a jewel. Each jewel reflects the light of all the jewels around it, and all of those jewels reflect others around them. In this way, the whole universe of jewels is ultimately reflected in every single jewel. This holographic image expresses our deep intimacy and interrelatedness with every being and every time in the universe.

In the Huayan "Fourfold Dharmadhatu," the first two aspects of reality are described as the *universal* and the *particular*, also spoken of as the ultimate and phenomenal, or real and apparent. The third aspect of reality is the mutual, nonobstructing *interpenetration of the universal and particular*. No universal truth or ultimate time exists apart from its active presence in a particular temporal situation, which completely expresses the whole truth of all times. The fourth aspect of reality is the mutual, nonobstructing *interpenetration of the particular with other particulars*, so that each particular event is fully present and complementary to any other particular time with the cooperative mutuality of all times.

Huayan theory and the *Flower Ornament Sutra* itself speak of ten distinct times: the past, present, and future of the past; the past, present, and future of the present; the past, present, and future of the future, and finally the combination of all these nine times.[5] The past of the present may also be the past of a future. The present of the future will be intimately connected to the future of our present, yet it is not necessarily predetermined or limited by our present future. We can reclaim the past in the present, and thus actually change our past, as well as our present, for the sake of the future. History is the changing process of defining the past for the present, and the stories we tell about the past in the present change the meaning of past events. We cannot bring back extinct species or detoxify nuclear poisons. But seeing those events as opportunities to change how we care for the world can change the meaning of this past and mitigate its effects, enhancing the possibilities of some other future. We can rewrite the history of the future in the present as well as in the future.

OUR BEING TIME

In the realm of *being time* elaborated in the writing of Japanese Zen founder Eihei Dōgen, time does not only flow from past to present to future. Time moves in mysterious ways, passing dynamically between all ten times and beyond. Time is not some intractable external, objective, or independent container we are caught in. We *are* time. When we fully express ourselves right now, that is time. We cannot avoid fully expressing our deepest truth presently in this being of time. Dōgen offers the consolation that even a partial, half-hearted exertion of our being time is completely a partial being time. He says, "In being-time there is the distinctive function of *passage*; there is passage from today to tomorrow, passage from today to yesterday, passage from yesterday to today, passage from today to today, and passage from tomorrow to tomorrow.

This transpires because passage itself is the distinctive function of time."[6] This multidirectional flowing makes it possible for beings to realize how they fully inhabit all times as the present time, rather than seeking some present as a restricted escape from regret for the past or anxiety over the future. Dōgen's concern matches Joanna's call for reinhabiting time "in a healthier, sane fashion." Joanna cautions that spiritual "injunctions to 'Be Here Now' can serve to devalue chronological time and encourage disregard for the future."[7]

Throughout his writings, Dōgen emphatically highlights the responsibility of practitioners. When we realize that we are ineluctably *being* time in this very body-mind, we can choose to be and act from our deepest and noblest intention. We can choose to express our being time in a way that connects with all beings here now, and also connects with all beings, all our ancestors, throughout the generations of past and future. We can be a time that accepts the support and guidance from all beings of all times.

BEING EARTH AND THE *LOTUS SUTRA*

Along with expressing the dynamism of temporality, Dōgen applies the vitality of reality to space as well. He clarifies space not as outer space or mere emptiness but as the reality of forms, the substance of our bodies and world. For us, this spatial quality lives in the spiritual depths and agency of the space of Earth. Our connection to all space and to all time is also our connection to Earth.

The ground of our being is the same ancestral ground that plants us in time. This truth is strikingly depicted in a story in the *Lotus Sutra*, arguably the most important Buddhist scripture in East Asia and crucial for Dōgen. Myriad bodhisattvas, enlightening beings, arrive from other dimensions or distant solar systems to hear Shakyamuni Buddha's teaching, and they ask if he needs their help to maintain this teaching in the future. From our vantage point, 2,500 years later, I imagine the question from Buddha that they are responding to as: "In the distant age of television, automobiles, internet communications, global climate breakdown, and toxic nuclear waste, how will those people hear the true teaching of universal awakening?"

The Buddha tells them not to fear, and suddenly from out of the empty, open space under the ground spring vast multitudes of noble, gentle beings dedicated to the emancipation of all creation.[8] The Buddha declares that these bodhisattvas practice diligently within the earth, forever guiding confused, worldly people. Moreover, they have all trained intently with him, even though many are apparently ages older than the Buddha himself. He is the ancestor even of those from his past.

In time, our connection to the earth is the connection to its natural rhythms. With patience we can find our own expression of these rhythms. Despite all of our tantalizing technologies, we cannot control or manipulate the deeper rhythms of the earth. Efforts to garner corporate profits from the earth's resources are now reaping disastrous consequences for all life. Attuned to the earth's rhythms, appropriate actions may become clear, and we may become ready to act helpfully. Our multiplicity of ancestors has bequeathed valuable guidance in finding our footing in this time-ground. Yunyan (780–841), an early Chinese predecessor of Dōgen, was once sweeping the temple grounds when his brother monk passing by commented, "Too busy." Yunyan responded, "You should know there is one who is not busy."[9] How can we recall the one not busy, and proceed with grounded, patient vision, rather than operating busily from the time frame of quarterly profit margins?

THE INCONCEIVABLE LIFE SPAN AND
THE FUTURE BUDDHA

When the underground bodhisattvas emerge in the *Lotus Sutra*, the Buddha is questioned about their provenance by Maitreya, the bodhisattva of loving kindness predicted to be the next future Buddha. This leads to the central revelation of the sutra, that Buddha truly only *appears* to be born, leave his palace, awaken, and pass away into nirvana. Actually, he has a vast, inconceivably long life span, described with astronomical metaphors that challenge our imagination and disrupt conventional conceptualizations of temporality. This lengthy life span is revealed only when it inspires beneficial action, and otherwise it remains hidden lest it encourage indifference to present conditions.

Dōgen sees the revelation of the Buddha's vast life span as "the one time in which the Buddha is living"—a striking, evocative phrase referring to this ultimate time outside of conventional time. Dōgen provides many references to Shakyamuni's inconceivable life span as vitally present in current wholehearted practice, fully illuminating the quality of all time as present in this being time. The significance of the enduring Shakyamuni is not merely that Buddha is immanent in the world but that his vigorous, inspiring practice continues through his successors.[10]

The problem of temporality is embodied in the figure of Maitreya, the future Buddha defined as not yet a buddha. As such, he expresses the unfulfilled aspect of the bodhisattva as a mere shadow of his future self. His predicted buddhahood is variously described in scriptural sources as being twenty-five hundred years from now, or perhaps not for hundreds of billions of years. Meanwhile he patiently contemplates the complexities of human consciousness and how we create suffering, a study that makes Maitreya the primary bodhisattva of the Yogacara branch of Mahayana, which describes levels and aspects of consciousness.

As a bodhisattva representing and sponsored by the future, Maitreya invites us to reenvision and reinhabit time itself. Buddha's view of time sees all times as included in the immediate present, here and now. Just as the bodhisattva path includes all beings, it includes all times. Maitreya encourages us to consider the historical as well as the existential future, and the relationship and implications of the future to our present situation. Maitreya serves as a protector of future beings, like Joanna, calling us from the promise of the future to revitalize our concern for future generations.[11]

Joanna has expressed Maitreya's Buddhist teaching and psychology in her study of contemporary Western systems theory, and also as an active spokesperson for deep ecology. In all of her work, Joanna powerfully brings the truth of Maitreya's contemplation of the future to bear on crucial dilemmas in our present world. Joanna has used the dilemma of nuclear waste and its multimillennial toxicity to offer a positive, hopeful vision of a long-term human future based on guardianship of nuclear waste and of our world with clear, spiritual awareness. Such guardianship could also apply to the dangers from climate breakdown through implementing some version of a long-term "Green New Deal." Joanna's insight and faith are that we can acknowledge and use the dire perils to our own and other species as opportunities for consciously taking responsibility for our world and our own garbage, living in a more caring, intentional manner. In workshops on deep time and future generations, Joanna encourages participants to envision themselves as beings from specific future times and places. She proclaims the fact that every being who will ever live on Earth is present here and now. This is true as a biological certainty, as all future life will collectively be produced from the DNA of present creatures. But also all future beings depend on our choices now for their lives and health.[12]

NOTES

1. For an expanded version of that paper, see Taigen Dan Leighton, *Zen Questions: Zazen, Dōgen, and the Spirit of Creative Inquiry* (Boston: Wisdom Publications, 2011), 243–53.
2. Joanna Macy and Molly Young Brown, *Coming Back to Life: Practices to Reconnect Our Lives, Our World* (Gabriola Island, BC: New Society Publishers, 1998), 136.
3. Taigen Dan Leighton with Yi Wu, *Cultivating the Empty Field: The Silent Illumination of Zen Master Hongzhi* (Boston: Tuttle, 2000), 49.
4. Joanna Macy, *World as Lover, World as Self* (Berkeley, CA: Parallax Press, 2007), 199–202.
5. Thomas Cleary, trans., *The Flower Ornament Scripture* (Boston: Shambhala Publications, 1984–93), 1029.
6. Norman Waddell and Masao Abe, *The Heart of Dōgen's Shōbōgenzō* (Albany: State University of New York Press, 2002), 51.
7. Macy, *World as Lover*, 171, 179.
8. Gene Reeves, *The Lotus Sutra* (Boston: Wisdom Publications, 2008), 279–81. For a detailed discussion of this story, including Dōgen's commentaries on it, see Taigen Dan Leighton, *Visions of Awakening Space and Time: Dōgen and the Lotus Sutra* (New York: Oxford University Press, 2007).
9. Thomas Cleary, trans., *The Book of Serenity* (Boston: Shambhala Publications, 2005), 91–94.
10. Leighton, *Visions of Awakening Space and Time*, 82, 86–87, 90. Joanna Macy's laudatory endorsement of this book included that it "reveals a transmission of the Buddha Dharma in which the utter reality of the phenomenal world is not to be questioned. Right now, when ecological crises imperil the future of conscious life, this work of scholarship is good news indeed."

11. For more on Maitreya, including Joanna Macy as Maitreya exemplar, see Taigen Dan Leighton, *Faces of Compassion: Classic Bodhisattva Archetypes and Their Modern Expression* (Boston: Wisdom Publications, 2012), 241–74.

12. Macy, *World as Lover*, 201.

LIBERATING THE SPIRIT OF THE ANCESTORS IN AFRICA

Liz Hosken

I WAS FORTUNATE TO MEET JOANNA in the late 1980s when I attended a workshop with her in the UK on despair and personal empowerment. I was astounded. Within a few hours, people from all walks of life, who did not know each other and would not call themselves "environmentalists," were sharing their pain for Earth, for other species, for special places, for the barren world their children would face. What was her magic, I wondered? How did she find the route into people's guarded hearts so quickly? Through her artful honing of questions and exercises, Joanna took us to the core of our common human experience—to re-member we are one species, one human family in the web of life, participating in an awe-inspiring, living planet, through whom we are deeply ensouled.

I have been honored to introduce the Work That Reconnects to friends and allies in Africa, where it is taking root with Joanna's ongoing guidance and support. I see this work as the vital medicine we need at this time to overcome the separations created through colonialism and anthropocentrism in their many forms. These deeply familiar patterns of domination are justified through superiority complexes of ideology, race, sexuality, gender, and religion. Yet as we face death everywhere—the deaths of cultures, species, ecosystems, and possibly life on our planet as we know it—we need to heal these wounds within the human family.

We need to come back to ourselves as earthlings, first and foremost, to nurture the possibility of life for future generations of all species.

RE-MEMBERING THE LAWS OF EARTH

Since that first workshop I took with Joanna in the UK in the 1980s, one of my dreams was for Joanna to come to my motherland, South Africa, to plant her magic in African soil. In 1987, I cofounded with Edward Posey the Gaia Foundation (Gaia) to revive biocultural diversity, regenerate healthy ecosystems, and strengthen community self-governance for climate change resilience. Twenty-six years later, in 2013, some African colleagues asked me to think about how they could build their skills in holistic methods for accompanying communities in a process of reviving indigenous ancestral knowledge. We recognized that after centuries of colonial and anthropocentric domination, there was a need to decolonize our minds and develop life-sustaining pathways rooted in our cultural diversity. The Gaia team responded to the challenge by calling on some of the remarkable mentors, friends, and colleagues who have journeyed with us over the years, including Joanna. Together we developed a training focused on deepening the understanding of Earth Jurisprudence (EJ), recognizing the laws of Earth as primary.[1]

A year later, we gathered together a group of dynamic young opinion-makers who were highly placed in their local societies and aware of the impacts of colonization and industrialization on their people. The first three-year course, completed in July 2017, was a powerful journey of discovery, de-schooling, re-membering their rich African heritage, and reconnecting with our living Earth. Graduates are now mentors for the second group, who are midway through their journey of EJ learning. The EJ course in Africa has been commended in reports by the UN Secretary-General, highlighting its important role in responding to the urgent need to bring about systemic transformation.[2]

Participants in the course come from seven African countries—South Africa, Zimbabwe, Benin, Cameroon, Ethiopia, Uganda, and Kenya. Most are working with rural communities through local civil society organizations concerned with ecological, cultural, and social justice. In a broad sense, these are people at turning points in their lives, disillusioned by the American dream promoted by the industrial growth economy. In these turbulent times, they are searching for ways to deepen their contribution in life-enhancing ways, while drawing inspiration from their African heritage and other traditional wisdoms.

HEALING FROM THE COLONIAL PAST

Coming Back to Life is a core text for our EJ trainings, and, with Joanna's guidance, we work with it in various ways. We begin with the spiral of the Work That Reconnects, where participants consider how African traditions nurture practices of gratitude. This takes them into a deep journey of reflection on their own roots and cultural practices. It reveals how gratitude is central for African traditions that understand reciprocity as a core life principle in honoring relationships with spirit/ancestors, animated nature/land, and human community.

The spiral of the Work That Reconnects also encourages us to face the pain of the Great Unraveling and not turn away. Witnessing and being conscious is essential, and, as Joanna teaches, it is likewise essential to know how to do so without unraveling ourselves. As EJ practitioner-in-training Shaun Dunn from South

Africa says, "Joanna's guidance highlights what our African philosophy of *uBuntu* teaches us, that we can connect with the pain of others. We can feel deeply and move through with reverence and love."

Fassil Gebeyehu, an EJ graduate from Ethiopia, says, "Joanna expresses the mystery of life and the complex interactions among Earth community members in a fresh and compelling way. I am particularly inspired by her deep exploration of how important it is to feel pain of the world in which I am part. I couldn't grasp this powerful thought until I encountered life-threatening experiences of my own. The experience opened my mind to dare to confront any uncertainty, to think about life beyond our physical being. Her wisdom on compassion, relatedness, gratitude, and seeing with fresh eyes are my lifelong companions."

As part of our training of African EJ practitioners, Gaia offers annual retreats where we draw on the text and the exercises in *Coming Back to Life* and start our day with *mysticas*, meditations on our relationship with the rest of nature. Participants take turns leading mysticas and reviewing each other's facilitation skills. Many have adopted elements into their own personal practice, which is at the heart of becoming a practitioner. Dennis Tabaro, an EJ graduate from Uganda, says, *"Coming Back to Life* is always near me. I keep reading it and incorporating the teachings into my practice. It gives me hope that future generations might have a chance if more of us practice coming back to life!" Appolinaire Oussoulio, a graduate from Benin, echoes this sentiment: "During my training in Earth Jurisprudence, I had the extraordinary opportunity to explore and practice the teachings in this book. Since then, it has become my faithful companion, connecting me to myself and to nature around me and helping me to facilitate others to do the same."

As part of the advocacy work, we encourage participants to explore using the exercises with their families, communities, and organizations. For example, Gertrude Pswarayi-Jabson, an EJ practitioner-in-training from Zimbabwe, was asked to open the regional meeting of the Alliance for Food Sovereignty in Africa (AFSA) in Senegal. She broke with convention for keynote speeches and instead introduced people to Joanna and the Work That Reconnects. She says, "I found Joanna's work deeply authentic, spiritual, and therapeutic. It has given me the strength and tools to deal with the dysfunctional system that is destroying all forms of life. It is so potent because it is packed with layers of truth that speak to the very core that makes us human. It goes beyond race, culture, religion, gender, class, and ethnicity, allowing us to freely surrender to the process of 'coming back to life.' As we are reborn, we make greater and more meaningful connections that restore and sustain life."

Fellow Zimbabwian Method Gundidza, an EJ graduate, draws on the Work That Reconnects when he is invited to open, close, or facilitate gatherings in South Africa on issues such as mining, post-extractivism, food sovereignty. He finds that people are deeply moved and want to know how they can learn more about the story behind the powerful experiences they have through the exercises. Method says, "Joanna's books are full of practical spiritual and nature-based exercises that now form part of my daily routine. I constantly refer to her books when invited to gatherings or in my work with communities. I take the opportunity to share an exercise with the groups whenever possible because they really speak to people's heart-minds."

The exercises are equally appreciated by communities on their own journey of reviving their indigenous knowledge and practices—core to coming back to life. Simon Mitambo, an EJ graduate from Kenya, reports that "each month we gather for a community dialogue with elders and begin with a mystica drawn from Joanna's exercises. The communities love the way the exercises stimulate their thoughts and affirm indigenous perspectives."

As these testimonies demonstrate, this singing of praise from members of Africa's growing Earth Jurisprudence movement, which I am honored to be part of, shows how the Work That Reconnects has a profound impact across countries, contexts and sociocultural backgrounds. The philosophy, analysis, and exercises open doorways to people's heart-mind, as Joanna would say. It is a revelation for many people in Africa to learn that there are philosophers and scientists in the Western and Eastern traditions who hold similar critiques of the dominant economic paradigm and colonial process and are aligned with indigenous Earth-centered thinking and spirituality. As Edonandji Gbegniho, a young poet, songwriter, activist, and EJ practitioner-in-training from Benin, says, "This work is so precious, because it reveals how and why we are disconnected. It fills us with energy to rediscover the joy of being part of our living Mother Earth. These exercises of liberation are contemplative while also rallying us to work for the cause of the universe, which is living and regenerative." Mersha Yilma, from Ethiopia, adds, "Joanna's teachings opened my mind and my heart, enabling me to experience love and communication with nature. This inculcated in me a desire to keep widening my circle of relationships with our more-than-human community of life. She opened my eyes to the 'beautiful self-organizing universe'—as she says, 'a wonder beyond words.'"

Joanna weaves many ways of thinking into a powerful and rigorous offering that helps us see with new eyes through an Earth-centered lens. This new perspective helps us understand the root cause of what we are living through now and demonstrates a way to navigate these unraveling times. Nnah Ndobe Samuel, an EJ practitioner-in-training from Cameroon, reflects on his deep gratitude: "My homage to incredible Joanna, who I have not met but I feel I know through her writings. I am so privileged to have been introduced to her through my EJ practitioners course. Her book *Coming Back to Life* has really reshaped my thoughts and practices as an environmental and social activist."

A particularly meaningful exercise for indigenous and traditional peoples, especially from Africa, is the Beings of the Three Times. It generates animated responses from communities and activists alike, because it affirms the recognition that ancestors of all species are present and participate with us in life. This understanding establishes a deep sense of gratitude for those who walked the path before us, and it engenders a sense of responsibility for those who are to come. The exercise helps us get a perspective on ourselves because it places us in the bigger context of our intergenerational and interspecies consciousness. This understanding is essentially what lies at the core of indigenous thinking and what holds us to be accountable.

For participants in our EJ training courses, the exercise not only affirms their traditions but opens up a possibility of connection between cultures—even to the Western world, which is generally experienced as a monolithic colonizing force. African ancestors and spiritual beliefs were and are still demonized in Africa, and nature was and is still seen as a resource for human exploitation. In contrast to this colonial past and its ongoing legacy, possibilities of solidarity and mutual respect can form around the core understanding of *ancestors*—a vital area for exploration and healing. As Mashudu Takalani, from Venda in South Africa, says, "I grew up having to hide my family practices of invoking the ancestors because people around us said it was demonic. *Coming Back to Life* has given me courage and a deeper perspective on the voice of the ancestors, affirming that this understanding is also held by other cultures and sciences. This opens the door for healing and solidarity in reconnecting across cultures and with Mother Earth, to bring hope for the next generation and rebuild life-sustaining ways together."

As Mashudu explains, the Work That Reconnects creates a context where African traditional knowledge and practices resonate not only with other indigenous, spiritual, and mystical traditions but also with newer developments in holistic, quantum, and postmodern Western science. This perspective is profoundly encouraging for those who are part of the movement reviving traditional African knowledge and decolonizing the mind—an ongoing practice of freeing ourselves from internalized prejudices against African and indigenous traditions, against those that are "other" than "us," and against nature herself.

Joanna's work brings together critical thinking and experience to provide a compelling context in which people from indigenous and other traditions can find themselves and feel part of a cross-cultural stream of consciousness that connects us through our wisdom traditions. This enables us to experience deep resonances for how we can each bring a crucial contribution at this time of the Great Unraveling. Such resonances create a sense of hope that, through the practice of decolonizing our minds, we can free ourselves from dominating, human-centered ways, meet each other as one species in the Earth community, and rebuild life-enhancing pathways together. This is now our vital task—for the sake of the generations to come and for all species.

Out of my experience in Africa has arisen the realization that there is potential for deep alignment in thinking and practice across cultures and disciplines. We can recognize that humanity's indigenous roots of belonging are held in common. In these challenging times, solidarity across divides and difference is fundamental for healing within the human family and in relation to the larger community of life. These two schisms are completely connected and interrelated. Nature "out there" helps us connect with our inner nature because we are an inextricable part of the whole. This understanding is deeply embedded in indigenous ways of seeing. Joanna's lifework provides food for the soul and tested practices to help us assist one another in "coming back to life." This is a most potent and meaningful gift at this time.

A final word of appreciation—as things get worse, Joanna's radiant joy and gratitude for the beauty of life is still with us, an inspiration to stay positive and determined as we practice the spiral of the Work That Reconnects. We witness and breathe through the pain and grief we feel for our living world as we continue the work of protecting and nurturing life-sustaining ways. It is a joy for me to see how her lovingly honed teachings are rippling across Africa, igniting and healing the heart-minds of growing numbers of people who honor her as a great elder of these times.

NOTES

1. Earth Jurisprudence is about recognizing nature as the primary source of law and ethics. Thomas Berry, widely considered the "father" of Earth Jurisprudence, worked closely with the Gaia Foundation to develop the core principles. See https://www.gaiafoundation .org/what-we-do/earth-jurisprudence.
2. Graduates of the first class were featured in Hannibal Rhoades, "Africa's First Class of Earth Jurisprudence Practitioners Graduate," *Ecologist*, September 4, 2017, https://theecologist.org/2017/sep/04/africas -first-class-earth-jurisprudence-practitioners-graduate.

DEEP ECOLOGY COURAGE IN NUCLEAR RUSSIA

Oleg Bodrov and Ludmilla Zhrina

PART I: OLEG BODROV

In Russia at the beginning of the 1950s, twenty secret cities were built. Half of the cities were engaged in creating nuclear weapons; the other half worked on building nuclear power plants. All life in these cities was regulated from the secret nuclear ministry (Ministry of Medium Machine Building) in Moscow. Information about nuclear accidents or about the impact of nuclear technologies on the environment had the status of "state secret." These cities were not marked on the maps.

Young physicists, builders, and engineers from leading universities in Russia were invited to staff the single-industry cities. These transplanted residents were not familiar with local cultural traditions, ways of life, or even the main occupations of the indigenous populations in the regions where the cities were built. The residents of the nuclear cities were dominated by a technocratic style of thinking. They perceived nature as a resource that should be used for the development of nuclear technologies for confrontation with the United States.

Thus within Russia there was another "Nuclear Russia" with its own secret citizens, secret laws, and a secret economy subsidized from the national budget. One percent of Russia's population lived in this "country." At this time, citizens of greater Russia could not come to "Nuclear Russia" without special permits. In fact, getting such a permit was like getting a visa to visit a foreign country. Only a few were able to obtain such visas. Russia was like the popular souvenir nesting dolls—a big *matryoshka,* inside which a small nuclear matryoshka was hidden.

After the Chernobyl accident in 1986, the disintegration of the Soviet Union, and the fall of the Iron Curtain between East and West in the early 1990s, there was a fundamentally new sociopolitical situation in Russia. Demand for further development of nuclear fissionable materials for the production of atomic bombs ceased. As citizens of Russia and other countries became aware of the damage caused by the Chernobyl meltdown, many began to oppose the development of nuclear energy. The accident at the Chernobyl nuclear power plant led to global contamination of our planet with radionuclides. Even as far as a thousand kilometers from the Chernobyl nuclear power plant, on the Baltic Sea coast near St. Petersburg, the secret nuclear city of Sosnovy Bor was contaminated by radioactive rain.

All this upheaval generated a sociopolitical and environmental crisis in the nuclear cities. The social infrastructure of such cities had been entirely supported by the generous budget of the nuclear ministry, and these funds were now greatly reduced. In fact, the cities were not cities in the conventional sense. Rather, they might be called the "bedroom shops" of nuclear enterprises. In the 1990s there were repeated strikes by nuclear workers over back wages as the standard of living dropped.

There was an urgent need to reset the nuclear cities on another socially and environmentally friendly basis. This meant developing new business, so that the cities' revenues could be generated from alternative sources and not from the national budget of Russia, which was in a deep economic crisis. It became obvious that we needed a new philosophy, a new way of thinking. We needed to find solutions at the local and regional level for those cities open to economic restructuring. It was necessary to take the initiative, to find support for alternative development.

Deep Ecology in the Beginning

In the spring of 1995 in St. Petersburg, Francis Macy, of the Center for Safe Energy in Berkeley, California, met with some environmental activists, including me. I was surprised that Fran looked at me with smiling eyes, spoke perfect Russian, and was interested in my work in the nuclear city of Sosnovy Bor. Here, five military reactors and four reactors for the Leningrad nuclear power plant (similar to Chernobyl) were being built.

I told Fran that I had worked as a physicist at the military Nuclear Institute of Russia studying the safety of nuclear reactors, and also as an ecologist studying their impacts on the ecosystems of the Baltic Sea. Unfortunately, I had to stop my career as a scientist because of my disagreement with the policy of secrecy and isolation of the nuclear community from Russian society. Fran was concerned about the safety of nuclear power plants in the United States, especially after the accident at Three Mile Island in Pennsylvania in 1979. In both Russia and America, we needed to find a new spiritual basis to avoid new accidents at nuclear power plants and to reduce the risk of using nuclear weapons, because of the very real threat to our planet.

Fran introduced "Chief Seattle's Message" as a possible spiritual basis for a new ecophilosophy. Fortunately, I, too, had once read this message, said to be sent from the leader of a North American Indian tribe to the president of the United States. Though I learned later that this may have been written by someone else, the message still rang true. It captured the main thesis of deep ecology philosophy—that humanity and every individual is part of the living planet Earth, and that each person needs to take care of the planet's health. It is a reflection of our own survival instinct.

At this meeting, and probably for the first time in Russia, the term *deep ecology* was used as a possible philosophical basis for the formation of a new mentality of the inhabitants of the secret nuclear cities. We hoped that this attitude could unite Russia and the US, creating a basis for a new life without confrontation between our nuclear countries.

Fran gave me some materials in English with the main principles of deep ecology. It was a precious gift! We agreed with Fran to hold a seminar on deep ecology on the southern shore of the Gulf of Finland near Sosnovy Bor. Schoolteachers and environmental officials from the former secret city would be invited to the seminar. In the nuclear city, inhabitants were used to living in an isolated society and not feeling that they were part of nature. We felt it was important to build a desire to reunite with nature, to become part of the "Tree of Life," to act to preserve this life, and not wait for all the problems to be solved by the atomic ministry as they had been for the past fifty years. It was important to involve teachers who could influence the formation of a new understanding of life in the new generation of Sosnovy Bor.

The first such seminar was held on May 26, 1996, in Lomonosov, a suburb of St. Petersburg. This day, perhaps, can be called the "birthday of deep ecology in Russia." The three-day seminar was attended not only by environmental activists and journalists but also by teachers working with children in Sosnovy Bor, and an official of the Environmental Committee. The participants were delighted because they realized the unity of the participants with nature and with one another. There were many articles written up in the local media.

Thanks to our coaches Fran Macy and Enid Schreibman, we came to feel that we were all part of our common planet Earth, that we (and not only our political leaders!) were responsible for the life and health of our common planet. This feeling increased after we visited the Nicholas Roerich Museum in Izvara village near St. Petersburg, where Roerich was born in 1874. Roerich was a philosopher, artist, traveler, and author of *Heart of Asia* and *Shambhala*, known not only in Russia but also in the United States and India. In the early 1920s, he even opened a museum in New York that still exists today. Soon after the seminar, Fran wrote to me, "The trip to Roerich's home opened my eyes wider to his contribution to us all in sensing the profundity of all being. He was certainly a deep ecologist long before the Norwegian philosopher Arne Naess first used the term." We came to understand that in Russia and America there are common values that unite us.

Working with the Center for Safe Energy, Fran came up with a proposal to hold a similar seminar at our center in Sosnovy Bor, including Russian psychologists, science teachers, and students. The American coaches and guests were invited to our home, the formerly secret nuclear city, to form together a new worldview for the younger generation—a worldview friendly not only to nature but also to a distant country, the US, commonly perceived as an enemy. Thus some of the inhabitants of a nuclear single-industry city became part of the family of deep ecologists on our common planet Earth.

After this seminar, Fran invited me, as the seminar organizer, to a ten-day training on deep ecology on Whidbey Island, Washington. Thanks to Joanna and Fran Macy, as well as John Seed and other coaches, within ten days I turned from a citizen of Russia into a citizen of planet Earth! This was a new stage in my life, a new spiritual basis for promotion of a nuclear-free Baltic region.

In St. Petersburg we translated and published the book by Joanna Macy and Molly Young Brown, *Coming Back to Life: Practices to Reconnect Our Lives, Our World.* This became a good basis for additional seminars on deep ecology for secondary-school teachers, not only in Sosnovy Bor and St. Petersburg but also in Petrozavodsk, Karelia. Each teacher received this book as a gift, along with an additional copy for school libraries.

The next step in promoting the philosophy of deep ecology was organizing a seminar for schoolteachers and representatives of nongovernmental organizations in Latvia, a neighboring country of the Baltic region. The mission of this seminar was to stimulate a new perception of the world—that we who live on the shores of our common Baltic Sea are a part of the sea as well as the fish and the forests on its shores. We affirmed that our sea unites us despite the political differences of our leaders. Through this seminar we came to a common understanding that our safety, the health of the sea, and our own health depend on those of us living on its shores. Thus the idea of deep ecology became part of the Baltic Sea region.

Deep Ecology in Russia Today

Since the early 2000s, the political situation in Russia has changed dramatically. With the coming to power of Vladimir Putin, the total "de-ecologization" of Russian legislation began. Large transnational projects began to move forward in Russia and on the shores of the Baltic Sea. Balancing environmental values with natural resource development was perceived by the political elite as a barrier to the economic prosperity of Russia.

In response to NATO's approach to Russia's borders, a new stage of Russian military-political confrontation with the US and

EU countries has begun. The line of confrontation runs right along the Baltic Sea. Politicians are trying to make enemies of the inhabitants of this environmentally sensitive and vulnerable Baltic region, where ninety million people live in nine countries (including Russia). On both sides of the confrontational line there is a militarization of consciousness. Military exercises are being conducted that imitate the use of nuclear weapons.

At the same time, the Russian nuclear business, with state political and financial support, is endorsing new nuclear power plants in Europe, Asia, and Africa.[1] This is being promoted as a positive process of technological cooperation and as a good alternative to direct confrontation, but it definitely is not! The production of fresh nuclear fuel for these power plants takes place in closed nuclear cities under the cover of undemocratic dual-use technology (military and civil). This means that civil society consumers in third world countries using electricity from Russian nuclear power plants are, in effect, helping to sustain the Russian nuclear military infrastructure (i.e., closed nuclear cities) installed during the Cold War.

Over the past twenty-five years, the cooperation between environmental organizations in Russia and those in other countries of the Baltic Sea region has created a strong Baltic antinuclear coalition to confront new nuclear threats. We know now that our health and safety and the health of our region depends on those of us living on its shores. We, the inhabitants of the region, must take responsibility for ensuring the safety of our common Baltic home!

PART II: LUDMILLA ZHRINA

For a good many years I have been a professor of biological sciences at the Pedagogical Institute in the Bryansk region of

Russia, where a large portion of my students have become school-teachers and administrators. The day I was defending my PhD dissertation at the University of Tartu—April 26, 1986—was the very day the Chernobyl disaster erupted. Bryansk is on the border of Ukraine, very close to the Chernobyl nuclear power station. At the height of the fires from the meltdown, strong winds carried intense radioactivity over Bryansk, especially drenching its western region and the city of Novozybkov. No one—not a single person—was evacuated. This powerful event has shaped my life and work ever since.

To help people understand radiation and to live with it as safely as possible, I immediately set about organizing a group we named "Viola." It would later be registered as an educational NGO under the post-Soviet government of Russia. Our first members were highly motivated educators in the natural sciences, and soon a large number of volunteers were helping in many ways. Our mission was and has remained focused on the education of all ages of the population on socio-environmental issues. The violet flower (*Viola*) is a protected plant in our region, listed in the International Union for the Conservation of Nature's Ecological Red Book. Its colors—purple, red, yellow, blue—are as varied as our members in religion, age, and background. We love this flower as our bright emblem.

My introduction to Deep Ecology work came in 1995 at the Kiev Eco-Forum, where I participated in a three-day training seminar taught by Fran Macy and Bill Pfeiffer. I knew right away that deep ecology would be folded into my work with Viola. Fran gave me a copy of *Thinking Like a Mountain* translated into Russian, to help me remember the insights and guide the practices we had just experienced. I could see that to feel part of the natural order of things, related to all beings in the web of life, would bring strength to people who felt abandoned and fearful after the meltdown. I believed that this Deep Ecology work could lower the stress of living with radiation, providing an alternative to self-isolation and generating an appetite for social collaboration.

Through Viola we found "cleaner"—that is, less contaminated—areas, where pregnant women and mothers with infants can take holidays, and where we hold summer camps for children. There, through games and gardening, the children learn to love nature and not be afraid of it. You will often find us doing the Elm Dance and expanding our ecological self with a Council or "Soviet" of All Beings. Viola also works with school children, starting in kindergarten, to help them develop a sense of trust in life and to grow habits of health, instead of being scared of what is dangerous. Many schoolteachers in the Bryansk region were students of mine at the Pedagogical Institute and were ready to integrate the use of radiation dosimeters into the class curriculum. The funds to purchase these dosimeters were raised by Joanna and Fran from their workshops, as they shared the Elm Dance and the story of Novozybkov. Using these dosimeters to measure radionuclides in the soil, pupils learn how to map and judge where best to locate each spring's gardens and playgrounds. This helps both families and children move from an identity of victim to one of investigator, giving them a sense of personal agency.

The production of written materials in clear, nontechnical language has been essential. Using leaflets, charts, posters, and books, I explain both the dangers of radioactive contamination and the ways we can protect ourselves from it. Perhaps the most useful of all is my forty-page booklet entitled *People, Save Yourselves from Radiation.* Here I share ways to distinguish internal from external exposure, how to clean soil for gardens, and the best foods to rid the body of radionuclides, including menus with recipes. When I heard about the Fukushima catastrophe in Japan, I took the train to Moscow and went to the Japanese Embassy to offer them this book. Whether or not Viola's experience has been shared in Japan, it certainly has had a wide impact in Russia, from the northwest to the far northeast, from the Urals to Yaroslavl, wherever people contend with radiation from nuclear energy or weapons making or dumping of waste. At their own expense, Viola's volunteers travel out by train to share the lessons we have learned.

In 2015, we had a second tragedy at Chernobyl: climate warming was causing the peat bogs to burn. Soon the forest itself in the exclusion zone around Chernobyl was afire, releasing the radioactivity that had been contained in the trees for almost twenty years. This "second Chernobyl" recontaminated western Bryansk, bringing as much radioactivity to Novozybkov as the first disastrous meltdown in 1986. Already this district has a very high mortality rate in people ages thirty to thirty-five. People who were small children when the initial disaster happened now have high rates of thyroid cancer, cancer of the reproductive organs, and blood diseases.

After the 2015 radioactive release, we called the school principals from Novozybkov and the other most contaminated cities of Bryansk—Zlynka, Klintsy, Krasnyaya Gora, Klimovo, and Starodub. We invited them to come to the university, where we explained to them the importance of supporting and working with the families, using all we have learned about keeping people motivated and active in protecting themselves.

I realize now that we in the NGO Viola are working not only for our own people in Bryansk and Russia but for our whole world. Everywhere contamination from nuclear energy and weapons making keeps growing in sheer amount and toxicity. The lessons we have learned belong to the whole world. May they be used, and may they serve to bring us together in this very important work.

NOTES

1. Ben Aris, "Russia's Nuclear Power Exports Are Booming," *Moscow Times*, May 9, 2019, https://www.themoscowtimes.com/2019/05/09 /russias-nucear-power-exports-are-booming-a65533.

CITIZEN AMBASSADOR

Linda Seeley

THE NAME EACH OF US IS GIVEN at our birth is important—it influences how we conceive of and present ourselves in this world. Fran's middle name—Underhill—fit him perfectly. A Tolkienesque name; humble, strong, mysterious. And along with his gender-ambiguous first name, he was born to stand beside, protect, and serve a courageous woman.

Francis Underhill Macy strongly populates my memory and dreamtime. I first encountered Fran at a Work That Reconnects intensive in Santa Cruz. On the first afternoon of the workshop, Fran walked into the sunshine-yellow classroom that we would inhabit for the next ten days. Tall, broad-shouldered, with a huge grin, shining brown eyes and a shock of bright white hair, he greeted each of us by name.

As Joanna told her stories and led the work, Fran chimed in from time to time. But he also participated fully, sharing his reactions to others' insights and struggles. Gradually I learned that he spoke fluent Russian and that, during many years serving the Peace Corps, he had been the assistant director for India, the director for Tunisia and Nigeria, and finally the director for all of Africa. He had founded the Center for Safe Energy, which supported antinuclear NGOs in Russia, and he'd arranged cultural exchanges between Ukraine and the US. He had also been a very early civil rights worker in the US. He was an idealist—a real one.

Fran had an easy laugh. He loved life and appreciated beauty in all its forms. He was fascinated by my work as a midwife, and he asked me endless questions about the emotional and spiritual effects of guiding the birth of a human into this world. He had three children of his own, and he was not allowed to be present at any of their birthing moments. Though he and Joanna had gone to great lengths to have a natural childbirth and found the one obstetrician in New York City that would support that, the rule of the time was "no men allowed." There was so much Fran wanted to know—how I felt when things were scary and how I knew what to do. His questions helped me appreciate my work in a new way.

On the full moon of January 2005, Fran and Joanna journeyed to Western Australia for the first thirty-day Work That Reconnects intensive. I met up with them in Perth, where we boarded a bus for a seven-hour ride to the Cove, an idyllic eco-resort in a *karri, tingle,* and *jarrah* forest, with each cabin handcrafted by the owners, Illya and Susan Cenin. We threw away our watches and went into deep time for a full month.

Early each morning, Fran and Joanna came down to the shore of the Wilson Inlet to greet the day with movement. Watching Fran move like a great blue heron as he focused all of his attention on the dawning horizon was spectacular. When he finished, he turned his head to the heavens and laughed out loud. The time at the Cove was like nothing else I have ever experienced. Joanna's teaching was inspired. She was channeling exquisitely insightful precepts, and our meditations felt as though we were one being, breathing and learning together in absolute union.

About halfway through the thirty days, I began to cry, and I couldn't stop. I wasn't sad or grief-stricken; in fact, I was overflowing. As I wept on the classroom floor, Fran sat behind me for a long time. He put his hands on my shoulders, and he didn't say a word.

He just sat there with me. Eventually I went back to my cabin where the great releasing continued. That evening Fran brought me a cup of tea. Again, no words were spoken. He sat with me, and then he left. I thought I might never stop crying. But finally, after forty-eight solid hours, my tears drained. I truly saw with new eyes. I was transformed. And a large part of that transformation came from Fran's trust. Fearless. Faithful. Grounded.

Amid all of his intensives with Joanna, Fran continued in his citizen ambassador role through the Center for Safe Energy with his cofounder, Enid Schreibman. They worked to bring citizen activists from the former Soviet Union and American activists together to organize in response to the nuclear arms race and the Chernobyl catastrophe. Fran was instrumental in organizing the program to provide Geiger counters to residents living near Chernobyl, and he facilitated dozens of exchanges between Americans and citizens of the former Soviet Union who were involved in renewable energy, psychology, and citizen activism. He traveled throughout Russia, Kazakhstan, Georgia, and Ukraine to build relationships and working groups. Fran knew that governments or paid professionals would never take heartfelt responsibility for managing nuclear waste. He understood that the only way to monitor radioactive waste was to train cadres of nuclear guardians, who would in turn pass the knowledge of the "poison fire" down to the following generation, and then on to the next, understanding that institutions and governments crumble but nuclear waste is forever.

In 2007, Fran joined Joanna for another thirty-day intensive, this one on the Oregon coast. Here he served as the "guidance counselor" for us. Each of the sixty participants had a thirty- to sixty-minute appointment with him, during which he listened to our stories, hopes, and apprehensions. He was the most gifted listener I've ever been with. As I explained my desire to retire from midwifery after thirty years' work, he queried me about my other interests—permaculture, biodiversity protection, and Mothers for Peace. I had served as legal intervenor in matters related to safety at the Diablo Canyon nuclear power plant since I moved to California in 1982. Fran helped me realize that committing my intelligence and my heart to that work—protecting the biosphere from nuclear poison—was probably the most soul-nourishing thing I could imagine. And I already had a head start on it. After the intensive, I went on a three-day solo trip to the coast, where it became very clear to me that Fran's counsel was solid. Right then and there I made a pact with myself to stay steady and learn as much as I possibly could about nuclear power and nuclear waste. I continue to this day, and I thank Fran again and again for his wisdom.

Fran and Joanna led a "Deep Time" workshop at Dancing Deer Ranch in Templeton on the weekend of January 9–11, 2009. He looked tired, but his spirits were high. When the workshop finished, Joanna, Fran, and I walked on the bluffs overlooking the Pacific Ocean in Cayucos, skies bright blue with puffy clouds pushing down from the north, and Fran soliloquized on his gratitude for Joanna's inspired teaching. Later that week, Fran's Center for Safe Energy hosted its yearly gathering for supporters. The following Tuesday, January 20, feeling jubilant after witnessing the first black man take the oath of office as president of the United States, Fran sat down on his bed to take a rest. With the latest copy of *The Nation* in hand, he lay back and, quietly alone, took his last breath. When his daughter Peggy found him, he was smiling. Fran died as he lived, with grace and beauty.

Joanna tells me that she wishes she could ask his advice, share political thoughts and opinions, work together during the

unraveling and reweaving of our world into a life-sustaining society. She misses him every day. I, along with hundreds of others,
hold him in my heart and memory as a homing device. "What
would Fran do? What would Fran say?" I frequently ask myself
when faced with a dilemma or challenge. Questioning myself
like that brings me back to compassion, inquiry, levelheaded-
ness, kindness—just as Fran showed for others in his big and wide
openhearted life.

THE JOURNEY OF A
NUCLEAR GUARDIAN

Kathleen Sullivan

IN 1985, WHEN I LEFT HOME AND moved out West to attend
university, I did not know that I was moving to a place located
eight miles from one of the world's largest concentrations of plutonium. Shortly after I arrived in Boulder, Colorado, my great
aunt, Anice Swift, took me on a drive down Highway 93. She
stopped in front of an industrial complex called Rocky Flats. At
the west gate of the plant site, on that bright September morning, she spoke with me about nuclear bombs, and when she said
"plutonium," she used a word I had never heard before. Anice explained to me that plutonium is a human-made radioactive material that causes cancer and generates mutations in the genetic
code of life, and that this invisible poison lasts for more than
240,000 years.

Coming of age during the Reagan administration, I was well
aware of nuclear weapons. I had marched in the streets for nuclear
disarmament with my mom, Sandra Sullivan; I had read books,
watched movies, and written letters. I was part of a generation uncertain whether we would make it to old age. Yet it was that moment, when Anice stopped her car at the nondescript plant site,
beautifully framed by the foothills of the Colorado Rockies, that
a certain obsession with plutonium began to take hold of my life.
It was during these formative years in Boulder, as a twenty-one-
year-old undergraduate, that I met Joanna Macy.

A few years into my Rocky Flats activism, on a snowy week-end, I went to hear Joanna speak at the Bethlehem Center near Boulder. I shared with her the rage I felt, the anger that fueled my activism, the fury I experienced when I thought about pluto-nium contamination along the Front Range and the radioactiv-ity borne of the nuclear weapons industrial complex throughout the world. Joanna shared my anger, and also awakened in me the joy of doing this work, the spiritual uplift that comes when taking on the mantle of a bodhisattva. "Yes, feel your anger and rage," Joanna told me, "and breathe that through as you fuel your motivation, your activism, and compassion." What a relief! I no longer had to avoid what I knew to be true. I had finally found a home for the matrix of emotions I felt as a young woman growing up in a world under threat. Seventy-thousand plutonium pits were not the only things Rocky Flats produced. Lifelong friendships, scholarship, love affairs, art, and activism were also the result of seeing that nuclear behemoth on a windy Coloradan plateau.

THE IDEA OF GUARDIANSHIP

Soon after meeting Joanna in 1989, I traveled to attend a Fire Group meeting at the Macy home in 1990. The Berkeley Fire Group had recently been formed; its monthly meetings were or-ganized around the three *s*'s: science, strategy, and spirituality.[1] Members would study the science of radiation together, learning about its harms and effects. They would discuss strategies for en-gagement, educate the public, and participate in public hearings with regulatory bodies. The five-hour meetings were designed to balance left and right brainwork, with experiential practice seen as essential for allowing the difficult information to penetrate. The term *poison fire* arose early in the Fire Group—a fire borne of human hubris, a fire that burns DNA, that must be capped and contained, protected from the biosphere. The idea of guardianship reflected the extraordinary longevity of radioactive violence and the need for future generations to understand what their ancestors created. It was the Berkeley Fire Group, exposing a deep denial of our obligation and agency in a post-Chernobyl landscape, that brought nuclear guardianship into being.

During my visit in 1990, I made a presentation about Rocky Flats and the disastrous "cleanup" effort underway. The Berkeley group had spent significant time developing the "Nuclear Guardianship Ethic," a guiding document outlining best practices for looking after radioactive waste and creating a culture of awareness and care. The group had also been developing a deep time practice, The Standard Remembering. This was written to help people imagine how our ancestors might recall the nuclear age, its origin, the arms race powered by advanced capitalism and collective insanity, and guardianship as the ground note for coming back to life.[2]

Later in Colorado, I shared what I had learned with Judith Mohling, a veteran of Rocky Flats activism. Based on guardianship principles, Judith and I co-created the Rocky Flats Ethics Study Group—a series of meetings between activists and staff from the US Department of Energy, Environmental Protection Agency, and Colorado Department for Public Health and the Environment. These off-the-record gatherings were in part modeled after the Fire Group's three *s*'s. We offered research and presentations on monitored retrievable storage of radioactive materials, used deep time practices to bring future beings to the minds of the decision makers, and strategized how to get these power brokers into one room to consider our moral responsibility. This focus on the ethics of Rocky Flats "cleanup" operations would later lead to the Rocky Flats Nuclear Guardianship Project.

Nuclear guardianship offers a radical realization of our responsibility throughout time while also presenting a plan for looking after nuclear waste in a way that honors our interdependence with all life on Earth and our connection to future generations. Nuclear guardianship requires that the storage of radioactive materials be in a monitored, retrievable configuration, using the safest industrial standards such as the current practice of hardened on-site storage. Materials need to be routinely repackaged, as no human-made vessel can outlive the radioactivity they temporarily contain—hence the idea of storage for periods of fifty years at a time.[3] This is a time frame people can understand and plan for. By guarding the radioactive materials, by monitoring and correcting any found problems, this is how we can, in a purposefully low-tech manner, continually isolate the radioactivity from the environment. Such storage, not disposal, should occur where possible at the site of generation, avoiding the further risk of contamination in the transportation of nuclear wastes. It is also important that guardian sites not be hidden from view but remain *in mind* through public education and community involvement, further developing people's commitment to the responsible care for radioactive wastes, perhaps humanity's most enduring artifact for future generations.

Nuclear guardians look directly at the fact that plutonium remains carcinogenic and mutagenic for some 240,000 years. No system of language or civilization, no work of art—*nothing* can outlive plutonium. The true age of plutonium is more akin to the upwelling of magma into mountains or to the creation of oceans. It is more of an earth age—glacial time, geological time, what Joanna calls deep time. Through art, poetry, movement, and storytelling, a guardian's vital role is to imagine what the physical practice of guarding will entail, as well as to own our connection to and responsibility for future generations.

GUARDING THE KNOWLEDGE

Nuclear guardianship is as much about guarding the knowledge and memories of what we have done, or what has been done in our name, as it is about physically guarding the poison fire. And this "what has been done" has been muddied from the start due to the secrecy and lies that typify the global nuclear establishment. Guardians must be vigilant in guarding knowledge—especially in this perilous age of "alternative facts." Joanna describes this aspect of guardianship:

> When we see how facts are manipulated and misrepresented— as we are, in fact, deluged with lies—the extraordinary gift of consciousness, the attentive mind, and the mindful heart become perhaps the most precious of gifts. . . . What more important task do we have but to guard these things for the sake of future beings—to carry them forward?[4]

Still we are told that deterrence and its attendant, near-constant modernization, keeps us safe and that we now need to ramp up nuclear power production in order to address global climate disruption. But no one in any of these camps, from defense strategists to deep greens, has fully considered the stream of waste borne of nuclear power, which lasts virtually forever and will mutate the perfection of life. How could anything in connection to nuclear violence be our protector or provider?

For my part, the pursuit of knowledge guardianship took the form of doctoral research at Lancaster University. I focused on nuclear guardianship using Mary Shelley's novel *Frankenstein*, with plutonium cast as the monster. In 1818, Shelley gave us the concept of monster in the natural world, while the father scientist flees his responsibility—a driving narrative that epitomizes the fundamentals of nuclear science to this day. We are still led to believe that scientists in pursuit of knowledge cannot be held responsible for what they unleash. It is rather the *products* that present as catastrophic—Promethean technology absent from its masters. Nuclear guardianship reverses this narrative by taking full charge of what we have created.

During my years in the UK, much research and writing on guardianship was generated and disseminated by the Fire Group. Tabloid-sized publications called *The Nuclear Guardianship Forum* were produced in the early to mid-1990s, filled with scholarly articles, poetry, art, and process ideas. Fertile imagination and collaboration across disciplines characterized the early nuclear guardians in our quest to understand the poison fire. Fran was the primary editor for the *Forum*, and over three years produced four editions.[5] During this time, Fran founded the Center for Safe Energy. Through his love of Russian language and culture, Fran built a bridge to people in former Soviet Republics concerned about the devastating effects of nuclear weapons development and the ongoing (still ongoing) Chernobyl disaster.

In 1994, I assisted Joanna and Fran in a series hosted by Stephen and Martine Batchelor as part of the Sharpham Colloquia Programme at Sharpham House in Devon, England. We convened a group of highly regarded scientists, journalists, and activists to discuss the moral challenge of radioactive wastes. In the paper that resulted, we argued that responsible care for nuclear materials was an extension of our moral responsibility and an expression of moral courage. Together we studied and added our revisions to the "Nuclear Guardianship Ethic." Helpful new suggestions concerning the clarity and power that each statement conveyed were incorporated into what we consider an ever-evolving, living document. As recently as 2015, we continued to revise the ethic, this time seeking counsel from the Rocky Flats Guardians.[6]

Mixed oxide fuel (MOX), the industry euphemism for plutonium-laced nuclear fuel, was a growing concern for Fran in the mid-1990s. In 1998, as part of our guardianship work, we brought together an international group of leading activists, academics, and scientists to Eaglehurst Manor in England to discuss a global response to MOX technology. Of particular concern was a proposal to transport the deadly fuel elements by boat between the UK and Japan. Nuclear guardians, along with our partners in the Plutonium Free Future movement, were part of the effort that made sure the mass trade in MOX fuel never really took hold.

GUARDING THE MEMORY

In order to pursue the idea of guardianship as part of an oral tradition, a tradition of storytelling, I moved from London to Brooklyn in 1999 and began working with high-school students, developing the Nuclear Weapons Education and Action Project through Educators for Social Responsibility. We brought the history of nuclear weapons use in World War II to students and also told the stories of current nuclear risks. Our in-class workshops often incorporated Joanna's interactive methods, in particular Open Sentences and deep time work.

In 2000 I was selected as an NGO consultant to the United Nations Study on Disarmament Education, in recognition of my work in New York City schools. When the UN report was launched in 2002,[7] the Japanese ambassador to the Conference on

Disarmament invited me to Japan to offer disarmament education workshops in high schools in Tokyo, Hiroshima, and Nagasaki. Using Joanna's techniques, I found ways to engage Japanese teenagers—a far different group than the rambunctious New York City youth I had become accustomed to. During this first pilgrimage to Japan, I befriended many atomic bomb survivors—*hibakusha*, as they are called in Japanese. I learned that hibakusha not only suffered mental and physical anguish from surviving a nuclear attack but also were subjected to discrimination at the hands of fellow Japanese. In 1945, little was known about the effects of radioactive contamination, and rumors spread that radiation exposure was akin to an infectious disease. Already traumatized by their experience of the "unforgettable fire," they fell victim to discrimination and were often deemed ineligible for work and marriage. Sadly, discrimination against hibakusha continues to this day, and it has been compounded, or perhaps renewed, by the ongoing radiation catastrophe at the Fukushima Daiichi nuclear power plant.

Over the years I have been back to Japan numerous times, making two documentary films, *The Last Atomic Bomb*, highlighting the lesser known stories of Nagasaki survivors; and *The Ultimate Wish: Ending the Nuclear Age*, weaving the connection between Fukushima evacuees and Nagasaki hibakusha. Story guardianship came into sharp focus in 2008 while I was working with the Japanese NGO Peace Boat. I was invited on the first Global Hibakusha Voyage, which brought over a hundred atomic bomb survivors around the world to share their stories. Witnessing their enthusiasm and urgency to share their experiences, I recognized them as nuclear guardians.

After this extraordinary journey, and in honor of our beloved Fran's untimely death in 2009, my colleague Robert Croonquist and I initiated the Francis Underhill Macy Hibakusha Stories Initiative to guard the memories of the first wartime use of nuclear weapons.[8] Over the years we have brought hundreds of hibakusha to New York City high schools, reaching more than 45,000 students. We have also organized Nuclear Guardianship Sails near Indian Point nuclear power plant, for New York City youth to engage with the "Nuclear Guardianship Ethic," learn about the catastrophic risks of nuclear power, and become familiar with radiation detection at the many sites throughout the city once engaged in the Manhattan Project.

The window of opportunity to hear the firsthand witnesses of Hiroshima and Nagasaki is quickly closing. Thus we encourage participants who have met hibakusha to become the guardians of their testimony. Students learned about and produced *kamishibai*, a traditional Japanese art form using a series of drawings to tell a story. They also have composed music and songs, taken portraits, written poetry and one-act plays—all based on a real person who survived nuclear hell. Many are moved to tears listening to hibakushas' stories and can feel the honor and weight of their duty to keep the knowledge alive.

EVOLVING A CULTURE OF CARE

The Hibakusha Stories Initiative has always incorporated the arts in its programming, primarily the art of storytelling. We have collaborated with musicians, artists, filmmakers, playwrights, photographers, and dancers to create new ways to share the culture of care, the culture of nuclear abolition, and the culture of guardianship. Art moves and motivates people. To commemorate the seventieth anniversary of the atomic bombings, we produced the concert *WITH LOVE to Hiroshima and Nagasaki: A Concert for Disarmament,* a sold-out music and art performance on May 2, 2015. In December of the same year, Hibakusha Stories was part of a team at Pioneer Works in Brooklyn to bring Iri and Toshi Maruki's monumental oeuvres, *The Hiroshima Panels*, to the United States. Not as well known in the West, but comparable to Picasso's antiwar masterwork *Guernica*, *The Hiroshima Panels* is a deeply moving portrayal of the agony and suffering visited upon the more than three hundred thousand people who died in Hiroshima and Nagasaki. Keeping with Japanese tradition, the panels are painted on folding screens made of wood and paper using mostly black ink, with powerful flashes of crimson red and sky blue to highlight certain elements of the painted scenes.[9]

The installation also included a set of black-and-white archival photographs of Hiroshima and Nagasaki, artifacts from the aftermath of Nagasaki (a melted glass bottle, burned roof tiles, disintegrating buttons from a school uniform), and a black-box room screening *Hellfire: A Journey from Hiroshima*, the 1986 Academy Award–nominated documentary of Iri and Toshi Maruki at work. Over the six weeks of the exhibition run, we presented disarmament education programs to hundreds of high school and university students from the New York City metro area. Students interacted with visiting hibakusha and responded to the panels and artifacts with their own art, poetry, and performance.

Recent works include collaborations with Ari Beser, digital storyteller and grandson of the only person on both planes over Hiroshima and Nagasaki—Jacob Beser, an electrical engineer who essentially turned on the bombs. We weave together music, testimony, and film to share hibakusha stories to a wide audience. We are currently making a film of the song cycle *Journey to Peace*, a harrowing and inspirational tale of a remarkable Nagasaki hibakusha, Chieko Watanabe. Her journey from despair to empowerment resulted in 1950s activism that would affect the lives of all hibakusha looking for health care, compensation, and dignity.

The teachings of nuclear guardianship require that we guard the knowledge and the stories, using art to engage others, to wake us up to our mutual interdependence and our mutual vulnerability. Instead of hiding ourselves from the poison fire, or hiding it from future generations, we can, as Joanna says, "put our mind on it." To put our mind on it, we learn how to build community, and we learn that we need each other to do the work well. We get to appreciate our true age—that we are born of all life, with four billion years' authority. And in this expansive space, we encounter a radically different notion of time—from the beginning into the far future, deep time, instantaneous and glacial.

THE NOBEL PEACE PRIZE

On July 7, 2017, the Treaty on the Prohibition of Nuclear Weapons was adopted by 122 member states of the United Nations. It has been my honor and privilege to support my dear friend, Hiroshima survivor Setsuko Thurlow, in her participation throughout the years of the Humanitarian Initiative—from our work in intergovernmental conferences in Vienna and Nayarit, Mexico, to the Open Ended Working Group on Multilateral Nuclear Disarmament at the United Nations in Geneva and the resulting ban treaty negotiations at the UN in New York in March and June–July of 2017.[10] Setsuko was given the final word on July 7, after the conference president Elayne Whyte Gómez gaveled in the world-changing nuclear ban treaty. When Setsuko finished her impassioned intervention, every person in the conference room rose to their feet in respect for this incomparable woman.[11]

The Francis Underhill Macy Hibakusha Stories Initiative of Youth Arts New York is a member of ICAN, the International Campaign to Abolish Nuclear Weapons, 2017 Nobel Peace Laureate. ICAN's work to foster the Treaty on the Prohibition of Nuclear Weapons was the primary reason for our Nobel Prize. As guardians, Hibakusha Stories helped craft language on future generations for the preamble of the treaty. Our team traveled to Oslo to assist Setsuko, who received the Nobel Peace Prize on behalf of our campaign.

Sitting in the Oslo City Hall, as the Norwegian royal family and the Nobel Committee processed into the flower-decked and ornately painted great room to the refrain of trumpet fanfare—I traced my steps from that moment back to the Bethlehem Center decades earlier. I owe this incredible journey of a nuclear guardian to the singular courage and compassion of Joanna and Fran Macy, two spiritual warriors with a wide embrace who have carried countless bodhisattvas forward into the Great Turning.

NOTES

1. The Berkeley group stayed active for six years; another Fire Group in Germany continued to meet over decades.
2. Joanna Macy, *World as Lover, World as Self* (Berkeley, CA: Parallax Press 1991), 234–37.
3. See Molly Young Brown, "How Can We Face the Challenge? 50 Years at a Time," *Nuclear Guardianship Forum*, no. 3 (Spring 1994): 1, 10, https://ratical.org/radiation/NGP/50yrs.html.
4. Alan AtKisson, "Guardians of the Future: Interview with Joanna Macy," *In Context*, no. 28 (Spring 1991):20–25.
5. See The Nuclear Guardianship Forum: On the Responsible Care of Radioactive Materials, https://ratical.org/radiation/NGP/index.html #HTML.
6. See www.rockyflatsnuclearguardianship.org/about for the principles of the Nuclear Guardianship Ethic.

7. United Nations General Assembly, *United Nations Study on Disarmament and Non-Proliferation Education*, August 2002, https://www.un.org/disarmament/topics/education.

8. See Hibakusha Stories, http://hibakushastories.org.

9. See Maruki Gallery for *The Hiroshima Panels*, http://www.aya.or.jp/~marukimsn/english/indexE.htm.

10. For details, see "Humanitarian Impact of Nuclear Weapons, Reaching Critical Will, http://www.reachingcriticalwill.org/disarmament-fora/hinw.

11. Again teaming up with Amber Cooper-Davies and Sam Sadigursky, we produced an animation of Setsuko's speech, *If You Love This Planet*, http://www.icanw.org/campaign-news/short-film-if-you-love-this-planet.

FINDING OUR WAY FORWARD AFTER FUKUSHIMA

Yuka Saito and Hide Enomoto

ON JANUARY 14, 1991, the United States invaded Iraq, launching the first Gulf War. A young graduate student named Tamio Nakano was in class with Joanna Macy at the California Institute of Integral Studies (CIIS). That day Joanna canceled her lecture and had everyone sit on the floor to share their feelings about what was happening. For Tamio, it was a turning point. He joined others in local nonviolent protests and organized meetings for Japanese people living in the wider Berkeley area, so they could have openhearted conversations on war and peace in their native language. When he returned to Japan, he became one of the initiators of the Japanese deep ecology movement, using an early translation of *Despair and Personal Power in the Nuclear Age* by Noriko Senda. Later, Tamio played a critical role in inviting Joanna and Fran Macy to Japan.

In 1994, having heard about Joanna from Tamio, I (Hide Enomoto) joined one of her CIIS workshops and later came to offer the Work That Reconnects in Japan. In 2014, I (Yuka Saito) took a course with Joanna and Sean Kelly at CIIS. Shortly after, I became part of the second cohort for the people-of-color facilitator training at Canticle Farm in Oakland, California. Following the early footsteps laid down by Tamio Nakano, we carried the work further in Japan, both of us called strongly by the Fukushima triple disaster of March 11, 2011.

PART I: YUKA SAITO[1]

I sometimes wonder why I am so uncomfortable being with someone in pain. At least as I have experienced it in Japan, our modern culture does not teach us how to deal with pain. Instead, it teaches us to be cheerful and uncomplaining all the time. Whether it is a friend with cancer, or one whose mother has just died, or one whose relative was a comfort woman, I have learned to keep my distance.

So, to begin with, I did the same thing with the pain around the Fukushima Daiichi disaster. This time, however, something happened that changed me completely. As Joanna Macy likes to say, many heroines and heroes are thrown into adventures unexpectedly and unprepared. She was right. My journey started just like that, with a message from a Japanese woman from Fukushima.

Fukushima Aftermath

The woman was Kinue Suzuki, a mother and soon-to-be grandmother in her sixties. She was about four feet tall and maybe sixty-five pounds. She had suffered her whole life with congenital rickets. When people first see her, they find it hard to believe that she is the one who helped three seriously disabled people and their caretakers escape from Fukushima city within three days after the disaster. She organized transport, found places to bring people, made sure they had wheelchair accessibility, made many phone calls for financial support, packed everything they needed, and then, in the middle of the night in total darkness, drove as far away as she could from Fukushima Daiichi.

In Kinue's message to me, she said, "Despair has been eating me alive. I need to raise myself up from here. Can you help me?" A woman as strong as Kinue was needing my help . . . how could I possibly help her? I was very honored that Kinue contacted me about offering a workshop. And yet I was also terrified by the thought of working with evacuees fleeing from radiation. Just imagining the burdens they had been carrying since the disaster was overwhelming.

Kinue suggested meeting beforehand with several other evacuees so I could listen to what had been troubling them. On one beautiful October morning in 2016, eight of us gathered in Kyoto Tower. When we talked and listened to each other face to face, I realized that they were ordinary people, just like me. They were desperate, sad, angry, tired, courageous, humorous, and bold. Don't all these characteristics also describe who I am, at least some of the time? After all, the evacuees are also children of Earth, going through life's challenges, just like me.

The two-day workshop for evacuees affected by the radiation from Fukushima Daiichi was a strong event. We talked, we cried, we laughed together. We even danced the Elm Dance with two wheelchairs in the circle. There was one beautiful moment when the pale winter light came through the big windows, casting silhouettes of us swaying on the floor. The music and the silence both embraced us. One by one people shared their stories: "I have been angry all the time for the past five years. But I don't know how long I can continue to be this way. Last year I started learning massage because of my sons who are still living near Fukushima for their jobs. I am preparing myself for the possibility of something bad happening to their health."

Another woman said, "I am worrying about my father who still lives in Fukushima. I insisted on him leaving there with me, but he didn't listen to me. I felt so bad that I had to leave him behind alone, but I just could not stay in Fukushima with the intense anxiety I felt every day. What hurts me the most is not the contamination per se but separating from him, feeling guilty all the time, and feeling the indifference of others."

One participant struggled with what to say to her children: "I can't explain why they can't go back to Fukushima where their father still lives for his work. I don't want to scare them. Five years is long for all of us, and sometimes I want to go back to Fukushima and live how we used to live! But, of course, my mind is clear. I can't bear to worry about my kids getting exposed to radiation every day. Now I need to replenish my spirit every day and tell my kids to be patient while I am working hard as one of the plaintiffs suing those responsible for the disaster."

Kinue Suzuki had been managing a facility in Fukushima Prefecture that supports people with disabilities to become independent. After the accident, many people with disabilities in Fukushima had no choice other than to stay. She said, "It feels like I have abandoned them. That accident threw me into the depths of despair. I became ill with thyroid cancer. The Work That Reconnects helped me begin by firmly embracing despair as despair, not trying to ignore it and jump to hope."

As I listened to them, my fear and anxiety melted like ice. I felt myself resonating with their love, sadness, confusion, and guilt. I could know how it feels because I had experienced all those feelings in my own way. What I needed in order to be with their pain was just to be open as who I am. It was that simple. It seemed their truth-telling cracked the shell of my fear.

Taking the Work Further

In Japan, every year at the end of the year, one kanji character is chosen that expresses that year in a single word. In 2018 that word was 災, meaning "disaster" or "unfortunate event" (combining the characters for "water" and "fire"). In addition to earthquakes, typhoons, and heat waves, there were other forms of disaster this year, such as sexual harassment by authority figures, discrimination against women applying to medical schools, tampering with public records by government officials, and the pressured return order for those who evacuated from Fukushima. The current Japanese government has also been using all means to influence public opinion while trying to change Article 9 of the Constitution to allow active participation in war.

At the same time, amid these dismal events, there is a growing movement in many parts of the country to accelerate the speed of the Great Turning by providing the Work That Reconnects, often called "Active Hope," based on the title of Joanna's book with Chris Johnstone. Participants in WTR workshops have been very responsive to extending their sense of time to a distant future and taking responsibility for future beings. They share the pain they carry forward from a difficult past, and through the Work That Reconnects they come to understand that our survival depends on the choices we make in solidarity with the vast web of life.

Sachiko Iejin Kang, a Japanese woman of Korean ancestry, told the story of facing her mixed ancestry: "At the age of ten, my mother told me out of the blue never to tell anyone that we are Koreans. She said that we would be discriminated against if we did. I was very surprised, and I became frightened. Since then, I have been thinking about the Japan-Korea issue, and when I learned about the spiral [of the Work That Reconnects], I thought that I could overcome various obstacles. When I do the exercises, I am encouraged and even energized. So, now I am sharing them with my friends, for they are my allies in working to make this world better."

One woman, Shigeko Suzuki, spoke of "a pain within me that I can't heal no matter how hard I work to heal it. My mother was born near the end of World War II and was always hungry when she was small. Even today, my mother can't go out unless she has some food in her bag. Her fearful thought, *The world is dangerous, and it will not give me enough*, has been handed down to me even though I was born in the era of abundant food. I believe that the world is not a kind place and will not provide enough. This is my pain. But I do feel hope for this pain because I've learned that it shows where I need to look and what needs to be healed."

Several Japanese facilitators have adapted the Work That Reconnects to the business world as a route to changing society. Naokazu Harada has been offering workshops for young people between ages eighteen and twenty-two who want to become entrepreneurs. He says, "I ask them to think about what the essence of a business is and what it would mean for their business to contribute to people and Earth. They are not yet completely involved in the Industrial Growth Society, so they can still easily connect with the feelings and dreams of their childhood and regain their sense of connection to Earth. I want them to know the importance of the sense of connection before entering the political economy."

Ai Sanda works at a big company in a big city with politicians, local leaders, business executives, educators, creators, and all sorts of people who could have big social impacts. In the business industry, companies develop mid- to long-term plans, providing a vision for growing business in the next three to five years. In contrast, she said, "When I spoke with people from rural areas, I found that their sense of 'mid- to long-term' was a hundred years or a thousand years!" For Sanda, when people who can have big influences on policies, education, or public opinion are themselves changed, the whole system can change in twenty to thirty years. "What I want to do is change the direction our social system is heading."

In 2015, Chris Johnstone and Joanna Macy's book *Active Hope* was translated into Japanese. Six of Joanna's books have now been published in Japan. *Coming Back to Life*, which I am translating, is scheduled to be published in late 2019. Once this WTR facilitator's manual is available in Japanese, there will be more opportunities for Japanese people to experience the Work That Reconnects. I am currently working to promote Joanna's teachings and practices throughout Japan as a workshop facilitator. The three issues I have chosen to focus on are treatment of victims of the Fukushima nuclear disaster; lingering pain in relations between Japan, China, and Korea; and the empowerment of women in Japan. Here in the US, in 2015, I and several of my friends in Berkeley resumed the group meetings first begun by Tamio Nakano. We offer a space once a month for native Japanese speakers to meet and consider topics of current concern. This space also serves as a bridge for East-West cross-pollination around ideas and practices related to the Great Turning.

PART II: HIDE ENOMOTO

My journey to Joanna Macy's work began with my thesis project at CIIS, which I called "Creating Meaningful Work" (CMW). I deeply resonate with Joanna's thinking that in order to solve the problems that we are facing in our world, we need to change how we relate to ourselves, to one another, to nature, and to our world. So many of us are trapped in the current system of work and are so busy just trying to get through the day to make a living that we don't have any time or any energy left over to do what's needed to heal our world. The goal of the CMW workshops is to liberate people from this entrapment so they can engage in their "real work"; that is, living out the purpose they have been born with, which not only enables them to live a better life but also empowers them to create a better world. I believe that this will be one of the leverage points to make the Great Turning happen.

I first began offering CMW workshops in Japan in 1997, after I had been certified in San Francisco as a professional coach.

I wrote a book about coaching that sold very well, which led me to set up a coach training company in 2000. I was feeling an acute need to train more people in coaching skills, so more people would be empowered to bring their very best to whatever they choose to engage in. However, I had a lingering feeling that coaching alone was not enough. If society isn't organized in a way to empower people, then it is very difficult for people to sustain the changes they make through coaching. I started asking myself, *What does an empowering society look like, and what can I do to create that?*

This question eventually led me to Findhorn, one of the world's leading eco-villages, located in Scotland. I moved there with my family in 2005 and stayed for two and a half years. This period was one of the toughest in my life because I couldn't seem to find the answer to my question. Then I came across transition towns (TT), a concept within the local citizens' grassroots Transition movement for community resilience, and Awakening the Dreamer (ATD), an initiative of the Pachamama Alliance. Later I learned that Joanna had a big impact on both of these movements, and I felt that my life journey had mysteriously come full circle.

In the spring of 2008, Joanna came to Findhorn as one of the speakers for the conference, "Positive Energy." I hadn't seen her in the nearly twelve years since I left the US, and I was so excited to see her again. I shared with her my life journey since we had last seen each other, and she said she was glad that our paths had crossed again. Soon after this reunion I became very busy setting up both TT and ATD in Japan. Seeing the need to refamiliarize myself with the Work That Reconnects after my ten-year gap, I signed up for an intensive with Joanna at the Land of the Medicine Buddha in California. All this time, I never forgot what I had learned from Joanna, and going through the WTR exercises with Joanna was like coming home.

Facing Fukushima

It was not until the land of Japan was shaken hard in March 2011 that I started thinking about offering the Work That Reconnects myself. Somehow I had been holding the Work as something sacred and felt that I didn't have enough depth to lead a workshop. However, as I witnessed the aftermath of that enormous earthquake and tsunami and watched the sense of hope for the future crumble as people learned of the irreversible impacts of nuclear fallout from Fukushima Daiichi, I felt a sense of urgency to reintroduce the Work to Japan.

In June 2013, I returned to Findhorn to attend a weeklong workshop offered by Joanna. During the workshop we did a Truth Mandala. I was the only Japanese among more than one hundred participants from all over the world; I knew I had to speak to what had happened in Japan two years before. When the time came for me to step into the circle, I picked up the rock representing fear. I began speaking: "I remember the day when the nuclear power station in Fukushima blew up. . . ." Then, all of a sudden, a big swell of emotion came up and completely took over me. I could not speak, no matter how hard I tried. I just cried my eyes out. Another part of me was totally calm and was observing myself. I was wondering, "What is going on with me? This is not just my feeling. Maybe I'm connected with the feeling of people in Fukushima." I had been feeling hesitant to offer the Work That Reconnects because I thought I would never be able to understand the level of despair that the people in Fukushima and other stricken areas of Tohoku might be feeling. But after the Truth Mandala, I realized that I had been coming from the paradigm of separation. The reason that I was overtaken by the overwhelming sense of despair is because we are all connected.

The famous phrase was ringing in my ears, "If not now, when? If not here, where? If not us, who?"

Shortly after this experience I had a chance to sit down with Joanna personally at "The Original Garden" in Findhorn. I shared my determination to start offering the Work That Reconnects in Japan. She didn't say much and instead invited me to join her in meditation. Even though we were just sitting there quietly, I remember the warm feeling pouring toward me from Joanna. And that feeling expressed much more than any words could have expressed. In that rich silence I felt I received her blessing. A few months later, I offered my first "Active Hope" workshop in Japan, mostly for those who had been involved in either TT or ATD. To my great relief, it received a very positive response, and since then I have offered countless workshops, including two in Fukushima.

Taking the Work Further

The publishing of *Active Hope* stirred up quite an interest among Japanese people, increasing demand for workshops all over Japan. I soon realized that the number of people who could offer this workshop was not enough to meet those demands. Then I thought of taking Japanese people who could be potential facilitators of the Work That Reconnects to the US for a special intensive with Joanna. She graciously accepted this idea without hesitation, and in June 2016 almost thirty Japanese people flew to the US and spent a glorious week at River's Bend. It wasn't easy to make this happen, as I was responsible for all enrollment and travel logistics, but there was no doubt in my mind that it had to happen.

At this point I was determined to let go of "holding the torch" for the Work That Reconnects in Japan and let the new people take the lead. I was feeling called to somewhere else, and I knew I would need to create space for something new to emerge. When I shared my determination with Joanna, she showed some sadness in her face for a moment but then encouraged me to follow my heart. On the last day of the intensive, she spoke to me directly in front of the whole group, telling me, "You go forth!" I was grateful that Joanna took the time to offer this personal blessing and, like a true teacher, gave me a strong and loving push on my back.

A few years earlier I had heard that the Coaching Training Institute (CTI) was planning to offer its leadership program in China for the first time. I asked CTI if I could lead this program, as I felt it could be a doorway for me to do something about the pain I was feeling about the Japan-China conflict over a small island in the East Asian Sea. I was able to lead the program in 2015 and 2016, and through this experience I fell in love with the people in China. In Shanghai I had the opportunity to make a TEDx presentation, and the topic I chose, "Your Pain Is a Gift," was based on what I had learned from Joanna over the years. About five hundred people were there, and the response was overwhelmingly positive. I felt I was being called to China, and the following year I moved to Shanghai. There I offered four "Active Hope" workshops, two in Shanghai and two in Beijing, along with six "Creating Meaningful Work" (CMW) workshops. One of the participants from an "Active Hope" workshop, Shan Wu, fell in love with the Work That Reconnects and decided to join the intensive offered by Joanna in June 2017. Another group of people is working on translating *Active Hope* into Chinese.

Through working with people in China, I have realized that there is deep pain around losing the connection with their ancestral wisdom in Taoism, Confucianism, and Buddhism as a result of the Cultural Revolution. Now that China has become the world's second largest economy and people's material needs are being met, especially in the big cities, more and more people are finding themselves in what might be called a "spiritual void." Considering the growing political and economic presence of China in the world, I think it is important that the Chinese people be exposed to wisdoms they can rely on, so they can be responsible not only for their own lives but also for the entire planet.

Conclusion

The events of March 11, 2011, served as a powerful springboard for the Work That Reconnects in Japan. With such widespread suffering and loss of hope, the workshops we were able to offer provided a chance for us to share our grief and despair. The impacts of the radiation will be felt on the land and people of Japan for many generations. We truly hope that other WTR facilitators will spread the work far and wide and help ease this terrible burden on the Japanese people. Our hearts have broken open as we have met those struggling to find a way forward under these difficult conditions. In this way, the work is inspiring our paths as unlikely heroes on the bodhisattva journey.

NOTES

1. Many people have supported my effort in this writing. I am grateful to Ken Anno, my bodhisattva brother and fellow student of Joanna, for providing a draft English translation. I am also grateful to Sean Kelly, my husband and guide in integral ecology, for his careful editing. I thank everyone who shared their stories with me. Due to space limitations, I unfortunately could not draw from the stories of Takehiko Akatsuka, Ken Anno, Kensyu Kamura, Kohei Saul Kuwahara, and Yasumori Tsukada.

NOTHING IS IMPOSSIBLE

Daniel Ellsberg

ON OCTOBER 10, 1976, the Continental Walk for Disarmament and Social Justice was approaching the culmination of a nine-month walk from the West Coast to Washington DC, advocating every night in towns along the way for a process of nuclear disarmament. A core group of about thirty had walked the whole way, arriving each night at prearranged shelters volunteered by churches and others and conducting teach-ins or rallies on the dangers of the nuclear era in a local church or school. The concept of the walk was that the main body of marchers each day would consist of people who joined the core group the morning after the local discussion, walking from their own town to the next one along the route.

This actually came about. On almost every link between towns, the locals outnumbered the core group, in some cases by hundreds. Many of these participants, carrying banners and handing out leaflets, had never marched in a demonstration before. They were taking part in a rolling protest against the US-Soviet nuclear race by a relay race of walkers that involved, by the end, many thousands of midcountry Americans.

I had promoted the action from its inception, held fundraisers for it in some of the larger towns, and joined it for three or four days at a time at several links across the country. Now, after marching for the final four days, I was part of the main body as it was joined by two feeder marches converging in Washington.

It was a bright day, with large white cloth doves on poles, flying above thousands of marchers with hundreds of banners in the sunlight.

I was walking next to a friend I'd made on the march, Selden Osborne, who had walked the whole way across the country as the oldest member of the core group. He was sixty-four, which seemed old even to me at the time. (I was forty-four at the start. He had a grandchild born during those nine months.) At last we walked in sight of the Capitol, and I said to him, "Selden, what do you tell people along the way when they ask what you hope to accomplish on this walk?"

He said, matter-of-factly, "I tell them I want to participate in a miracle. It will be a miracle if the United States decides to disarm. And it will be another miracle if the Russians join them."

After a few more paces, he added cheerfully, "Fortunately, miracles are possible."

I wasn't used to hearing such propositions in secular circles. One aspect in particular struck me at first. "It's an interesting concept, Selden," I said. "A 'miracle' that requires human participation." I tried to think of an example.

Within moments I thought of what was going on in my own household on the other side of the country. My wife, Patricia, was three months pregnant in San Francisco. In her womb a new human being, our son, was developing. And for that to be possible, two humans had to come together to beget . . . a miracle.

That was true for every person who had ever lived. And every animal. Yes, that process was not unpredictable for humans, or even unexpected. Yet miraculous. As is the existence of life itself, and the conditions for it.

Still—*social* miracles? I took it for granted that Selden was not talking about a divine intervention, nor, since his youth, violent revolution. (Though now a pacifist, and still a Marxist, he was for-merly a Trotskyist who in the Depression year 1933 had graduated from Stanford College with a BA and had immediately chosen to spend his working life as a longshoreman under Harry Bridges on the San Francisco waterfront.) He meant, I took it, a nonviolent transformation of society so sweeping and sudden as to be—in the eyes of experts and laypeople alike—virtually unimaginable not long before it actually occurred. Not merely "extremely unlikely" but *impossible.*

And from the perspective of nearly everyone in the world, that is exactly what happened thirteen years later, beginning the night of November 9, 1989, when citizens of Berlin, mainly Easterners, dismantled the Berlin Wall with hammers, picks, and their bare hands, without interference from East German soldiers or police. I've never heard of a single person on Earth in the early years of the 1980s who imagined there was the slightest possibility of that coming about by the end of that decade.

Countless American youngsters—such as our son, Michael, then twelve years old—were hauled in front of the family TV to see it as it happened, told to watch and remember. All across the country, dumbstruck parents such as us were trying to impress on our children's minds that they were seeing something astonish-ing, impossible, a miracle. What followed in the next two years seemed just as miraculous: the peaceful dissolution of the Warsaw Pact, unification of Germany, and the end of the USSR.

All that could have been—"should" have been—the catalyst for the particular miracle Selden sought: US and Russian nuclear disarmament. But that has not yet occurred, nor anything really approaching it. What's worse, I can point at this moment to no sub-stantive, specifiable reason to hope that the danger will disappear in the next decade or more.

Now, thirty years after the Berlin Wall came down, both the United States and Russia are engaged in "modernizing" their nuclear "triads"—alert forces consisting of land-based intercontinental ballistic missiles (ICBMs), long-range strategic bombers with air-launched cruised missiles, and submarine-launched ballistic missiles (SLBMs)—*each "leg" of which* constitutes a doomsday machine, capable of killing nearly all humans on Earth. The prospect of global "nuclear winter" was modeled by environmental scientists in both nations in 1983 and confirmed by peer-reviewed studies in the last decade. As of now, the catastrophic effects of a US-Russian nuclear war using even a small fraction of current operational warheads are scientifically as predictable as human-caused climate catastrophe if current levels of carbon emissions are continued. (The same models are used.)

Explosions near or in cities (as most of the alert forces are targeted) would cause firestorms that would loft more than one hundred million tons of smoke and soot into the stratosphere, where it would not rain out. A thick layer of black particles would quickly envelop the planet, reducing sunlight reaching the earth by 70 percent and producing Ice Age conditions on the surface for much of a decade. Starting almost immediately, *no* harvests would be possible for much of that time and most vegetation (and animals dependent on it) would die. Some humans would probably survive, living on mollusks and fish in the Southern Hemisphere, but nearly all others—and *all* members of the other, less adaptable, large animal species—would starve to death in less than a year.

Some three thousand thermonuclear weapons in the two countries are still maintained on constant high alert. (There are no ongoing or currently projected negotiations or plans to reduce them further.) The ICBMs in particular—vulnerable to destruction in their silos by the opposing ICBMs—are subject to a "use them or lose them" mentality on each side. They are all poised to launch on ten-minute warning of incoming attack—radar or satellite warnings that have frequently proved to be false. These weapons—anachronistic for half a century, since the advent of large submarine-based missile forces, not targetable by ICBMs—are the hair trigger on the doomsday machines. Moreover, each side threatens and readies both its strategic and tactical (short-range) nuclear forces for "first use" in the course of any armed conflict, "if necessary." Any limited use of tactical nuclear weapons against each other would almost inevitably escalate, with commanders of each strategic force feeling a desperate urgency to preempt before the other side does.

Given the scale of the alert forces, their targeting, the launch-on-warning policies of their ICBM leg, and the first-use policies proclaimed by both sides, the otherwise dramatic reduction in size of the two arsenals *has not diminished in the slightest degree* their characteristic as doomsday machines *or* the magnitude of the risk this poses to the destruction of civilization, the near-extinction of humanity, and the total extinction of nearly all other large animals. This unstable two-sided apparatus of extermination has endured three decades beyond the ending of the Cold War that purported (falsely) to require and justify it. In fact, a new cold war with Russia is in process of reconstitution, as are the entire doomsday machines in both countries, at a cost of half a trillion dollars each in the next decade.

To change this system—to dismantle the doomsday machines in the US and Russia—will take a transformation in our respective political economy—and values, attitudes, priorities, incentives, leadership—comparable to that in the dissolution of the communist state in the Soviet Union. Not *more* likely, I'm thinking at this moment, than that seemed, or was, over the previous seventy years. Nor, by the same token, *less* likely.

That is to say, that transformation in our nuclear policy—our threats, our "assurances" to our allies of first use if necessary, our unstable weapons systems and operations—looks to me unlikely, in almost any specified time period, but *possible*. Not impossible. Almost nothing in human affairs can be said confidently, reliably, to be impossible. Life is not that certain.

Given the stakes—everything, from the perspective of humans and (as Joanna Macy calls us to attend) all other forms of life—can it be worthwhile, then, to commit one's life and encourage others, as Joanna has done for decades, to enlarge that small but positive probability: to participate in Selden's "possible" necessary human miracle?

Of course.

Joanna Macy speaking at Marlboro College,
Vermont, 2015 (photo by Joan Beard).

PART FIVE

ON THE MOVE TOGETHER

The legacy of Joanna Macy's work has only grown more relevant as time goes on. Now, more than ever, the planet hovers on the brink of collapse, with social and environmental disasters on the rise and governments struggling to respond. Citizens and neighborhoods can barely meet local needs while climate and resource refugees stream out of their homelands in search of safe havens. The "work of our time" seems to multiply in focus and scale as ecological and political systems erode beyond repair. In her stories, Joanna encourages us to let go of the need for certainty, and even for hope. *"Not knowing* rivets our attention on what is happening right now. And this present moment is the only time we can act, and the only time, after all, to awaken."

Radical uncertainty requires considerable courage. It is not for the faint of heart. As the work moves forward, we are invited to see impermanence itself as a refuge, the ground of practice and action. This is far easier in the company of collaborators focused on the three dimensions of the Great Turning: holding actions, life-affirming alternatives to business as usual, and shifts in consciousness. We are summoned to work from love, from a place of fearlessness, to open to what is right before us.

From a broad planetary view, Sean Kelly asks us to consider "unfinished business"—what most needs to be addressed to correct long-standing acts of tremendous harm? He suggests repentance and reparations for the long history of genocide of native peoples and enslavement of African peoples. Paula Green draws on Joanna's work in her peacebuilding work in war-torn countries, where healing and repair are desperately needed. Sarah Vekasi offers facilitation, de-escalation, prayer, and mediation in her role as eco-chaplain to energy-extraction resisters. The writers in this section make it clear that there is still much to do, that the world deeply needs our efforts and attention.

As the work passes on beyond Joanna Macy into the hands of hundreds of leaders and facilitators of all ages, questions remain. Can the principles and practices of the work be applied to issues between the global North and global South? Can tenderness and intimacy restore a world "dried up by the wounded masculine," as Zilong Wang asks? Is this work still relevant in addressing the scale of despair today, what Matthew Fox calls "the most dangerous of all sins?" All of these questions call for love and compassion, or in Joanna's words, seeing the "world as lover, world as self." This wild and passionate love for the beautiful planet, the universe we call home, is already alive in our hearts. Joanna invites us all into the profound practice of mutual belonging, rooted in the living body of Earth. These gifts will carry us into the future. These gifts are her legacy to us and to future generations of bodhisattvas, serving with joy to benefit all beings.

—STEPHANIE KAZA

OUTCOME UNCERTAIN

Joanna Macy

IN 1979, AFTER RECEIVING my doctoral degree and teaching for
a semester at American University, I set off in June for a year of
participant research with the Sarvodaya Shramadana movement
in Sri Lanka. I was eager to see how the Buddha Dharma was inspiring grassroots social change as an alternative to the Western
industrial model of development. For the holiday break we had
arranged a family meet-up in India. I headed north to find Fran,
Peggy, and Jack, along with two of his close friends from Tufts in
New Delhi, where we concocted a sweet peripatetic Christmas together. Plans had been made for Christopher to join the others to
visit me during the spring in my Sri Lankan village. The discoveries I was making with Sarvodaya were already so rewarding that I
was looking forward to all I would share with them.

From Delhi we took the train to Pathankot, where Khamtrul
Rinpoche's car waited to drive us "home" to Tashi Jong.[1] Here in
the foothills of the Daula Dhar range, his once ragtag community of refugees had acquired land and built a splendid temple
with monastery for over a hundred monks. This little corner of
Tibet-in-exile included housing for yogis and the lay community
as well as an active handcraft center. By then, our friendship with
the monks was some fifteen years old. Our first glimpse of the
prayer flags against the slopes of the Himalayas and the shouts of
the children as we approached were both familiar and as magical
as ever.

There was a lot to catch up on. Choegyal Rinpoche and Dor-
zong Rinpoche, now in their midthirties, were eager to hear about
my work with Theravada Buddhism in Sri Lanka and how Sarvodaya was using the Dharma to inspire social change. Choegyal especially was intrigued by Sarvodayan principles and practices of
self-help. Seven years later, when I joined him in his homeland of
Kham, he would apply them in planning the Eastern Tibet Self-
Help Project. As an artist, Choegyal was always ready to look at
power in new ways; hierarchy made him uncomfortable. At the
time, Khamtrul Rinpoche was away in Bhutan, and Choegyal was
serving as president of Tashi Jong, albeit a bit reluctantly.

In the afternoons I would wander into the carpet-making
center and sit there listening to the weavers' songs and watching
the patterns emerge. Afterward, Choegyal and I would meet in
his office and talk.

Through the letters that flowed between us after I first left India in 1966, Choegyal had accompanied me through the assassina-
tions of Dr. King and the Kennedys, the war in Vietnam, and my
awakening to the menace of nuclear power. To Choegyal, the tragedy that befell Tibet was but one aspect of a more widespread disintegration. It challenges us, he said, not only to take the Dharma
seriously but also to share it in fresh ways. He nodded as he listened
to my reports; in return he spoke of ancient prophecies, many attributed to Padmasambhava, who brought Buddhism to Tibet in
the eighth century. From friends in the lay community of Tashi
Jong I had heard references to a particular prophecy twelve centuries old, coming true in our time.

Toward the end of one long afternoon I asked, "Rinpoche,
can you tell me anything about a prophecy concerning the coming of the Kingdom of Shambhala?" He let the room fall into a
long silence before responding to my query with the prophecy it-

self. I watched his face, listening to every word, arrested by his description of the Shambhala warrior. I understood it as a metaphor for the bodhisattva, the one with the boundless heart. Outside the office window, quiet descended, the carpet center closed, an office clerk popped his head in to say goodnight.

When he finished, we sat quietly for a bit. Then I bowed my deep thanks and took my leave. I ran down the hill through the gathering dark, past the closed doors of the school, down the path to the lodge where my family would be getting ready for dinner. I burst through the door, "You all won't believe the prophecy that Choegyal just told me!" And then and there I spoke out loud the words still echoing within me. In each of the many times I would speak these words, I would feel held by the power of their message.

"There comes a time when all life on Earth is in danger. Barbarian powers have arisen. Although these powers waste their wealth in preparations to annihilate each other, they have much in common: weapons of unfathomable devastation and death, and technologies that lay waste to our world. It is now, when the future of all beings hangs by the frailest of threads, that the kingdom of Shambhala emerges.

"Now you cannot go there, for it is not a place. It exists in the hearts and minds of the Shambhala warriors. But you cannot recognize a Shambhala warrior by looking at them, for there is no uniform or insignia. They carry no banners to show whose side they're on. They build no barricades on which to climb, from which to threaten the enemy, or behind which to rest and regroup. Shambhala warriors have no home turf of their own. Always they move on the terrain of the barbarians themselves."

By this time, I found myself deep inside the words.

"Now comes the time when great courage is required of the Shambhala warriors—moral and physical courage. To dismantle these weapons—in every sense of the word—they must go to where they enter into the corridors of power, where the decisions are made. The Shambhala warriors know they can do this because the weapons are *manomaya*, mind made."

I could feel in my body how this understanding of manomaya was absolutely critical. It felt like a key that opens the path to action.

"These weapons are made by the human mind; they can be unmade by the human mind. The Shambhala warriors know that the dangers that threaten life on Earth do not come from satanic deities or extraterrestrial powers. They arise from our own choices, our habits, and relationships. So, now, the Shambhala warriors must go into training."

I asked Choegyal, "How do they train?"

"They train in the use of two weapons."

"What are they?" I asked. Then I showed the family how he held up his hands the way they had seen the monks hold the ritual objects of *dorje* and bell in the lama dances.

"One weapon is compassion, the other is wisdom. Both are necessary. We need compassion, because it provides the fuel, it moves us to act for the sake of all beings. What it boils down to is not being afraid of the suffering of our world. This is necessary, but by itself, this weapon is too hot—so hot it can burn you out.

"So we need the other weapon as well—insight into the dependent co-arising of all things. It lets us see that the battle is not between good people and bad people, for the line between good and evil runs through every human heart. We realize that we are interconnected, as in a web, and that each act with pure motivation affects the entire web, bringing consequences we cannot measure or even see. However, by itself, wisdom can seem too cool to keep us going. So, we need the heat of compassion as well, our openness to the world's pain. Both weapons, or tools, are necessary to the Shambhala warrior."

As I finished, Jack looked puzzled. "But Mom, didn't he tell you how it was going to turn out?" I laughed and said, "If Choegyal had told me how it was going to turn out, I wouldn't have believed any of it. And don't you believe anyone who tells you they know what's in store for us."

After I began offering workshops, I occasionally included a telling of the Shambhala prophecy. As I saw its impact on the listeners, I shared the prophecy more often, though I still avoided writing it down, sensing that it belonged to an oral tradition. It was when I learned that some people had published what they heard me say in their own books, that I decided to formalize it in my own writings in the words I had recalled from the start.

Over the years I've realized that one of the most useful insights for people today is the exchange I had with Jack. I've emphasized the importance of not knowing the outcome, because I see how the desire for certainty can distract our attention and warp our perceptions. Liberated from the need for certainty, and even hope, we can more fully inhabit the present moment. Not knowing rivets our attention on what is happening right now. This present moment is the only time we can act and the only time, after all, to awaken.

NOTES

1. The Eighth Khamtrul Rinpoche was head of the Dragon Kagyu lineage in Kham, Tibet, and his people were the Tibetans who changed my life, an enduring relationship to this day.

MOTHER OF ALL BUDDHAS

Joanna Macy

UNDER THE TALL REDWOODS DEEP in the Santa Cruz mountains, people were parking cars and bringing their bags into the lodge. It was August 1980, and I had been invited to a Quaker conference center to conduct a weekend workshop titled "Despair and Empowerment"—and I wished I were somewhere else. I felt totally unprepared.

When I left for Sri Lanka a year and a half earlier, *New Age Journal* had published an article of mine called "How to Deal with Despair." I had written it to distill what had opened for me on the Charles River Bridge when grief for the world overwhelmed me, and what had followed the next year at the Society for Values in Higher Education conference at Notre Dame University. The article was published just weeks before I left for a year of fieldwork with the Sarvodaya Shramadana movement in Sri Lanka. Letters responding to the article had followed me there, often with requests to lead this despair work. Well, I thought, maybe one or two workshops when I return to the US, then back to finish the Sarvodaya book and search for a university teaching position, the only career I could imagine for myself. So I accepted one invitation that could fit with plans to fly home by way of the Pacific.

Shown to the room reserved for me, I hid there until dinner time, shuffling through the few papers in my bag not left behind in the rush of departure. I looked at them as if I might find workshop instructions or the article on despair work, but I only found my journal, an unfinished letter to Bhikkhu Samitha, and a few Sri Lankan newspapers with their huge headlines about my departure. It all swept over me again, a loss that was still fresh and raw, still unreal.

I held the letter close as I remembered that last day. I had awakened early with the thought that only a month remained of this precious village life. After showering by the well, hauling bucket after bucket of water to pour over my head, I motorcycled to the port city of Galle. I went to visit young and heartful Samitha, a Sarvodaya monk and my favorite friend for discussing what was happening in the world. That day I wanted to complete my notes on his work to create a community clinic for mothers and infants. But when we sat in a quiet corner of his open-walled, palm-shaded vihara, another matter surfaced. He wanted to understand why at our last meeting I had referred to him as a bodhisattva. I knew that for Theravada Buddhists that term was reserved for earlier incarnations of the Buddha himself. "Do you have a different understanding?" Samitha asked.

"Well, yes." And closing my eager notebook, I told him of the scriptures arising at the turn of the first millennium, heralding the dawn of Mahayana Buddhism and celebrating her, the Perfection of Wisdom, the Mother of All Buddhas. I explained that her teachings were called the Second Turning of the Wheel of Dharma, because her wisdom evokes the radical interconnectedness—indeed the interbeing—of every one of us in the web of life. "Samitha, when I see how hard, how faithfully you are working for the poor and the young, instead of sitting in your temple receiving alms, I can't help knowing that the Mother of All Buddhas calls you a bodhisattva, a Buddha-to-be."

It was getting dark when I rode the ten miles back to my village. In the warm evening along the irrigation canal, there were so many moths and mosquitos I had to slow down to keep from breathing them in. Nearing home, I paused below the temple—my temple—to gaze at its reflection in the quiet pond. Everything in that hushed night felt as known and close to me as my own larger body. When I got to my house, the light was on and there, on the table, was an officially sealed envelope addressed to me and delivered by courier from the Office of the President of Sri Lanka. Opening it, I read the words and time stopped. Even with multiple readings it made no sense: my visa revoked, my children's visas as well, with three days to leave the country.

Danya, the Sarvodaya coordinator living nearby, appeared at my side and took charge. "Joanna Akka, don't question, just move. Do what you need to do, and I will see you through this. To get tickets before the airline office closes, we must drive tonight to Colombo." I had just a few hours to pack, to say goodbye to my friends here, and to give them my typewriter and motorcycle. I drove all night with Danya to Colombo. The next day I spent the afternoon with the first secretary at the American Embassy. Everyone was trying to find reasons for my being declared *persona non grata*, the first American ever deported from Sri Lanka. It seemed that the conservative Tamil faction with influence on the president had taken issue with the nonviolent direct-action workshops I had led with Peggy and Jack in the Tamil north and that they and their friends had been invited to stay on to lead for another two months while I returned to my Buddhist village in south. They had been welcomed in the community and well supported. But the civil war that would ignite in three years was already polarizing the Sinhalese and Tamil populations. Our work was seen as inflammatory by the conservative Tamils; they must have wanted us out of the country.

As I sat in my room in the Quaker Center, trying to gather myself for the weekend event, I had no clue if I would ever be allowed to return to Sri Lanka and the Sarvodaya community I so loved. Nor could I even imagine that the president would someday invite me back. I felt uprooted from the work that was so important to me and from a sense of who I was. But one thing was clear. I might not remember how I once defined despair work, but despair itself was fresh and real, and I was close to being engulfed by it.

In the main room, several dozen people who had given up a whole weekend to be here were now settling themselves on chairs, sofas, and cushions, waiting for things to begin. Still in shock from the deportation, I greeted everyone and invited them into some moments of silence. In the stillness moving over us, I thought of the concerns that brought these people here: the hunger of children, the chainsaws in the forests, the reactors' radioactive emissions, the exquisitely precise construction of warheads to incinerate whole cities. Those realities were, like the Mother of All Buddhas, beyond the reach of our senses. In this lovely old lodge, we could not see or hear or touch the bombs or hungry bellies, but their experience of relatedness to them was strong enough to bring these people here. Prajna Paramita, the deep space of our interbeing, was at least as real as the fears and greed that made the bombs and clearcut the forests, and as real as the caring in the hearts of these people.

As soon as I thought of her, there she was—Prajna Paramita, the Mother of All Buddhas. Big and invisible, she was holding me in her lap. Instead of kneeling at her feet or sensing her towering high above me, I found myself cradled by her. I could feel her shielding my back and breathing through me. Here, in the very embodiment of pratityasamutpada, the core of the Buddha's teaching, I felt held by a vast maternal presence. I settled into the power of her presence and authority, and felt myself open to her love for these people, her bodhisattva sons and daughters.

In that moment at the first workshop, my life fell open, and the Mother of All Buddhas wove herself into the fabric of my being. I never did seek or accept a full-time teaching position. I simply stepped out into the world. Since then, when I face a roomful of strangers and feel at a loss, she shows up as soon as I invite her, holding me in her presence. Each time I need her, I find her anew—fresh, luminous, and empty of preconceptions. Sitting in her lap, time and time again, I experience our mutual belonging in this beautiful and suffering world, and know that there is ultimately nothing to fear.

FOR LOVE OF GAIA

Sean Kelly

I RECENTLY HEARD JOANNA in an interview where she imagines a reporter stopping Frodo as he journeys through Mordor on his quest to destroy the ring of power.[1] The reporter asks, "Are you hopeful or optimistic that you will make it to Mount Doom?" Joanna has Frodo reply with a gesture as if waving a pesky fly out of one's face, saying, "Get out of here! I don't have time for this!" In other words, confronted as we are with the prospect of civilizational collapse and mass extinction, stopping to determine whether or not one has hope is a distraction from the matter at hand. If we imagine Frodo as having relinquished hope, or at least having suspended the question of hope, it is clear that he has retained a steadfast *faith*—faith in the absolute value of his mission and in the virtues this mission unconditionally affirms, in this case: fellowship, truthfulness, the essential goodness of creation, love. Joanna's lifework, her friendship, and her partnership have wakened my heart-mind to the possibility and promise of a new kind of faith, a faith grounded in our interbeing with the living body of Gaia.

In the first years that I co-taught with Joanna at the California Institute of Integral Studies (CIIS), it was still possible for me to imagine that, seven generations from now, we would have beaten the odds and succeeded in making the transition to a life-sustaining civilization. By the last time we offered the course on the Great Turning at CIIS, and in the times since that

305

I have facilitated practices from the Work That Reconnects, the odds have shifted dramatically.[2] While I remain as committed as ever to the fundamental values that inform the idea of the Great Turning—at the center of which is a view of the human as embedded within and called to protect and celebrate the web of life and wider Earth community—I can no longer in good faith hold to any expectation that we will halt the accelerating Great Unravelling, or Great Dying, as others call it. Despite this lack of expectation, this absence of hope, I am also just as committed to enacting the three dimensions of the Great Turning that Joanna has identified: *holding actions* to slow, if not halt, the unraveling; promotion of *Gaian structures* as life-affirming alternatives to the ways of business as usual; and the *shift in consciousness* associated with the growing awareness of our deeper Gaian identity and our interbeing with all that is.

PLANETARY INITIATION

For the past two decades, a few colleagues and I have been characterizing our collective moment as one of being poised on the threshold of planetary initiation.[3] In all traditional societies, major life transitions (puberty, grave illness, becoming a tribal leader) are marked by rites of passage or initiation, the purpose of which is to deconstruct an old identity and summon a new one. In this case, the initiation is planetary, not only in the sense that it involves all members (and species) of the Earth community but also in that the new human identity being called into being is itself planetary, or Gaian, in character. In even stronger terms, some of us are open to the possibility that the new, planetary identity in the making is not only a question of human transformation but that Earth, or Gaia herself, is waking up to herself through this human transformation, in some sense transcending the human as well.

As in many traditional rites of passage, the planetary initiation underway seems to involve and even require a confrontation with death. However we might measure the success of the initiation, it would appear that it cannot proceed without some kind of death, or at least without some kind of near-death experience. Exactly what form this near-death experience might take, or what might lie on the other side of the threshold, only time will tell. The important point is the insight that we are being swept up in a highly charged archetypal process of transformation. Though we have no certain vision as to outcome, we know from the nature of the archetypal process involved that avoiding, denying, or otherwise diluting the full force of the planetary near-death experience being constellated risks aborting the new identity struggling to be born.

UNFINISHED BUSINESS

It is a common experience for individuals who have come to terms with a terminal diagnosis, having passed the stages of denial and crippling fear, anger, and despair, to be gripped with a vital passion to attend to "unfinished business." While this may include unrealized goals or aspirations common to many so-called bucket lists (visiting long-dreamed-of travel destinations, undertaking physically risky adventures, finally attending to a neglected passion, etc.), more typically such business has to do with making peace with others and oneself—with seizing this last opportunity to "make things right." This can take the form of a confession or other kinds of truth-telling, such as asking for forgiveness, offering forgiveness to others, or making amends for harm done.

If we transpose this passion to the level of the collective, whatever reconciliation might be achieved will doubtless demand a great deal of moral courage and, alongside the desire for peace, a passionate commitment to truth and justice. Though our histories already include long and unbroken traditions of struggle for liberation, we can perhaps see the mounting wave of holding actions and proposals for more Gaian structures—from the Black Lives Matter and Me Too movements to the many expressions of "Blockadia" (such as the iconic action at Standing Rock), the Extinction Rebellion and Sunrise movements, and calls for a Green New Deal—as evidence that a growing segment of the population is prepared not only to make peace but to make things right.

And there is still much that we can do well in whatever time we have left. Along with planetary hospice work and the many struggles for liberation, for saving what we can of our lands and forests, our precious waters, and the dwindling numbers of our other-than-human siblings, I imagine at least two pressing matters of unfinished business in my adoptive country of the United States of America: genuine repentance for the genocide of this land's indigenous peoples and for the treatment of those who survived, and an honoring of promises made; and genuine repentance for the sin of slavery, acknowledging the critical role of enslaved Africans and their descendants in building whatever greatness this country once enjoyed, and reparations to those now alive who still suffer from this sin.

GAIA MANDALA

The call to planetary initiation has brought us to the edge of an abyss. In terms of Tolkien's epic tale, however, this abyss is not only the Crack of Doom, above which Frodo and Gollum stand poised as the dark power of Sauron threatens to engulf Middle Earth, but also one that opens onto the western seas that stretch out from the port of the Grey Havens, beyond whose waters lies Valinor, the Undying Lands. All of the major world religions have their own versions of this beyond, their various kinds of heaven, including a highest or best heaven that is our true origin and destiny. Whatever we might intuit regarding the great Mystery of this beyond, we now know that we share a common origin and destiny as living members of Gaia, this living Earth and our only home.

To guard against self-deception and the temptation of escapism, any talk of "beyond" in these end-times must be accompanied by an unshakable resolution, such as the bodhisattva vow, to abide in the here and now, as hellish as it might be or become. It is as though the way to the Undying Lands runs through the center of Gaia as a kind of Earth-sized mandala. I am thinking here of the practice from the Work That Reconnects known as the Truth Mandala. Participants convene around a sacred circle and, as the spirit moves them, are invited to enter into one or more of the quadrants, where they can speak and honor their pain for the world. This ritual is not merely cathartic, for what emerges in the end is the insight that this pain is an expression of a deeper solidarity with the greater life in which we are embedded. Our anger, Joanna reminds us, is rooted in our passion for justice. It takes enormous courage to be honest about our fear. The deprivation and powerlessness we feel is a signal of our interdependence, and we only grieve that which we love and to which, despite the loss, we still feel bound.

THE FULLNESS OF TIME

In the spiral of the Work, the stage of *honoring our pain* for the world allows for, and is followed by, that of *seeing with new eyes*. Here the teachings and practices are designed to facilitate an experience of our deeper identities as living members of Gaia, the living and sacred Earth. A key expression of this way of seeing involves an exercise of the moral imagination whereby one enters into what Joanna calls the "fourth time" (a term she borrows from Tibetan Buddhism). This is a time within which we can reclaim our solidarity with all of our ancestors—human, other-than-human, and cosmic—as well as with the future beings, all of whom "surround us like a cloud of witnesses."[4]

In the practice called Harvesting the Gifts of the Ancestors, for example, one is guided into an embodied identification with the lives of countless generations who walked before us—those who, in their own times, faced so many hardships, were the vehicle for countless forms of creativity, knew victory over evil, and whose lives even now ring out like a mantra of blessing. We experience not only our human ancestors but all of our cosmic and Gaian kin, the fruits of whose evolutionary adventures we rehearsed in our mothers' wombs and have enfolded in each of our cells.

In the practice called The Seventh Generation, we sit face to face with a future being, or we ourselves temporarily embody this future being, from whose perspective we are graced with new and vivid insights pertaining to our present time of the Great Unraveling and Great Turning. Here I note that, in more recent facilitation of the Work, some of the future beings have delivered messages from a postapocalyptic world. Though still speaking to us with gratitude and compassion for our roles in these end-times, these new voices, at least, no longer sing songs of the success of the Great Turning. Instead they invite us to reimagine the nature of the Great Turning in ways that do not depend on hope or some imagined outcome.

And if our future as a species is short, if the abyss we are hurtling toward promises not only a collective near-death experience but a transition through the Great Dying already upon us to the Great Silence that would seem to follow, then what? We are brought back to our earlier consideration of a terminal diagnosis and unfinished business. From the meta-perspective of the fourth time, one could say that the length of time remaining is not so critical because all moments in some sense abide eternally; each moment possesses its own intrinsic, and in some sense infinite, value. In this way we can begin to intuit the eternal significance of our actions in these end-times—the love declared, the wrongs confessed or forgiven, the struggles entered into on the side of the true, the good, and the beautiful. That these actions might be our last—and, of course, the same holds true for our individual lives—makes them all the more precious.

And how precious our Joanna, beloved daughter of Gaia, who calls us to walk together, arms linked in ever-widening circles of life and love. Loving for the sake of the greater life and living for the sake of love. In the absence of hope, faith and love abide, but now as before and always, the greatest of these is love.

NOTES

1. "Power of Community Online Summit: Climate Change and Consciousness," February 2019. See https://summit.ecovillage.org/ for access.
2. See, for example, Catherine Ingram's courageous essay "Facing Extinction," which, after presenting hyperlinked summaries of many of the most recent studies, offers wise counsel on living in end-times from her own deep engagement with the Buddha Dharma. http://www.catherineingram.com/facingextinction.
3. See Richard Tarnas's 2001 essay "Is the Modern Psyche Undergoing a

Rite of Passage?" (http://www.jung2.org/ArticleLibrary/Tarnas.pdf),
which foreshadows themes developed later in his *Cosmos and Psyche: Intimations of a New World View* (New York: Plume, 2006).

4. Joanna Macy and Chris Johnstone, *Active Hope: How to Face the Mess We're in without Going Crazy* (Novato, CA: New World Library, 2011), 160.

HEALING OUR BROKEN WORLD
Pathways to Peacebuilding

Paula Green

SARAJEVO, THE CAPITAL OF BOSNIA, endured a siege of 1,425 days between 1992 and 1996. Serb forces assaulted the city from the surrounding hills, compelling residents to risk their lives in search of food, water, or medicine. Fourteen thousand were killed during the siege, the longest in history.

In returning to Sarajevo after an absence of twenty years, I noticed that the bullet holes in the buildings had been repaired. My Bosnian colleague said, "We know how to patch our buildings but we cannot seem to patch our broken hearts." How could I, called back to facilitate workshops for the mixed ethnic groups whose parents' generation had experienced that war, offer any wisdom or insight that might shift their laden hearts? What heals, I asked myself, what adapts, and what remains of scar tissue to serve them as wounded healers? What legacy from Joanna's lustrous teachings could help me?

In Afghanistan, the circumstances for women in the workshops and on the streets were so dire that I could barely maintain my own equanimity. I remembered Joanna proclaiming that our troubled historical moment is a great time to be alive because we are so needed for the turning of the world. That phrase would come to mind as I struggled to be responsive, enabling me to support a group of brave women political leaders in their role in turning their exceptionally troubled world toward the light. I hear

Joanna's words: *Don't give in or give up. You are required, essential, and significant.* I watch the reaction such a message evokes. I know it matters.

Life guided me toward international peacebuilding. It points me in the present moment of grave dangers to my own country to bring my experience with peacebuilding home to the United States. But first I had to go forth. I served in many regions of the world, leading seminars, facilitating workshops, and encouraging dialogue between those whose communities had waged war in the hopes that together they could learn to wage peace. Most importantly, I sought to plant seeds that the next generation would water.

In the years when Joanna was carving out her path as a workshop leader who would synthesize Buddhist teachings, systems theory, deep ecology, and social activism, I was reordering the ingredients of my own professional life to combine Buddhist teachings, humanistic psychology, intergroup relations, and peace and justice activism. I immediately recognized Joanna as a guide and exemplar to my own future: a prophetic teacher, expansive thinker, and revolutionary synthesizer. I was fortunate to have stumbled into Joanna at that formative stage of my life, and even luckier to have found such a powerful woman role model.

TRANSFORMATIVE PEDAGOGY

In all my work, in Asia, Africa, Eastern Europe, and the Middle East, Joanna's inspiration, courage, and creativity as a teacher and facilitator stayed with me. I adapted many bold and dramatic exercises from her books *Coming Back to Life* and *World as Lover, World as Self.* The processes and meditations I shaped from her teaching proved healing for many whose minds and bodies were ravaged from the impact of violence and catastrophe. In the early days I carried *Coming Back to Life* with me, seeking exercises that would fit my purposes of gently supporting group members to release their pain, recognize the fragility and broken hearts of those they were taught to hate and fear, and discover the source of empathy within themselves. I learned to evoke Joanna's positivity, engaging it to carry hopefulness for my participants from war zones until they could believe in hope themselves. Sometimes that carrying felt almost literal and absolutely necessary. There are times when we cannot turn on the lights by ourselves.

In the context of postwar peacebuilding, the possibility of shifting one's energies from despair to empowerment can open a way forward for those whose lives have been flattened by armed conflict and feel permanently in despair. Guided by Joanna's genius at brilliantly designed experiential activities, I sought to convert words and theories into rays of hope to go directly into the hearts of participants. I often think of her approach as a call of consciousness to move from protected anxiety for the small self to expanded concern as a member of the collective Self.

In Joanna's work, concepts are not delivered by words alone, or even by words predominantly. The intellectual underpinnings are acted out, so that bodies, minds, and spirits inhabit first the despair and then the journey to awakening and finally to empowerment. This radical approach to workshop pedagogy, developed so artfully by Joanna, comprises the journey from theory to practice, and from understanding to activism. Compelling exercises encourage people to express their pain for the world, discover or recover their power, learn to reframe it as compassion, experience the solidarity of group courage, and arouse their dedication on behalf of life. The scale of one's vision can encompass the globe or the village, however appropriate to one's scope and distress.

My own experience confirms that this is a superb method for transformation. Participants in peacebuilding workshops share the anguish of experiencing their communities and nations becoming battlefields. They discover very importantly that no one wins in war, that victim and perpetrating communities are both wounded, albeit differently, and that creating peace on the ashes of shattered hopes takes enormous courage, will, and trust of the other. One Sri Lankan participant, recognizing the truth that all parties are harmed by war, remarked, "We are all in one great pot of suffering."

Like Joanna, I believe in the power of groups as precious and essential islands in time, correctives for the hyper-individualism of modern life. Groupwork enables us to recognize that we are not alone in our fear and fragility, that others will partner with us along the path of healing and restoration. It helps us see that who we call "enemies" can become colleagues in the struggle for peace and justice, and that we can find generativity and bravery through our collective efforts.

In 1994, the international community stood by as genocide destroyed Rwanda. Close to a million people of the Tutsi ethnic group were murdered by members of the Hutu ethnicity in a period of just one hundred days. One year later, I entered the region as part of a group invited by the churches to begin a process of healing that has continued unabated for twenty-five years. I witnessed extraordinary courage in subsequent programs as Hutus and Tutsis, slowly over time, rediscovered each other's humanity through rituals that evoked the ancestors, reawakened positive past memories, and cast images for a possible shared future. Engaging their shared cultural and religious traditions, they sang, danced, and worshipped together, voices harmonizing as they began the hard, almost endless journey of reestablishing trust and safety. Many of these former participants now serve as wounded healers, continuing the process of mending all that had shattered.

In Myanmar, formerly Burma, my history goes back to the founding of the International Network of Engaged Buddhists in Thailand, through which I was asked to be a member of a delegation investigating the results of a 1988 military crackdown on protesters seeking freedom and human rights. Over the decades I engaged frequently in that country, both in leading workshops and in accompanying groups seeking to respond to the oppression and marginalization of activists and minorities. Most recently, colleagues and I facilitated group members representing the four alienated and misunderstood religions of their country— Buddhists, Muslims, Hindus, and Christians—as they encountered one another face to face for the first time. We and they were astonished by the bonds and reciprocal care emerging through circle exercises, meditations, role plays, team games, and more— all of it inspired by Joanna's practices to reconnect our lives, our world, and especially our hearts.

For the past twenty years, I have led a program for peacebuilders called CONTACT (Conflict Transformation Across Cultures), held each summer on the campus of the School for International Training in Vermont for a fully internationalized group. More recently we have added another program for South Asians in Kathmandu, Nepal, as many can no longer obtain US visas. Imagine these groups of fifty to sixty each, from perhaps twenty different countries, a half dozen religions; all colors, sizes, shapes, cultures, ethnicities; and a Tower of Babel's worth of languages—and all of them traumatized by war. We spend two to three weeks together in a residential learning community, plunging into undreamed of spaces of encounter while we discover what it means to be upstanding, responsible, resilient, compassionate human beings ready to transform hatred and despair into hope and possibility.

Perhaps our most creative adaptation of Joanna's rituals is a daylong investigation of the cycles of revenge and reconciliation. Participants place their bodies on a room-sized circular replication of the stages of revenge, which is surrounded by another circle representing the stages toward reconciliation. Walking slowly in silence to the sounds of a shakuhachi flute, these war-impacted participants tap into their deepest honesty to situate themselves on anger, revenge, guilt, grief, confronting losses, meeting the other, promoting tolerance, and more. All day we tell stories, comfort each other, build caring relationships to replace enemy images, and begin to repair the broken world. By day's end, a community woven of empathy and generosity emerges, holding all suffering in a common thread and acknowledging that we have enlarged the boundaries of our compassion.

BUDDHIST TEACHINGS AS TOOLS FOR TRANSFORMATION

Much of my work as a professor of peacebuilding focuses on unpacking the multiple and bewildering drivers of violent conflict. While integrating numerous theories, I also introduce Buddhist insights into the root causes of suffering from which all harmful actions spring. The three poisons of greed, hatred, and delusion cloud and sway the mind. Greed, hate, and the mistaken belief in otherness afflict the mind and result in unskillful behaviors that cause unending harm and violent conflict. Greed expresses itself as desire, envy, craving, lust, clinging, and entitlement, including the desire for land, water, oil, and other goods and resources, thus fostering control and dominion. Hatred manifests as anger, all the "isms" of prejudice, abhorrence, and dehumanization, and the arrogance of false superiority. Delusion, or ignorance, references the mistaken notion of separateness or separate self, enabling the fallacy that one can harm others without harming oneself. In workshops, we identify where these mind states manifest in our own behavior and in our societies. Beyond the endless words written to grapple with the roots of violent conflict, this 2,500-year-old analysis from the Buddha stands out as a coherent and accessible framework.

All humans have basic human needs that vary little over centuries and circumstances. When individuals and communities cannot meet their basic survival requirements through any available means, they commonly resort to violence rather than succumb to death. Marginalized groups who are denied any channels to obtain water, food, or land cannot survive. Communities that are threatened by lack of security and safety cannot protect their members. Those whose identities are vilified by media or manipulative leaders cannot satisfy the need for belonging and basic dignity. When demagogues representing dominant countries or religious groups make decisions from minds filled with the three poisons of greed, hatred, and delusion, irreparable harm and suffering occur. Interpersonal violence and the organized violence of armed conflict arise.

Incorporating Joanna's strategy for experiential learning in our workshops, we engage in role plays and other exercises to internalize these conditioned mind states and their consequences. Our imaginations and our moving bodies experience how it is to be victimized and also to be those creating the victimization. We viscerally learn, as Walt Whitman said, that "we contain multitudes." Thich Nhat Hanh echoed this insight in his poem "Please Call Me By My True Names": "I am the twelve-year-old girl, refugee on a small boat, who throws herself into the ocean after being raped by a sea pirate, and I am the pirate, my heart not yet capable of seeing and loving."[1]

As group members engage in exercises to identify these toxins, their destructive potential becomes obvious, as do the antidotes to each of the three poisons. We recognize that there can be generosity rather than greed, kindness rather than hatred, and interconnection instead of separation. Each can be kindled in the heart, habituated in the mind, and become a pathway for personal responsibility and healing. Understanding the mind states as causes of suffering and of violence helps empower the learner, the learning community, and those beyond to recognize how human conflicts arise and how we can endeavor to more skillfully manage our impulses and reactivity. These insights into our behavior help answer the question, articulated by Bosnian group participants, of how "we who lived and intermarried together so well could have destroyed each other in armed conflict so thoroughly."

The core Buddhist teachings on interdependence and impermanence also inform my teaching and enrich my relationships. In workshops I sometimes adapt Joanna's meditation on the Web of Life to share the insight of interdependence. This meditation, garnered from systems theory and Buddhist tradition, helps us experience our interexistence and our essential, nonnegotiable need for one another. For those among the millions cast aside by hate and conquest, this meditation brings comfort and belonging. If each being is a jewel in the vast net, each has value and dignity, respect and honor. For those who have not been discarded, here is an opportunity to widen their own net for greater inclusion, to offer love and safety to the marginalized, where it is most needed.

Because so many of those I encounter have been harmed by warfare and its consequences, the sorrowful present can feel permanent and unchanging. In the River of Life exercise, participants use art materials to draw and map their lives thus far and, in sharing their drawings with others, to explore how experiences, whether valued or feared, continually arise and pass away. That which is present, no matter how painful or glorious, will not last. Experiencing its temporality awakens hope and helps those who are wounded by circumstances to envision a future, which can then be added to their river-of-life drawing. Like a river, everything changes and flows; joys, sorrows, and wars are all impermanent.

In this work and the work of so many others, we are reweaving the threads of respectful, ethical, interdependent communal life. Our common bonds tear further apart at our peril. As hardships multiply on our fragile planet, our need to act together with generosity and loving kindness on the home front and world stage will increase. Joanna's deep-seated hope in the Great Turning offers an invitation to choose life, to join and expand an impassioned experiment in radical inclusion and visionary effort to create a sustainable civilization. What better tribute to her long decades of labors than to encourage future generations of healers and peacebuilders to "go forth on your journey, for the benefit of the many, for the joy of the many, out of compassion for the welfare, the benefit, and joy of all beings."[2]

NOTES

1. Thich Nhat Hanh, *Being Peace* (Berkeley: Parallax Press, 1987), 64.
2. Attributed to Gautama Buddha and quoted in Joanna Macy and Molly Brown, *Coming Back to Life: The Updated Guide to The Work That Reconnects* (Gabriola Island, BC: New Society Publishers, 2014), 191.

THE EAGLE, CONDOR, AND QUETZAL

Adrián Villaseñor Galarza

THE WORK THAT RECONNECTS (WTR) has drawn from the life experience of its root teacher, Joanna Macy, and associates since the first public workshop over forty years ago. By aiming to show the essential interdependence that nurtures our being, the Work helps participants see themselves as Earth in human form. After all, Earth is what sustains all living beings. The inspiration to act on behalf of Earth originates from just such a realization. Still, an important question to ask is whether the Work's gifts of empowerment, clear vision, and belonging can be summoned in the global South in spite of its North American origins. How do people of the global South, in particular Latin America, encounter and benefit from this Work? Based on my experience, I consider the relevance of working on behalf of the historically repressed in the context of a much-needed North-South dialogue.

Since 2004, I have been acquainted with Joanna's work in deep ecology and her lucid ability to integrate systems theory and spiritual insights. I had the pleasure of meeting her in 2009, when she asked if I would be interested in translating into Spanish the facilitators' manual, *Coming Back to Life*. My response was a resounding yes! The prospect of working directly with the planetary grandmother and delving deeper into her work alongside my doctoral studies was music to my ears. The Spanish translation has been available free online since 2010,[1] and Joanna has remained a guiding beacon in my own life. In addition, I've since published the first Work That Reconnects anthology for and from Latin America that spells out key theoretical foundations of the Work with various undertakings of activists and educators throughout the Americas.[2]

NORTH AND SOUTH

The healing power of truth-speaking is particularly relevant in the global South, including Latin America. Grief and pain have intertwined in many ways in Latin American communities and their prolific ecosystems due to the destructive history of systematic exploitation of humans and nature over the last five hundred years. The liberation theologian Leonardo Boff has long focused on the relation between North and South, claiming that the welfare and progress sold by the (Northern) industrial system rests on a cosmology of control and domination of Earth that impoverishes and enslaves the South.[3] Echoing Boff, Pope Francis has more recently proposed that "a true ecological approach always becomes a social approach; it must integrate questions of justice in debates on the environment, so as to hear both the cry of the earth and the cry of the poor."[4]

Given the historical oppression of Latin America and the peoples of the South, there is widespread intergenerational trauma from repression of psychic and somatic intelligences that might be transformed through the Work That Reconnects. It has been my experience facilitating the Work that within such systematic abuse and historical repression lies tremendous impetus for change and liberation for the benefit of Earth. The Work also aids in building an enhanced sense of community by forging virtuous alliances among participants. In the Americas, as well as globally, there is an urgent need to establish a mutually beneficial dialogue between

North and South, both geographically and likewise within our-selves, if we are to co-create a brighter future for all.[5]

In 2014, I began offering Work That Reconnects workshops in Mexico with a renewed impetus. After finishing my doctoral studies and completing the Spanish translation of the first edi-tion of *Coming Back to Life*, I felt the time was ripe to contribute to the emotional resiliency and psychospiritual unfolding of several permaculture sites and organizations throughout the country.

The first of such sites was a family project named *Tierramor* (For Love of Land), a pioneer permaculture farm in the state of Mi-choacan. The founders, Marina Ortiz and Holger Hieronimi, had experienced Joanna's work years back with Helena ter Ellen, and we had known each other since a 2007 workshop with permaculture cofounder David Holmgren. From 2014 to 2016 we organized four multiday workshops at Tierramor that were fundamental in rein-troducing the Work to permaculture circles in Mexico. Through the newly formed *Instituto Bioalkimia* (Bioalchemy Institute), a number of presentations and weekend workshops followed in Gua-dalajara, Mexico City, Queretaro, Huasca de Ocampo, Morelia, Chiapas, Valle de Bravo, Veracruz, Playa del Carmen, and Bacalar.

The Work gained enough traction that we were able to of-fer the first ten-day Latin American intensive training in 2017. We collaborated with *La semilla colectivo* (The Seed Collective), a grass-roots initiative dedicated to conscious nutrition and education, to provide a solid alliance for expanding into the next phase of the Work in Latin America. Alongside Jaime Carral and Ana Karla Enríquez, founders and members of *La semilla colectivo*, we orga-nized two ten-day intensives in Mexico, with a third one planned for follow-up. At the same time, we joined forces with Javiera Car-rion and Grifen Hope from *El manzano* (The Apple Tree), a pioneer regenerative and transition school, to introduce the Work to Chile.

The first ten-day intensive took place there in 2018 with a second in early 2019. The aim is to offer these trainings once a year, and there is active interest from Brazil and other countries.

We've launched a website specifically about the Work in Spanish and created a WTR Facebook group in Mexico and Latin America.[6] Overall, the response from participants and organizers has been inspiringly positive, though few people had heard of the Work before attending. Already in service to Earth, most participants long for a deeper perspective to clarify their purpose and strengthen their commitment as they face the dark emotions associated with our planetary moment.

BLOOMING TOGETHER

From the original wisdom of the Americas comes the prophecy of the eagle and the condor, envisioning North-South dialogue and integration. "We were waiting 500 years. . . . Now, in this age when the Eagle of the North and the Condor of the South fly together, the Earth will wake up. The Northern Eagles cannot be free without the Southern Condors. Now it is happening. Now is the time."[7] The eagle and the condor represent the brightest human potential, and their flight exemplifies the growing integration of Earth-based knowledge taking place in our times. The wisdom keepers of Mesoamerica add the quetzal to the prophecy, stating that the brightly colored bird serves as a bridge between the North (eagle) and South (condor) of the Americas.

The pre-Hispanic myth of Quetzalcoatl, or "Feathered Serpent," provides further information on how to virtuously balance polarity. Quetzalcoatl, a legendary figure in Mesoamerica, has been revered for thousands of years and has held a central role as a chief deity of ancient Mexico. This figure represents the integration of the serpent (the South) and the quetzal (the North), offering an expanded expression of human identity. Similar to the alpha and omega of the Greek alphabet that refer to the Christ figure, the quetzal and the serpent symbolize the origin and final destination of all creation. Quetzalcoatl stands as a representation of the luminous totality that arises from the harmonious integration of North and South.

From the original peoples of Mesoamerica emerges an ancestral tradition known as *xochiyáoyotl*, or "flower war" or "war of flowery hearts." In its postclassical expression, this war consisted of engaging in battle in order to take prisoners from the opposing side to offer later to the gods. However, in the earlier classical period, the flower war was a symbolic-ritual activity. The flower warriors enter into battle with themselves in order to make their hearts bloom. Equipped with the "weapons" of flower and song (*in xochitl in cuicatl*), these warriors aimed to reconnect with the sacred spark of creation within.

From my experience, the Work That Reconnects has been a welcome medicine in Latin America. Through various intensives, weekend workshops, courses, and lectures, I've witnessed firsthand how participants fall back in love with themselves, with one another, and with the living Earth. Equally, the Work inspires people to reclaim their own cultural legacy, which makes their actions all the more sound as they take part in the Great Turning. In the case of Latin America, reclaiming our cultural legacy and weaving it into contemporary proposals that address pressing socioecological needs makes the Work That Reconnects a potent formula for transformation. For participants, this often translates into empowerment, resilience, and courage to speak up for Earth.

Like the flower warriors of old, following in the footsteps of the Feathered Serpent, these people partake in the adventure of awakening to the flowering Earth within by way of two weapons. The first is our song of truth in relation to the systematic abuse inflicted upon Earth. It speaks of the erosion of our humanity as well as the many opportunities to celebrate our mutual belonging. The second weapon is the realization of our rootedness in our precious planet-home. With this weapon we uphold culturally sensitive stories, myths, and fresh developments that inform our identity both as unique individuals and as planetary citizens. Having now emerged in the land of the eagle, the Work itself calls for strengthening relations with the many voices of the condor and the quetzal in order to magnify its gifts and fortify its powerful reconnective message.

NOTES

1. The Spanish translation of the first edition of *Coming Back to Life* was made available for free in 2010. Equally available to all with internet access, the translation of the second edition was recently released and can be found here: http://www.living-flames.com/libros.

2. Adrián Villaseñor Galarza, *El Gran Giro: Despertando al florecer de la Tierra* (self-pub., Createspace, 2015).

3. Leonardo Boff, *Ecología: grito de la Tierra, grito de los pobres* (Madrid: Trotta, 2006).

4. Pope Francis, *Laudato Si*, Libreria Editrice Vaticana, May 24, 2015, para. 49, http://w2.vatican.va/content/francesco/en/encyclicals/documents /papa-francesco_20150524_enciclica-laudato-si.html.

5. Adrián Villaseñor Galarza, "Teachings from the Deep South: North-South Contributions to Integral Education," *Integral Review* 7, no. 1 (2011): 86–94.

6. The Work's website in Spanish: www.eltrabajoquereconecta.org.

7. Maria Monachesi, *Profecías Incas: Asombro y sabiduría en épocas de cambio* (Buenos Aires: Kier, 2008), 122.

ON THE ROAD
FOR THE GREAT TURNING

Sarah Vekasi

WE HAD BEEN MARCHING FOR DAYS, single file, walking left of
the white line along a twisting and hilly West Virginian road.
It was early June of 2011, and nearly four hundred people were
following the same footsteps that unionizing coal miners had
taken before us on their way to what became the Battle of Blair
Mountain in the summer of 1921. We sang union songs and songs
of resistance and carried hand-painted signs that declared our
intent: "Save Blair Mountain," "Protect Our Heritage," "Stop
Mountaintop Removal." All of us managed to stay along the side
of the road, off the road but still on the pavement when we could
manage. We walked this way in order to comply with the stipula-
tion from the state police who were trying their hardest to thwart
us at every turn, the same state police originally founded to fight
the Mine Wars on behalf of the coal mine owners. We had already been turned away from our sleeping place each night of
the week. So we had persevered together, with folks volunteering
to drive us back and forth each night to our rented warehouse in
Marmet, West Virginia, where we, like the union miners ninety
years before us, began our journey.

From front to back our march stretched over half a mile. The
weather was hot and sticky, with occasional thunder and lightning
storms fierce enough to send us all into the woods. I was wearing
my hand-embroidered hat labeled "Eco-Chaplain" to help folks

find me when they needed someone to listen or to help de-escalate a situation. Around my waist I had my eco-chaplaincy bag with my bell—small enough to carry but loud enough to garner attention in a crowd—tissues, bandages, a red blessing cord for each of the marchers, a notebook to help me remember who asked for what and to document incidents, a small camera, and a handmade prayer book with songs, hymns, scripture, and prayers from different traditions common in central Appalachia.

By the time we were marching to Blair Mountain, I had been working full time as an eco-chaplain in West Virginia and central Appalachia for several years. We had chosen to do the march because of the rich history that place imbues. Blair Mountain is in Logan County, just over the line from Boone County. Enough blood was shed in the fight to unionize in 1921 that you can still find old bullet casings and guns from the battle up on Blair Mountain. In any other region it would be a national park and its history would be taught in all our schools.

We were marching in the miners' footsteps because Blair Mountain was under imminent threat of destruction from mountaintop removal coal mining. This kind of coal mining is a particularly horrific process wherein the entire surface of a mountain is blown up with explosives. Trees, animal carcasses, soil, and water are bulldozed into the nearest valley, effectively destroying the entire watershed, and then the last remaining coal is scraped off the newly barren surface. The coal is washed in a toxic slurry that is left on-site in enormous impoundments. It is a disaster for Appalachia's land and people. In the midst of a national campaign to stop this toxic practice in central Appalachia, and a push by labor historians to declare the Blair Mountain battlefield a protected historical preservation site, a coal company had somehow secured permits to blast off the top of the mountain for surface mining. It would destroy one of the last remaining intact mountains in West Virginia and simultaneously bury its history.

By the fifth day of the march we were dirty and sweaty, but spirits were high. We were getting close to Blair Mountain. Earlier that day we had passed the union hall; union folks along the route with family members who fought in the original battle had offered us a sanctuary in which to set up our mobile kitchen, portable toilets, and have a meal and a break. As we began to cross the road and walk down the twisting driveway into the fog-covered field, I could sense the importance of the moment.

My official role in this march—and in the movement broadly speaking—was as an eco-chaplain. Eco-chaplaincy is something that I coined and created before I met Joanna Macy, and it met up with the Work That Reconnects in the beautiful way that working toward the Great Turning often can. I had opened the march with an interfaith service and facilitated group dialogue nearly every morning and night as we navigated our feelings and came to consensus about how to go forward through police obstacles. I had mediated between organizers and been available for individual and interpersonal pastoral counseling at each break. By day five everyone was familiar with their eco-chaplain.

In this moment as we all began to gather, I started to feel the fullness of the task at hand and to connect with the living expanse of time between the coal miners' march ninety years before us and our journey. While the cooking crew set up and the medics attended to folks in need, I settled into a kind of presence that is easy to miss but quite profound if you can catch the moment—a moment when time connects between ancestors and us, and there is a felt sense that there will be stories of our time for our descendants.

One of the roles I step into as an eco-chaplain, when appropriate, is that of large-group facilitator and storyteller. After we had eaten, but before going on, I gathered our entire group in circles upon circles and asked permission from the group to open up to the big picture of what we were doing. In large activist events where we have to stay vigilant about *what* we are doing in order to stay safe, the *why* can get forgotten. One of my purposes as an eco-chaplain is to help folks stay in intention throughout the work. My role, as I define it, is to help people remember their own calling and purpose, and to find strategies to help come back to this intention when we get wrapped up in the drama of it all.

In this foggy field, on this hot June day near the foot of Blair Mountain, in a field where we know the union men gathered before the battle, I helped the group return to our original focus by encouraging time for silence and listening to the natural world. I followed this with an invitation to pay attention to the specific history that took place there. I welcomed our local historians and residents into the circle to share what they knew about the history of that place and the current situation in their home. One of our ballad singers offered a song that cut through the fog and reached through time itself.

I responded with a facilitation technique I learned from Joanna Macy—the simple and profound Open Sentences we had been using to help share information, process feelings, and come to agreements about how to proceed when we were in danger. In this situation, I invited each person to come into their own presence in the place and their own personal intention. With participants in pairs, I offered a set of prompts, each time the first person repeating the words and completing the sentence while their partner listened. At the end of the sequence, the partners switched roles, proceeding with no cross talk or conversation.

> Listening to the land around me, I notice . . .
> Knowing we are in the same field the union met in on their
>   way to Blair Mountain, I feel . . .
> My intention in participating in this great march is . . .

After a short process period all together and another song, we continued marching with ballad songs, singing and holding our flags high. We arrived at the base of Blair Mountain later that evening as a group that knew the fullness of what we were doing. While we were steeped in exhaustion and exhilaration, we were also steeped in our own story, in the purpose of our march and the fullness of time that brought so much gravity to the moment. That is how we were able to release trauma as we experienced it. When over a thousand more people joined us the next day from all over the country for the final march to the top of Blair Mountain, we were clear about why we marched and what it meant to our ancestors and our descendants, and we were able to share that with the many people who joined us.

PASTORAL CARE FOR RESISTANCE WORK

Eco-chaplaincy is something I created to build support systems into movement spaces. It stems from my own experience as a direct-action activist, a tree sitter, a community organizer, and later as a Zen monastic. Eco-chaplains are embedded within movements of resistance, just as the military has chaplains who attend to everyone in their unit, and hospitals have chaplains who attend to patients and staff. In an ideal world, chaplains are people who know their own root faith tradition well enough to be able to separate their own beliefs from those to whom they minister. We are trained to use religious and even nonreligious language that is most appropriate for the individual.

Good chaplains, and all eco-chaplains, need to be people who are well trained in the arts of deep listening, empathy, mediation, facilitation, de-escalation, prayer, and world faith traditions; people who are comfortable with anarchist communities and atheists and all manner of spirituality. It is a fascinating field with a lot of potential. Chaplains are seen as pastoral care providers, religious representatives, change agents, and healers. Chaplains are the only officers in the military who are allowed to disobey an order on moral grounds.

On any given day as an eco-chaplain, I might deliver a formal religious service, sit with individuals for pastoral counseling sessions, help mediate conflict between organizers, and/or create a community-based ritual to help honor the moment. During the six days of the march to Blair Mountain, I must have used every single tool in the eco-chaplain's tool bag.

Eco-chaplaincy was still in its infancy when I had the incredibly good fortune to meet Joanna Macy. She was invited to deliver a talk, followed by a full workshop, at Naropa University in the spring of 2006, where I was studying for a master of divinity degree. I will never forget that night—every single word Joanna spoke was amazing. I finally understood the notion of a Buddha-field! I felt as if I was the only person in the large packed room—as if Joanna were just speaking to me, articulating ideas that I had long experienced but could not succinctly explain. The Great Turning! The Great Unraveling! Rooting down in gratitude first so we can honor our pain for the world! And then we see with new eyes while we go forth! Yes! My roommate secretly signed me up for Joanna's workshop (I had no resources), and another friend of Joanna's paid for me to follow up with the intensive training she was offering that week. The Work That Reconnects was the piece I needed for eco-chaplaincy to cohere. It is hard to coin a term and dream into a profession that doesn't yet exist. Spending that time with Joanna helped deepen my theories and turn them into practice at an exponential rate.

I followed up by creating the time to attend the amazing thirty-day "Seeds for the Future" retreat with Joanna and Fran Macy and sixty incredible facilitators on the Oregon coast a year and a half later. It helped me deepen into this work so that the spiral of the Work That Reconnects and the ideas of the Great Turning would come to live at the center of my knowing.

As a facilitator of the Work That Reconnects, I have had the honor to bring people through the spiral as I learned it from Joanna, to experience firsthand the power of the Work. The spiral of the Work That Reconnects is pure genius. I have been able to use this work in the field countless times in unpredictable ways that are nearly always spontaneous. The Open Sentences practice was one example that helped bring folks into gratitude, intention, and presence in that ancestral field in West Virginia. When we finished the march, I facilitated a going-forth exercise where each person was offered a blessing cord to tie around their wrist to remember our story, our strength, and our solidarity as they spoke their commitment out loud. I am always aware of the spiral in my work in the field and often use it to help navigate a way forward when the work seems entrenched. As the years continue, eco-chaplaincy as a field grows deeper and more poignant. Eco-chaplaincy is needed, proven to work, and so much stronger because of Joanna Macy's influence.

We learned last winter that Blair Mountain will be registered again on the National Register of Historical Places. Some of the mountain is gone forever from surface mining, yet some of it remains, in part due to our march and in bigger part to the ceaseless effort of locals and march organizers to protect it and keep the history alive. We have our grief and our celebration. Resistance work demands a long time frame—it includes our ancestors and our descendants—even as we focus on the immediate threats. I have found that embedding pastoral support and spiritual presence into our movements can help prevent burnout and help us recover from the inevitabilities of caregiving activist fatigue. Most importantly, it can help remind folks to walk in dignity, hold this work in divinity, and continue with all the power available to us in a Great Turning.

A PILGRIM RETURNS
TO CHINA

Zilong Wang

WITHIN WEEKS OF MOVING TO San Francisco, friends led me to discover a hidden gem across the Bay in Oakland called Canticle Farm. Many of the dozen diverse people living there were students of Joanna's, and they shone a special light. "Ye shall know them by their fruits." I immediately signed up for an upcoming Work That Reconnects workshop, offered regularly on-site, complete with delicious home-cooked vegan food using garden vegetables. It was a blessing to meet Joanna the person (through her community) before encountering Joanna's teachings, for her very being had already convinced me of whatever she teaches. Within months I found myself moving to Canticle Farm, where I stayed for two years, joining just about every single retreat Joanna offered.

I left China at age seventeen to study in Germany and then the US. After graduating from Hampshire College, I received a job offer to work in a management consulting firm in San Francisco. I thought I should learn something about the United States before joining the corporate world, so I came up with the idea of bicycling across the country, despite my extremely limited experience on a bicycle! I became a monk-like pilgrim, seeking shelter and food from strangers all along the way, seeing the country from the perspective of a "foreigner."[1]

It had been a five-year "Journey to the West" in pursuit of knowledge and individual growth. I was well educated to take up a role in capitalist society, yet I felt a strong calling to service and activism. My pilgrimage seemed to lead me increasingly to a sense of angst and emptiness. Then, at the westernmost edge of the world, across the Golden Gate Bridge, I came upon Joanna and her work. To someone with roots in classical Chinese culture, Joanna's teaching was instantly familiar and yet refreshingly scientific and revolutionary.

The ensuing apprenticeship with Joanna—and friendship, if I may—launched me onto a five-year "journey to the East," surrendering to wisdom and universal love. I decided to quit my job and the green card process, and I proceeded to embark on another bicycling pilgrimage from San Francisco back to China, pedaling across sixteen countries over two and a half years.[2] Joanna was the first person I approached when the pilgrimage calling arose within me. I saw her as a bridge person, spanning science and spirituality, East and West, scholarship and activism, poetry and analysis, ancient traditions and future possibilities. Returning to China, I wondered if I, too, was destined to be a bridge person between East and West, taking up some of the same challenges.

Joanna's blessing and guidance has been with me on each turning of the wheel along this less-traveled path. Now, at age twenty-seven, I find myself back in China, settled as a resident volunteer and apprentice at a Zen monastery. The vibrant community consists of over forty young people about my age, many of whom are also familiar with Joanna's work from their own explorations. With their support, I am taking the Work That Reconnects into China and making an offering of it to those with concerns for the future of our planet.

As the other authors in this volume have abundantly noted, Joanna is a gift of our time. And as a woman, mother, and grandmother, Joanna, like a life-giving river, showers wholeness, tenderness, and intimacy upon a world so dried up by the wounded masculine. "Who Joanna is" makes "what Joanna teaches" all the more evident, relatable, colorful, and empowering. She walks the walk, together with all of us.

When thinking of Joanna, the first memories—as warm as the home-cooked food at her dinner table—are the small moments being with her in her Berkeley living room or during tea breaks at various retreats. I remember hanging up her basket of laundry together in her sunlit garden, as she told stories of her late husband, Fran, and their adventures around the world. I remember cooking dinner and washing dishes with her in the kitchen. I remember seeing how her grandchildren came in to casually chat with their grandma. In today's America, the fact that her children and grandchildren enjoy living close by is proof enough of her virtues. As a "nonresident alien" according to immigration, I was especially touched to be welcomed into Joanna's life as one of her own children—a gift she generously offered to many of us from abroad.

I remember going on a stroll with Joanna through her Berkeley neighborhood. She would hold on to my arm, not really for strength or support but just to let me know that I was loved and trusted. She would stop to contemplate a lovely flower and then turn and say, "Isn't is good to be alive?"

In a workshop or retreat, when our hearts were all heavy with the pains of the world, Joanna would be the first to laugh at her own silliness and our self-righteousness. She would often jump up to dance to the music—there is no way to stop her from still "rocking out" at age ninety with her new titanium hip bone. She would sprinkle the day with poetry reading, group singing, body movement, nature walks, and silent journaling to remind us to create beauty and to embrace life with passion but not be overserious.

I found Joanna to be quick to examine her own privileges and their accompanying blind spots, and to give space to those who are usually silenced or invisible. The conversations around race and power have been candid and forefront in many retreats and in the ongoing development of the Work That Reconnects. During one retreat, when the race conversation was centering exclusively on "black and white" struggles in the US, I was grateful that Joanna made extra effort to listen to those of us from abroad who were neither black nor white and were quietly finding the conversation disorienting and divisive.

As the root teacher of the Work That Reconnects, Joanna has been generous, flexible, and freely giving of this body of work from the very beginning, making it open-source at the "source code" level. Once, during an eleven-day intensive for dozens of WTR trainers, someone asked whether a trademark aspect of the workshop could be modified. Joanna's co-facilitator (who was leading the discussion) quickly answered, as we all expected, "No." But to our surprise, Joanna chimed in, "Well, yes!"

When facing something new or uncertain, Joanna is often the first to say, "I don't know." "It's okay." "Maybe, let's try." Again and again I witnessed how Joanna is not dogmatic or protective about the outer form of her lifelong work and gives license to all of us to adapt and re-create with our own imagination. It has been a living lesson in nonattachment and emergent properties.

Given her accomplishments, Joanna could have easily made herself into a guru—and a rich one. Yet she chooses to be a spiritual friend who is just as willing to listen—or even bow—to you. She will ask you about your life with full attention: "And now, tell me about your family. What are your parents like? How is your job going?" Many times I have been surprised by how she remembers the details of my personal stories that I had forgotten I had told her.

When I am facing major life decisions, Joanna is among the first people I turn to, not just for her guidance as a teacher but also for her deep listening as a friend who makes the effort to enter into my world. It seems that many of my most important friendships have generated from the karmic nexus around Joanna, which, I have learned, is true for many of her students. The relationships that grow out of the Work That Reconnects often turn out to be deep, lifetime bonds. In this work we share at such depth that we come to know each other intimately and with great care for each other's spiritual journeys.

Looking at the web of life in terms of the most meaningful human relationships, it might be obvious that our dear bodhisattva sister has indeed "been circling for thousands of years," and perhaps has been them all—"a falcon, a storm, and a great song."[3] We are gathered into this constellation in this lifetime, through this work that stimulates this ancient memory. And just to keep it interesting, she says, "I still don't know," with an ever-playful twinkle in her wise eyes.

Joanna's teachings and the Work That Reconnects will, no doubt, reach ever more people in coming years. In my own world, I witness how the Work is increasingly hitting a chord with young people in China, despite the language barrier. Yet Joanna's most precious legacy might be the invisible transmission of her energy, her presence, through the hearts of those who have been blessed with the gift of walking the path with her. It is now our turn to join in the "widening circles that reach out across the world."

NOTES

1. John Brant, "Zilong Wang and the Cosmic Tale of the White Dragon," *Bicycling*, October 28, 2015, https://www.bicycling.com

/rides/a20048898/zilong-wang-and-the-cosmic-tale-of-the-white
-dragon.

2. More stories here on my travel blog—www.JourneyE.org.

3. Anita Barrows and Joanna Macy, trans., *Rilke's Book of Hours: Love Poems to God* (New York: Riverhead Books, 1996), 48.

NOTES FROM A ZEN MONASTERY

Susan Moon

I'M MUSING AND WRITING ABOUT Joanna from Tassajara, a Zen monastery deep in the coastal mountains of California. Along with sixty-five other monks and laypeople, I am ten days into a three-month practice period, spent mostly in meditation. In my case, because I'm on the kitchen crew, zazen is punctuated by periods of chopping bok choy. Today, a day off, I sit at a small table in my tiny room, looking out the window at the rain pelting down and the swelling Tassajara Creek. I am writing by hand on a yellow legal pad—no laptops or cell phones allowed here. (What a blessing!) I feel as though I'm in a time outside of time, in a world beyond the world, but Joanna's teaching of interconnectedness reminds me that there is no such time and no such place. All time and all worlds are woven together in Indra's net.

Sometimes I wonder what good it is doing for me to come here, away from the suffering of the world. But I know Joanna understands. She told me she did a three-month silent vipassana retreat years ago. I'm here to explore what it means to be a human being. There is suffering here too—the suffering caused by self-clinging. Perhaps I can let go of some of that before I return to the so-called real world.

Anyway, Joanna's way is not the monastic way. Her practice is in the gritty smoky world of tar sands and broken treaties, teaching and collaborating with others for the sake of life on planet Earth.

Shortly after she and her husband, Fran, moved to San Francisco in the early 1980s, I connected with her in the antinuclear movement. At the time, many convert Buddhist centers in the West, including my beloved Berkeley Zen Center, felt that it was inappropriate for a Buddhist sangha to support anything as "political" as nuclear disarmament. I acknowledge they had a point; they wanted people of every political view to feel welcome.

These were the early days of the Buddhist Peace Fellowship (BPF), established in 1979 precisely to bring together activism for peace and justice with Buddhist practice. Joanna joined early in 1982 and served on the board with Gary Snyder and Rio Imamura for some years. As an activist and a Zen student, I was grateful to the Buddhist Peace Fellowship, and grateful to Joanna for showing up in the Bay Area and bringing together these two seemingly separate parts of my life.

The first time I met her was at a "Despair and Empowerment" workshop. Joanna helped me realize that my own despair about my children's future and the future of life on Earth was the very thing I had to walk right into in order to find my way to action. This was revolutionary for me at the time. I saw that I was not alone in my grief and fear, and this gave me courage. Joanna was personal and open, speaking of her own fear for her children, and this drew me to her. Her passionate voice and her bright eyes encouraged me.

I was already a student of Zen, but it seemed I needed Joanna to point out to me a basic value of Buddhism: seeing things as they are, *including* the suffering. Turning away from what is difficult doesn't work. What is difficult keeps blocking your way until you go right through it, like the next dharma gate that it is. (Easier said than done!) For me, Joanna exemplified not turning away and "sustaining the gaze."

In 1990 I started working at the Buddhist Peace Fellowship as the editor of the newsletter, which soon became *Turning Wheel* magazine. This job, which I loved, gave me lots of opportunity to work with Joanna and get to know her. We published articles by her and interviews with her. But in my first year as an inexperienced editor, I made a bad mistake. Joanna had just started the Nuclear Guardianship Project, and I wanted to put a short piece about it in *Turning Wheel*. I learned that she was teaching out of the country and wouldn't be back until after the issue had gone to press. Unable to contact her—this was before the days of email—I decided, in my great enthusiasm for nuclear guardianship, to write a short description myself. When she returned and saw the published piece, she gave me a well-deserved scolding, something along the lines of "How could you do that without asking me? You make me sound like a New Age dreamer. I'm afraid people won't take the project seriously." She taught me a basic rule that every editor should know: "Don't put words in other people's mouths." I followed the rule assiduously after that.

In the next issue, Joanna wrote her own piece, correcting my mistakes and saying what she wanted to say. She forgave me, and we went on to have a fruitful and mutually supportive relationship as writer and editor, and beyond that, as friends. Years later, she asked me to do some editing for her, so maybe she even forgot about my mistake. Except, oh dear, I've reminded her now!

For many of the seventeen years I worked at BPF, Joanna was a board member, and even when she left the board, she remained an elder and guide for the organization. Her ability to be ready for whatever came up, to be fully present, not to turn away from discord, stood BPF in good stead. And she was local, an added boon.

In my early days at BPF, I was one of three staff members. But as the membership, staff, and projects grew, so did the stress.

Mostly things went well, but a couple of times we had major crises in connection with changing staff positions, different priorities, and a limited budget. You could call it nonprofit-itis. Joanna was always there for us, amazingly. I remember one time when things seemed to be falling apart completely and our condition as an organization looked terminal. Everyone was mad at someone—and I don't mean the same someone. At our weekly staff meetings we skated on thin ice and sometimes fell through. There was weeping. Honestly, I don't even remember what the issues were, though that probably says more about my memory than about the importance of the issues. In any case, we were desperate.

We had an emergency meeting of the staff and board in the big living room of a board member's home, and Joanna came. It must have been painful for her to see this organization that she had nurtured, that was close to her heart, floundering like a small boat in a big storm. But as soon as she came into the room and sat down in an armchair as if she meant to stay awhile, I felt better. I think it was at her suggestion, though I could be wrong, that we unrolled about twenty feet of butcher paper across the living room rug. Everyone was invited to pick up a marker and write down something they loved about BPF—a meaningful part of our history, a successful accomplishment, or something that BPF had given us. We filled the paper with phrases, memories, diagrams. And then we read over this spontaneous people's history of BPF and felt a renewal of hope. Joanna said, "We're the Buddhist Peace Fellowship. Let's remember Buddhist; let's remember peace; let's remember fellowship."

Joanna has consciously tried to show up for younger women as a strong woman, active in the realms of civic, spiritual, intellectual, and family life. She remembers how much she missed such examples when she was young. She has done this for me. At seventy-six, I'm hardly a "younger woman," but Joanna has long been an important role model for me—she still is. She is half a generation older than me, just right for being both an elder and a friend. Once, a stranger who met us at a demonstration asked if we were related because, she said, we resembled each other. I was delighted. No, we said. But that wasn't true; we *are* related.

Years ago, when I was having a rough time, I was questioning Buddhism because I wanted to appeal to someone along the lines of God to help me, and there was no God in Zen. So I went to Joanna, not because I thought *she* was God but because I thought she'd understand and help me. She had been a devout Christian when she was young and was a serious practitioner of both Tibetan and Theravada Buddhism. She took me seriously. She said it was fine to be a Buddhist and to believe in God at the same time. She reminded me that there are deities to appeal to in Buddhism as well, such as Tara and Kuan Yin. She encouraged me to visit a Baptist church in Berkeley where the socially engaged preacher was a friend and the gospel music was inspiring. I went one Sunday and the service recharged my faith. I took this spirit with me back into the zendo.

Joanna's courage encourages. Like going with Fran to Chernobyl, meeting with traumatized residents in the neighboring villages, doing despair and empowerment work, dancing the Elm Dance with them, and coming home to tell Americans what they had seen. If she can do it, I can do it too. Well, if not Chernobyl, at least I can be a little bit braver, thanks to her example.

Joanna is a real person in the world I live in, bringing her bright passion to everything she does, sharing bran muffins at her kitchen table or reading a Rilke poem out loud. As I write about her on my yellow pad, in this rainy-day monastery, she's with me, widening my horizons and enlarging my sense of the possible.

OUR COMPASSIONATE NATURE

Matthew Fox

I AM THRILLED TO REFLECT WITH other writers on the gifts that Joanna Macy leaves for future generations and social movements. She has done so much and leaves so much that I am sure this volume, like my own modest essay here, leaves more unsaid than said. But, of course, that is a very Buddhist thing to do. It is important that we acknowledge the limits of language, which can barely scratch the surface of things—things, after all, that include time and space and our personal times and spaces that we live while on Earth. These things are very deep, deeper than words, deeper than concepts, yet our language is often on the surface. This is why Meister Eckhart, whom D. T. Suzuki celebrated for the "closeness of his way of thinking to Mahayana Buddhism," says that "to speak of divine things we must necessarily always stammer."[1] Thus, committed to stammering, I will nevertheless make an effort to recall some of the gifts that Joanna Macy brings to the number one moral issue of our time—the eco-crisis.

It has been my privilege to work with Joanna on numerous occasions and in numerous locales over many years. So, I speak not only from having read her works—all of which were ahead of their time, remain timely, and are full of prophetic insight and verve—but also from working together side by side and elbow to elbow. She has been a very special teacher to me, ushering me into the wisdom of her Buddhist lineage including, of course, the many practices of that lineage that she shares with students. She is always practical, always keen on practice as well as theory. While systems theory and Gaia theory are important to her, so too are spiritual practices that cleanse and strengthen the heart.

Who is Joanna Macy? I see her as a bodhisattva, a person committed to the long haul of awakening our species to our Buddha nature or, from my tradition, our Christ nature, or, from Judaism, our image-of-God nature. This nature we might summarize in one word as *compassion*. Our compassionate nature. The Dalai Lama reminds us that we can do away with all religion but we cannot do away with compassion. Compassion is "my true religion, my simple faith."[2] I find that same truth echoed in the prophet Isaiah and in the Jewish teaching that compassion is the secret name of God. And in Jesus: "Be you compassionate as your Creator in heaven is compassionate" (Luke 6:36). One might say that Jesus let the secret out of the bag, as did the Buddha and many other teachers, of the depth of our being. Meister Eckhart asks what the human soul is and concludes, "The soul is where God works compassion."[3] Joanna Macy is a teacher of compassion. All beings are deserving of our compassion. She teaches not only by words but by example. Her activism is all about putting compassion into action. I think it can be said that all of her teachings and writings are stories of encouragement for our compassionate natures. They all contribute to our vocation to compassion.

Another name for Joanna Macy is prophet. Rabbi Abraham Joshua Heschel defines the prophet as "one who interferes." Joanna interferes. She interferes with injustice wherever it manifests itself—as sexism, as extractive capitalism, as racism, as adultism, as endangering Earth and its marvelous diversity of species. She interferes with despair and fear by teaching us how to confront them directly and effectively. She also offers medicine for our moral ailments through her teachings on active hope. She interferes with anthropocentrism (what Pope Francis, in his encyclical *Laudato Si* on "the care of our common home," rightly calls our narcissism as a species). She interferes by waking us up. She interferes by encouraging us to take our moral outrage at what is happening at human hands in the despoiling of Mother Earth and steer it to effective action, thus melting violence into nonviolence, reptilian brain energy into mammalian care.

She interferes with excessive talk and excessive theorizing and even argumentation about change by offering practices that deal with the inner person. In this way, she also interferes with the grave danger of projection that haunts our species and our communities from the Left as well as the Right. She blends the inner work with the outer work—a blending that is so needed in our time. As Meister Eckhart puts it, "The outward work can never be small if the inward one is great, and the outward work can never be great or good if the inward is small or of little worth. The inward work always includes in itself all size, all breadth and all length."[4] Joanna's teaching marries the inner and outer work and reaches to expand the size, breadth, and length of our souls and imaginations.

One more name I would ascribe to Joanna Macy comes from Clarissa Pinkola Estés—the Wild Woman. Estés reminds us that the Wild Woman's main occupation is invention. "As in all art, she resides in the guts, not in the head."[5] Joanna Macy is a woman in pursuit of invention and in touch with her guts—her moral outrage and her passion for Earth and its creatures are heartfelt and gut-felt. That is, after all, where true compassion lies—in the guts and not just in the head or even the heart. This is how she has been so significant as an artist in moving people through practices and rituals to tap into their hearts and guts to get to the place where the struggle for justice can carry on. It is part of the Wild

Woman, according to Estés, to "thunder after injustice."[6] Joanna does that. But her thundering is a quiet kind of thundering, a Buddhist kind of thundering. And it is very effective.

How effective is her thundering after eco-injustice? Consider her and John Seed's profound ritual, the Council of All Beings. Many times have I seen groups and individuals moved deeply by that ritual as they become animals who speak to the complacent world of humans, waking us up to their pain. Breakthroughs and conversions happen. Consider how Joanna and John's book *Thinking Like a Mountain* (co-written with Arne Naess and Pat Fleming) moves us from a preoccupation with our own species to a realization of our interconnectedness with all being, and how reciting the holy litanies contained therein reminds us of the extinction and suffering of creatures around the globe in our time and at our hands.

Consider her first book with Molly Young Brown, *Despair and Personal Power in the Nuclear Age*, and her recent book with Chris Johnstone, *Active Hope*, which contain many practices for facing but not succumbing to the reality of our deepest fears. On a windswept sandy landscape in northern Scotland over twenty years ago, Joanna, Fran, and myself led a Stations of the Cross ritual on Good Friday. Retreat participants created their own images at numerous crossing points to grieve the loss of animals, the poisoning of the air and waters, the suffering of Gaia, AIDS, and more. Joanna and Fran had just returned from their trip to Chernobyl, which lent a strong charge of reality to the whole ritual.

Consider her amazing solution to the intractable problem of what to do with our poisonous nuclear residue: Not to bury it in the ground where it can continue to damage Earth, her waters, and her creatures for hundreds of thousands of years but to bury it above ground so that all can be reminded of our power for evil. Not to let it be out of sight and out of mind but to set it up in sacred sites guarded by trained, committed citizens who will stand vigil and teach future generations of the dangers of our species and its inventions when we ignore Gaia. Consider Joanna's workshops, so often attended by young activists, that offer encouragement and support to carry on the work of spiritual warriorhood to which they feel so deeply called.

In our times, many are tempted to despair, to succumb to an apocalyptic mood or a doomsday message. Joanna's recent books offer an alternative path, one that embodies and incarnates practice into a way of hope. The four stages of the Work parallel perfectly the four paths of Creation Spirituality that have been at the heart of my lifework also: gratitude (*via positiva*), honoring the pain of the world (*via negativa*), seeing with fresh eyes (*via creativa*), and going forth (*via transformativa*).[7]

Despair is not to be underestimated. It is a profound human condition—one so great that Thomas Aquinas in the thirteenth century warned that "the worst thing a person can do is to teach despair."[8] And that despair is the "most dangerous" of all sins—injustice is the worst, but despair is the most dangerous. Why is that? Because when one is in despair, one cannot love oneself, much less anyone or anything else. From her earliest to her most recent writings, Macy has taken on the "most dangerous" of sins, those of despair and indifference, and she has offered healing medicines for both. Among these is to see the world as lover, world as self (the title of yet another book). How can we save what we do not love?

Joanna has faced the doomsday mentality of our times, first with nuclear war and now climate change and the war against Earth. Her own work is a reminder that the word *apocalypse* can be translated as "revelation." Joanna's work converts the dangers of apocalypse to revelations—about oneself, one's courage, one's contribution to be made, one's relationship to the greater community, and that community's responsibility and potential for growth and positive service.

It was from Joanna that I first learned about deep ecology, and from that insight I created a term of my own, *deep ecumenism*. Deep ecology includes the spiritual dimension of the fight against eco-injustice in all its expressions—from climate change to species extinction to the destruction of forests, soils, and waters. Joanna's life is a testimony to the spiritual warriorship of deep ecology. Her Buddhist lineage and practice, including her adaptation of many ancient practices to new expressions, has played an integral role in her teachings of resistance and resilience. Deep ecumenism is about including the spiritual dimension in interfaith efforts and learning and working side by side to fight injustice and eco-injustice. Joanna is herself a practitioner of deep ecumenism; she welcomes co-workers and co-practitioners from spiritual traditions other than her own. That is one reason she and I, a Buddhist and a Christian, have worked together so often.

Joanna Macy should also be praised for her generosity and for choosing cooperation over competition. I do not just praise her for being willing to travel over the years, many times to many lands, to instruct and carry on the teachings of survival with grace in the midst of despair. I also praise her for her constant willingness to learn, to be a hunter-gatherer for justice and for ways to honor our Earth and our holy existence. I thank her for her many generous endorsements of my and others' books over the years, where she has taken the time to study our writings and has spoken truth to power just by the succinct blurbs that she offers. She sees herself in a community of learners and teachers, and that is so important today. Sadly, it is also often quite rare. Academia today does not breed cooperation and community as easily as it breeds competition and one-upmanship. Joanna is beyond such ego traps. She works from a deeper platform, one that honors relationships and seeks to find common ground. She works from a feminist and not a patriarchal consciousness, unlike most of academia. And she works from her rich Buddhist lineage.

In Joanna's passage about my concept of "Original Blessing," one sees her deep ecumenism in action.

Original Blessing is a revolutionary event in the spiritual life of our people. It takes our habitual religious notions and turns them over, turns them around. Like a revolving wheel, it sweeps us back to the past and then up and over into the future—back to recapture treasures of forgotten wisdom, forward to fresh insights and creativity. This revolutionary event can be dated ten years ago, with the publication of *Original Blessing*, or dated now, or tomorrow, for it keeps on happening each day with each fresh encounter with what Matthew Fox is saying. Once set in motion, the wheel keeps turning.

The image of wheel comes naturally to me, for it is central to the Buddhist tradition, my spiritual path. It symbolizes the Dharma, the teachings of the Buddha about the dynamic interdependence of all things. When the Buddha gave his teachings, say the scriptures, he "turned the wheel of the Dharma." And his followers today keep the wheel in motion, like Tibetan people reaching out to spin their temple prayer wheels as they pass by.

Original Blessing reminds me of the Dharma wheel because it brings a similar shift of focus—a radical shift from substance to process. The Buddha shocked ancient India by refusing to acknowledge an immutable god, a divinity aloof from the world. He focused instead on the presence of mind in every action, every breath. His teachings did not call people to seek a supernatural haven for the sinful, suffering self, but to recognize their interdependence with this imperfect world and to follow a *magga* or path where the self dissolves into aware and compassionate intention.

The spirituality of Original Blessing has the same kind of revolutionary thrust. It delivers us from theological hair splitting and from preoccupation with our separate selves, however sinful or noble we may deem them, and summons us into an invigorating flow of spirit-experience. It suggests that we are not entities to be perfected so much as processes to be valued and enlivened. As Buckminster Fuller exclaimed, "I seem to be a verb!" As verbs we want trajectories, ways to go, paths for exploring and unfolding consonant with science and crisis.[9]

What I learn from examples such as this is how much a learner as well as a teacher Joanna is. She is always eager for truth as well as for justice. This shows how much Joanna is a heart person as well as an intellectual, fashioning creative solutions to pressing problems. (Thomas Aquinas said that "the proper objects of the heart are truth and justice."[10]) These are the touchstones of Joanna's work—a search for truth and justice. A teacher and hunter after both. The Great Turning that she calls for is a turning away from anthropocentrism toward an eco-conscious civilization.

I thank Joanna Macy for her teachings of deep ecology and so much else. May the profound work of this generous, courageous, wise, and Wild Buddhist Woman never be forgotten or ignored. It will flourish in generations to come. It will flow as sacred waters that nurture the hearts, souls, and minds of future beings—those spiritual warriors, bodhisattvas, prophets, wild women and men called to stand up on behalf of our beloved Earth.

NOTES

1. D. T. Suzuki, *Mysticism: Christian and Buddhist, the Eastern and Western Way* (New York: Macmillan, 1969), 11. The book was first published in 1957.

2. Dalai Lama, *Ethics for the New Millennium* (New York: Riverhead Books, 1999), 234.

3. Matthew Fox, *Passion for Creation: The Earth-Honoring Spirituality of Meister Eckhart* (Rochester, VT: Inner Traditions, 2000), 442.

4. Cited in Matthew Fox, *The Reinvention of Work* (San Francisco: Harper-SanFrancisco, 1994), 82.

5. Clarissa Pinkola Estes, *Women Who Run with the Wolves: Myths and Stories of the Wild Woman Archetype* (New York: Ballantine Books, 1992), 13.

6. Pinkola Estes, *Women Who Run with the* Wolves, 13.

7. I lay these four paths out in Matthew Fox, *Original Blessing* (New York: Tarcher, 2000).

8. Matthew Fox, *Sheer Joy: Conversations with Thomas Aquinas on Creation Spirituality* (New York: Jeremy P. Tarcher/Putnam, 2003), 186.

9. Personal correspondence, Feb 5, 2013, in which Joanna writes of uncovering these comments, "written probably twenty years ago," found within her copy of *Original Blessing*.

10. Fox, *Sheer Joy*, 420.

Joanna Macy at home in Berkeley, California, 2012 (photo by Adam Shemper).

Afterword

JOANNA MACY

In the dark times
Will there also be singing?
Yes, there will be singing.
About the dark times.
—BERTOLT BRECHT

ACROSS THE YEAR OF THIS BOOK'S PREPARATION, projections of widespread climate impacts now extend to the possibility of widespread societal collapse. I have been following closely the UN reports on climate change and biodiversity as well as the bold leadership of Greta Thunberg and the global school strikes she inspires. Uppermost in my mind is Jem Bendell's work on deep adaptation, which offers new ways to consider openly the prospect of collapse. These hard visions, which are not new to the Work That Reconnects, are central now to my talks and teaching as we look at what our future holds.

Shortly after reading the most recent Intergovernmental Panel on Climate Change (IPCC) report, I was on retreat at Spirit Rock Meditation Center, engaged in walking meditation. At one point my mind was stuck on an old memory, some minor embarrassment, and no mindful "noting" could loosen its grip. "Wait a minute," I thought, "I should know how to handle this." At that very moment, a strong voice came to me and thundered, "Just fall in love with what is!" As I heard these words, I saw two curtains closing. One was the IPCC report with its urgent orders to shrink our greenhouse gas emissions. The other was the election in Brazil, with the promised razing of the Amazon rainforest, dooming all hopes of carbon reductions. I stood immobilized, as if turned to stone, my whole body deadened by the eclipse of a livable future. And yet the message came, *Just fall in love with what is*—a clear call for acceptance.

Carl Jung once said that at the core of each life's journey is one question that we are born to pursue. For me, that question has been *How can I be fully present to my world—present enough to rejoice and be useful—when we as a species are destroying it?* The question came in the middle of my life, with the 1977 Cousteau Society symposium. It lurked inside me for fifteen months of silent grief until it broke me open at Notre Dame. The query was clearly my life koan. I learned then, in a circle of colleagues, that expressing our pain for the world can uncover a wellspring of solidarity and creativity.

Ever since, this question keeps surfacing in my heart-mind, and the responses keep coming. The most resounding have come through the four decades of group work. I remember saying to my husband, Fran, in the early 1980s, "Nothing in my life has prepared me for what I experience now: the sheer size of the human heart—it's so big I could walk into it." I continue to be stunned by the strength of community that springs up when people, through their anguish and their tears, open to the immensity of their caring. Courage flowers, and a team spirit so spunky that hilarity flowers too. I began to sense in this adventure the loosening of the hyper-individualism that for centuries—like some foot-binding of the spirit—has cramped our natural abilities and isolated the separate self to the point that it seeks release in mob mentality.

In the 1990s a name emerged for the purposeful and Earth-based solidarity we were experiencing and for the promise it carried—the Great Turning. The term soon came to signify the transition underway to a life-sustaining society—a transition as real and pervasive as the unraveling caused by the industrial growth society. While the Great Turning does take form in specific actions and achievements, it essentially lives within us as vision and commitment. In that sense, it reminds me of the Buddhist notion of *bodhicitta*, dedication to the welfare of all, often portrayed as a flame in the heart.

I think many of us assumed that we could achieve a life-sustaining society without the collapse of the global economy. But given the depth and breadth of destruction, breakdown now seems inevitable and may also be necessary for the emergence of a life-sustaining society. The Great Turning will be more important to us than ever, not only as a light at the end of the tunnel but as compass and map, as well as a supply house of skills and tools for nourishing our spirit, ingenuity, and determination.

We can start right away, while we can still easily communicate and work together. What we do now in our immediate communities as well as in wider "rough weather networks" strengthens our capacities, which will be ever more valuable as the consumer society falters and fails. Everything we learn from the self-organizing nature of Gaia will serve to guide and steady us. And to help us grasp the beauty and relevance of Gaia's laws, it is our great good fortune that we are beginning to listen to indigenous voices as they share, despite genocide and betrayal, their millennia-old Earth wisdom traditions.

The solidarity we grow in our work together will help us meet and move through the bardo of the breakdown of our globalized political economy. Bardo states are phases of transition from one form of existence to another, often described as changes in consciousness. In the Tibetan tradition, Akshobhya is the first Buddha you meet in the bardo. He is known for his mirror wisdom, which reflects everything just as it is. This is the bardo invitation: to not look away, to not turn aside, but to be fully present to what confronts us. The mirror wisdom is a radical teaching, calling for total attention, for depth of acceptance, a call to "just fall in love with what is."

This leads me to a state of utter gratitude. It is so great a privilege to be here in Earth at this time. I have the good fortune to drink from three great streams of thought—the Buddha Dharma, systems thinking, and deep ecology. Each gives me another way to know Gaia and to know myself. Each helps me be less afraid of my fears. I have had the joy of helping others experience this too, of seeing them take the Work That Reconnects further, building our collective capacities and our trust in reciprocity.

And who would not want to be here at this time? I would hate to miss out on this! I sometimes imagine Buddha-fields out there in the universe with long lines of people applying to be born on Earth now to take part in this evolutionary moment.

Being fully present to fear, to gratitude, to all that is—this is the practice of mutual belonging. As living members of the living body of Earth, we are grounded in that kind of belonging. We will find more ways to remember, celebrate, and affirm this deep knowing: we belong to each other, we belong to Earth. Even when faced with cataclysmic changes, nothing can ever separate us from her. We are already home. The practice of mutual belonging is the medicine for the sickness of the small self and can accompany us through the bardo, through the hard times ahead.

Our belonging is rooted in the living body of Earth, woven of the flows of time and relationship that form our bodies, our communities, our climate. The poet Rainer Maria Rilke expressed this sense of belonging in the closing lines of his "Ninth Duino Elegy":

Earth, isn't this what you want? To arise in us, invisible?
Is it not your dream, to enter us so wholly
there's nothing left outside us to see?
What, if not transformation,
is your deepest purpose? Earth, my love,
I want that too. Believe me,
no more of your springtimes are needed
to win me over—even one flower
is more than enough. Before I was named
I belonged to you. I seek no other law
but yours, and know I can trust
the death you will bring.

See, I live. On what?
Childhood and future are equally present.
Sheer abundance of being
floods my heart.[1]

When we turn and open our heart-mind to Earth, she is always there. This is the great reciprocity at the heart of the universe.

My gratitude to all, may we experience "sheer abundance of being" and know that we truly belong here.

NOTES

1. Anita Barrows and Joanna Macy, trans., *In Praise of Mortality: Selections from Rainer Maria Rilke's "Duino Elegies" and "Sonnets to Orpheus"* (Brattleboro, VT: Echo Point Books, 2016), 60.

Joanna Macy Biography

JOANNA MACY, PHD, author and teacher, is a scholar of Buddhism, systems thinking, and deep ecology. A respected voice in movements for peace, justice, and ecology, her scholarship is informed by six decades of committed activism. As the root teacher of the Work That Reconnects, Macy has created a groundbreaking framework for personal and social change, as well as a powerful workshop methodology for its application.

Her wide-ranging work addresses psychological and spiritual issues of the nuclear age, the cultivation of ecological awareness, and the fruitful resonance between Buddhist thought and postmodern science. The many dimensions of this work are explored in her thirteen books, which include a number of theoretical and facilitation guides to her group work, her doctoral dissertation on mutual causality, her personal memoir, and translations of Rainer Maria Rilke poems with commentary.

Based in Berkeley, California, Macy has spent many years in other lands and cultures, engaging movements for social change and exploring their roots in religious thought and practice. Since the early 1980s she has received countless invitations to teach the group work that she and a number of colleagues have developed. Much of the work emerged in her first extensive teaching tours in the UK, Germany, and Australia. She has also led trainings in Russia, Hungary, Japan, India, Sri Lanka, Ukraine, Belarus, New Zealand, Italy, Austria, Norway, Sweden, the United States, and Canada.

Hundreds of thousands of people around the world have participated in Macy's workshops and trainings across the past forty years. These methods, incorporated in the Work That Reconnects, have been adopted and adapted widely in activist movements, academic programs, and community organizing. In the face of overwhelming social and ecological crises, this work helps people transform despair and apathy into constructive, collaborative action.

Macy received a BA from Wellesley College in 1950 and a PhD in religion from Syracuse University in 1978. She married Francis Underhill Macy in 1953, and they raised three children together (Christopher, Jack, Peggy), with formative years during Fran's Peace Corps work in India and Africa. After years living in Washington, DC, and Syracuse, New York, Fran and Joanna settled in Berkeley, California, in 1987, where their children joined them and brought three grandchildren into the family.

Macy served as an adjunct professor at Starr King School of Ministry, the California Institute of Integral Studies, the University of Creation Spirituality, Naropa University, and John F. Kennedy University, with guest teaching at Schumacher College, UK. She received honorary degrees from New College of California, Starr King School of Ministry, the California Institute of Integral Studies, and Alice Lloyd College. In 2013, she was honored with the Bioneers Lifetime Contribution Award. To learn more, visit www.joannamacy.net.

Bibliography of Works by and about Joanna Macy

WORKS BY JOANNA MACY

Books

Macy, Joanna, and Anita Barrows, trans. *Rilke's Letters to a Young Poet.* Boulder, CO: Shambhala Publications, forthcoming.

——. *In Praise of Mortality: Selections from Rainer Maria Rilke's "Duino Elegies" and "Sonnets to Orpheus."* Brattleboro, VT: Echo Point Books and Media, 2016.

Macy, Joanna, and Molly Young Brown. *Coming Back to Life: The Updated Guide to the Work That Reconnects.* Gabriola Island, BC: New Society Publishers, 2014.

Macy, Joanna. *Greening of the Self.* Berkeley, CA: Parallax Press, 2013. eBook.

Macy, Joanna, and Chris Johnstone. *Active Hope: How to Face the Mess We're in without Going Crazy.* Novato, CA: New World Library, 2011.

Macy, Joanna, and Norbert Gahbler. *Pass It On: Five Stories That Can Change the World.* Berkeley, CA: Parallax Press, 2010.

Macy, Joanna, and Anita Barrows. *A Year with Rilke: Daily Readings from the Best of Rainer Maria Rilke.* New York: HarperOne, 2009.

Macy, Joanna. *World as Lover, World as Self: Courage for Global Justice and Ecological Renewal.* Berkeley, CA: Parallax Press, 2007.

Macy, Joanna, and Anita Barrows, trans. *Rilke's Book of Hours: Love Poems to God.* New York: Riverhead, 2005.

Macy, Joanna. *Widening Circles: A Memoir.* Gabriola Island, BC: New Society Publishers, 2000.

Macy, Joanna, and Molly Young Brown. *Coming Back to Life: Practices to Reconnect Our Lives, Our World.* Gabriola Island, BC: New Society Publishers, 1998.

Macy, Joanna. *Mutual Causality in Buddhism and General Systems Theory: The Dharma of Natural Systems.* Albany: State University of New York Press, 1991.

———. *World as Lover, World as Self.* Berkeley, CA: Parallax Press, 1991.

Macy, Joanna, John Seed, Pat Fleming, and Arne Naess. *Thinking Like a Mountain: Towards a Council of All Beings.* Gabriola Island, BC: New Society Publishers, 1988.

Macy, Joanna. *Despair and Personal Power in the Nuclear Age.* Philadelphia: New Society Publishers, 1983.

———. *Dharma and Development: Religion as Resource in the Sarvodaya Self-Help Movement.* West Hartford, CT: Kumarian Press, 1985.

———. *Despairwork.* Philadelphia: New Society Publishers, 1981.

Book Chapters

Macy, Joanna. "The Greening of the Self." In *Spiritual Ecology: The Cry of the Earth*, edited by Llewellyn Vaughan-Lee, 151–64. Point Reyes, CA: Golden Sufi Center, 2016.

———. "Earth Community: What It Tells Us about Faith and Power." In *Thomas Berry, Dreamer of the Earth: The Spiritual Ecology of the Father of Environmentalism*, edited by Ervin Laszlo and Allan Combs, 105–14. Rochester, VT: Inner Traditions, 2011.

———. Foreword to *Building Commons and Community*, by Karl Linn. Oakland, CA: New Village Press, 2007.

———. "Buddhist Resources for Despair." In *Not Turning Away: The Practice of Engaged Buddhism*, edited by Susan Moon, 162–67. Boston: Shambhala Publications, 2004.

———. "The Great Turning." In *Hope in a Dark Time: Reflections on Humanity's Future*, edited by David Krieger. Santa Barbara, CA: Capra Books, 2003.

———. "Joanna Macy." In *What Does It Mean to Be Human?* edited by Frederick Franck, Janis Roze, and Richard Connolly, 185–88. New York: St. Martin's Press, 2001.

———. "Faith, Power, and Ecology." In *This Sacred Earth: Religion, Nature, and Environment*, edited by Roger S. Gottlieb, 415–22. New York: Routledge, 1996.

——. "Working Through Environmental Despair." In *Ecopsychology: Restoring the Earth, Healing the Mind*, edited by Theodor Roszak, Mary E. Gomes, and Allen D. Kanner, 240–61. New York: Sierra Club Books, 1995.

——. "The Full Measure of Our Days: Time and Public Policy in a Postmodern World." In *Postmodern Politics for a Planet in Crisis*, edited by David Ray Griffin and Richard Falk, 33–48. Albany: State University of New York Press, 1993.

——. "Practicing the Presence." In *Earth and Spirit: The Spiritual Dimension of the Environmental Crisis*, edited by Fritz Hull, 41–42. New York: Continuum, 1993.

——. "Not to Escape, but to Transform: Enlightenment and the Concept of Paranimana in the Astasahasrika Prajnaparamita." In *Buddhist Heritage in India and Abroad* by G. Kuppuram. Delhi: Sundeep Prakashan, 1992.

——. "Planetary Perils and Psychological Responses: Despair and Empowerment Work." In *Psychology and Social Responsibility: Facing Global Challenges*, edited by Sylvia Staub and Paula Green, 30–58. New York: New York University Press, 1992.

——. "The Ecological Self: Postmodern Ground for Right Action." In *Sacred Interconnections: Postmodern Spirituality, Political Economy, and Art*, edited by David Ray Griffin, 35–48. Albany: State University of New York Press, 1990.

——. "The Greening of the Self." In *Dharma Gaia*, edited by Alan Hunt Badiner, 53–63. Berkeley, CA: Parallax Press, 1990.

——. "Buddhist Resources for Moving Through Nuclear Death." In *Heal or Die: Psychotherapists Confront Nuclear Annihilation*, edited by Kenneth Porter, Deborah Rinzler, and Paul Olsen, 111–23. New York: Psychohistory Press, 1987.

——. "Going Back into the World." *A Gathering of Spirit: Women Teaching in American Buddhism*, edited by Ellen S. Sidor, 52–56. Cumberland, RI: Primary Point Press, 1987.

Macy, Joanna, and Eleanor Zelliot. "Tradition and Innovation in Contemporary Indian Buddhism." In *Studies in the History of Buddhism*, 133–54. Delhi: B. R. Publishing, 1980.

Macy, Joanna. "Perfection of Wisdom: Mother of all Buddhas." In *Beyond Androcentrism: New Essays on Women and Religion*, edited by Rita M. Gross. Missoula, MT: Scholars Press for the American Academy of Religion, 1977.

Articles by Joanna Macy

2010S

Macy, Joanna. "The Community Awaiting Us: Flowers from the Rubble." *Kosmos* (Spring 2019): https://www.kosmosjournal.org/kj_article /the-community-awaiting-us.

———. "Coming Back to Life—Chapter One: To Choose Life," with Molly Young Brown. *Kosmos* (Summer 2015): https://www.kosmosjournal .org/article/coming-back-to-life.

Macy, Joanna, and Sam Mowe. "The Work That Reconnects: Mapping the Transition to a Sustainable Human Culture." *Tricycle* 24, no. 3 (Spring 2015).

Macy, Joanna. "Living and Leading with Active Hope." *The Occasional Papers of the Leadership Council of Women Religious* (Summer 2013): 19.

———. "Hearing the Call." *Resurgence and Ecologist*, no. 277 (March/April 2013).

———. "Soul-Centering Practices for Hard Times." *Radical Grace* 24, no. 3 (Summer 2011).

———. "Spiritual Practices for Times of Crisis." *Huffington Post*, June 4, 2011: https://www.huffpost.com/entry/spirituality-crisis_b_871311.

———. "Four Steps to a Better World." *In These Times* (April 2010): 56–61.

Macy, Joanna, and Gil Fronsdal. "Noun, Adjective or Verb? Two Scholars on Enlightenment." *Inquiring Mind* 27, no. 1 (Fall 2010): https:// www.inquiringmind.com/article/2704_24_macy-fronsdal/.

2000S

Macy, Joanna. "The Global Crisis and the Arising of the Ecological Self." *Journal of Holistic Health Care* 6, no. 3 (November 2009): 5–10.

———. "The Great Turning." Center for Ecoliteracy, June 29, 2009. https:// www.ecoliteracy.org/article/great-turning#.

———. "The Greatest Danger and the Radical Uncertainty of Our Time." *Yes! Magazine*, no. 45 (Spring 2008): https://www.yesmagazine.org /issues/climate-solutions/the-greatest-danger.

———. "The Great Turning as Compass and Lens." *Yes! A Journal of Positive Futures*, no. 38 (Summer 2006): 44–46.

———. "The End of Oil, Climate Change, and the Great Turning." *Inquiring Mind* 22, no. 1 (Fall 2005): 20–22.

———. *"El Color del Ser* (The Greening of the Self)." *PanNature, The Sangay Foundation,* June 27, 2004.

———. "Turning the Wheel." *Life Positive Plus* (Dehli, India) (October– December 2003): 54–56.

———. "All the Time in the World." *Earthlight*, no. 44 (Winter 2002): 24–25.

———. "The Meditation That Can End a War." *Inquiring Mind* 19, no. 1 (Fall 2002): 20–21, 29.

———. "Giving Voice to Earth." *Earthlight*, no. 46 (Summer 2002): 34–35.

———. "The Wings of the Bodhisattva." *Insight Journal* (Barre Center for Buddhist Studies) (Spring 2001): 34–36.

———. "9/11 and the Heart of the World." *EarthLight*, no. 43 (Fall 2001): 16–17.

———. "Mother of All Buddhas." *Inquiring Mind* 17, no. 1 (2001): 28–29.

———. "Wild Goose." *Orion* (Spring 2000): 12–14.

1990s

Macy, Joanna. "Coming Back to Life." *Timeline* 16, no. 5 (September/ October 1999): 6–11.

———. "The Great Turning." *Sojourn: Awakening Spirit, Culture and Knowledge* 3, no. 4 (Spring 1999): 42, 44–46.

———. "The Great Turning." *Wild Duck Review* 4, no. 1 (Winter 1998): 14.

———. "Challenge at the Millennium: Waking Up in Indra's Net." *Shambhala Sun* (September 1998): 36–43.

———. "Facing the Violence of Our Times." *ReVision* 20, no. 2 (Fall 1997): 47–48.

———. "Respect for Sentient Life." *Inquiring Mind* 14, no. 1 (Fall 1997): 9, 36.

———. *"Zeit der Groben Wende* (Time of the Great Turning)." *Connection* 34, no. 3 (1997): 12–17.

———. "To the Limits of Our Longing." *Permaculture International Journal*, no. 63 (June–August 1997): 35–38.

———. "Woman on the Brink of Time: Religious Studies and the Global Crisis." *Spring Journal* (Starr King School for the Ministry) (May 1997): 3–6.

———. "Collective Self-Interest: The Holonic Shift." *World Business Academy Perspectives* 9, no. 1 (1995): 19–22.

———. "For the Awakening of All: The Sarvodaya Shramadana Movement in Sri Lanka." *Gassho* 1, no. 4 (May/June 1994): http://enlight .lib.ntu.edu.tw/FULLTEXT/JR-AN/an141165.pdf.

———. "Rivers Running through Our Lives." Preface to *Lifelines*, edited by Birgit Engelhardt, 1994.

———. "Asking to Awaken." Joanna Macy and Donald Rothberg. *ReVision* 17, no. 2 (Fall 1994): 25–33.

———. "Schooling Our Intention." *Tricycle* 3, no. 2 (Winter 1993): 48–51.

———. "World as Lover, World as Self." *Lotus* (Winter 1992): 20–23.

———. "Deep Ecology or Shallow Environmentalism." *Human Potential* (Spring 1992): 10–13, 29–32.

———. "What's So Good about Feeling Bad?" *New Age Journal* (Spring 1991): 32–37, 91–95.

1980s

Macy, Joanna. "Breaking the Spell." *In Context*, no. 22 (1989): 20–23.

———. "Guardians of Gaia." *Yoga Journal* (Winter 1989): 53–55.

———. "In League with the Beings of the Future." *Creation Spirituality* (1989).

———. "Power." *Sage Woman* 2, no. 6 (Summer 1988): 5–7.

———. "Mother of All Buddhas: The Second Turning of the Wheel." *Anima Magazine* (Fall 1986).

———. "Gaia Meditations—At the Council of All Beings." *Awakening in the Nuclear Age: An Interhelp Journal* (Summer/Fall 1986): 10.

———. "Breathing Through the Pain of the World." *Journal of Humanistic Psychology* 24, no. 3 (Summer 1984): 161–62.

———. "Buddhist Approaches to Social Action." *Journal of Humanistic Psychology* 24, no. 3 (Summer 1984): 117–29.

———. "What about the Russians?" *Journal of Humanistic Psychology* 23, no. 3 (Summer 1983): 115–18.

———. "Taking Heart: Spiritual Exercises for Social Activists." *Fellowship* (July/August 1982): 3–6.

———. "Shramadana Means Sharing Energy." *CoEvolution Quarterly*, no. 25 (Spring 1980).

———. "Giving Energy." *Resurgence* 10, no. 5 (January–February 1980): 24–25.

1970s

Macy, Joanna Rogers. "Dependent Co-arising: The Distinctiveness of Buddhist Ethics." *Journal of Religious Ethics* 7, no. 1 (1979): 38–52. http://www.jstor.org/stable/40018242.

Macy, Joanna. "How to Deal with Despair." *New Age Journal* (June 1979): 40–45.

Macy, Joanna Rogers. "Systems Philosophy as a Hermeneutic for Buddhist Teachings." *Philosophy East and West* 26, no. 1 (1976): 21–32.

Macy, Joanna. "The Dialectics of Desire." *Numen* 22, no. 2 (1975): 145–60.

DVDs and Online Lectures

Macy, Joanna. "Deep Adaptation Q&A with Joanna Macy." Interview by Jem Bendell. YouTube, June 5, 2019. https://www.youtube.com/watch?v=k1wUY6945kY.

Ankele, John, and Anne Macksoud, dirs. *The Wisdom to Survive*. Woodstock, VT/New York: Old Dog Documentaries, 2014. DVD. https://www.resilience.org/resources/the-wisdom-to-survive.

Joanna Macy: The Work That Reconnects. Joanna Macy Intensives, 2006. Training DVD.

Macy, Joanna. "The Courage to See, the Power to Choose." Boulder, CO: Naropa University, October 17, 2014. Lecture. https://earthcitizens.net/honorary-mentors/joanna-macy.

———. "Choosing Life." Bioneers National Conference, 2013. San Raphael, CA. Lifetime Contribution Award acceptance speech. https://bioneers.org/joanna-macy-choosing-life-bioneers.

INTERVIEWS

Macy, Joanna. "Transforming Despair: An Interview with Joanna Macy." Interview by Mary NurrieStearns. *Personal Transformation.* https://www.personaltransformation.com/joanna_macy.html.

——. "Serving the Earth, Serving One Another." Interview by Allen White. Great Transition Initiative, August 2018. http://www.greattransition.org/publication/serving-the-earth-serving-one-another.

——. "Widening Circles—Joanna Macy." Interview by Emmanuel Vaughan-Lee. *Emergence Magazine,* April 5, 2018.

——. "Learning to See in the Dark amid Catastrophe: An Interview with Deep Ecologist Joanna Macy." Interview by Dahr Jamail. Truthout, February 13, 2017. https://truthout.org/articles/learning-to-see-in-the-dark-amid-catastrophe-an-interview-with-deep-ecologist-joanna-macy.

——. "Joanna Macy on How to Prepare Internally for Whatever Comes Next." Interview by Ecobuddhism. Films for Action, May 27, 2016. https://www.filmsforaction.org/articles/joanna-macy-on-how-to-prepare-internally-for-whatever-comes-next.

Macy, Joanna, and John Robbins. "Great Turning, Long Friendship." Interview by Barbara Gates and Wes Nisker. *Inquiring Mind* 31, no. 1 (Fall 2014): 16–18.

Macy, Joanna. "Living for the Future with Joanna Macy." Interview by Sam Mowe. *Spirituality and Health* (December 26, 2013): https://spiritualityhealth.com/articles/2013/12/26/living-future-joanna-macy.

——. *"Nichts und niemand kann uns je von Gewebe des Lebens trennen: die Tienfenökologin Joanna Macy."* Interview by Marietta Schuerholz. *Buddhismus Aktuell* 4 (October/November/December 2013).

——. "Allegiance to Life—An Interview with Joanna Macy." Interview by Sam Mowe. *Tricycle* 21, no. 4 (Summer 2012).

——. "Woman on the Edge of Time." Interview by Barbara Gates, Susan Moon, and Wes Nisker. *Inquiring Mind* 28, no. 2 (Spring 2012): 9, 11–13, 30.

——. "The Great Turning or The Great Unravelling? Maddy Harland in Conversation with Joanna Macy." Interview by Maddy Harland.

Permaculture, June 6, 2011. https://www.permaculture.co.uk/articles
/great-turning-or-great-unravelling-maddy-harland-conversation
-joanna-macy.

———. "The Way to Make Earth Sustainable with All Beings—An Interview with Ecophilosopher Joanna Macy." *Buddhism and Culture*
(Winter 2011).

———. "Joanna Macy: A Wild Love for the World." Interview by Krista
Tippett. *On Being with Krista Tippett*. Podcast audio, September 16,
2010. https://onbeing.org/programs/joanna-macy-a-wild-love-for-the
-world.

———. *"Am Tanz des Lebens Teilnehmen."* Interview with Joanna Macy. *Buddhismus Aktuell* 3 (July/August/September 2009): 6–9.

———. "The Great Turning for Global Healing." *Dharma World* 36 (April–
June 2009): https://rk-world.org/dharmaworld/dw_2009ajglobal
healing.aspx.

———. "Our Long Journey Together: An Interview with Joanna Macy."
Interview with Martha Boesing and Susan Moon. *Turning Wheel*
(Fall–Winter 2006): 29–32.

———. "Interview with Joanna Macy." *Dharma Vision Buddhist Community
Newsletter* 6, no. 5 (2005): 3–4, 7.

———. "Sustaining the Heart of Action Research(ers)—An Interview with
Joanna Macy." Interview by Hilary Bradbury. *Action Research* 1, no.
2 (October 1, 2003): 208–23.

———. "Doing the Work." Interview with Marianne Arbogast. *Witness* 15,
no. 1 (March 2001): 6–8.

———. "The Wisdom of Uncertainty: Living with the Shambhala Prophecy." Interview with Mary E. Gomes and Jürgen Kremer. *ReVision*
23, no. 2 (Fall 2000): 19–23.

———. "The Great Turning." Interview with Sara Ruth van Gelder. *Yes! A
Journal of Positive Futures*, no. 13 (Spring 2000): 34–37.

———. "A Conversation with Joanna Macy." *Spirit Rock Newsletter* (September 1999–February 2000): 1, 9, 24.

———. "An Interview with Joanna Macy, Environmental Activist, Educator, Speaker and Bestselling Author." *Share Guide: The Holistic Health
Magazine*, no. 43 (May/June 1999): 12–13, 26.

———. "Contemplation and Revolution: An Interview with Joanna Macy." Interview by Susan Moon. *Turning Wheel* (Summer 1998): 21–23.

———. "The Feminine Face of the Buddha" Interview by Barbara Graham. *Common Boundary* (March/April 1996): 28–35.

———. "Interview with Joanna Macy." *Wild Duck Review* 2, no. 1 (November 1995): 1–2.

———. "Ecology from the Inside Out." *Kindred Spirit Quarterly: The Guide to Personal and Planetary Healing* (Spring 1995).

———. "The Incredible Exploding Self." Interview by Wes Nisker and Barbara Gates. *Inquiring Mind* 11, no. 2 (Spring 1995): 6, 8, 14.

———. "*Wir Mussen Lernen, Den Shit Zu Begreifen, Den Wir Fabriziert Haben.*" Interview by Hans Joachim Ehlers and Christopher Baker. *Raum & Zeit,* no. 73, (January–February 1995).

———. "Positive Disintegration." Interview by Tensho David Schneider. *Tricycle* 2, no. 3 (Spring 1993).

———. "Guardians of the Future." Interview by Alan AtKisson. *In Context* 28 (Spring 1991): 20–25.

———. "Guarding the Earth," Interview by Barbara Gates. *Inquiring Mind* 5, no. 2 (Spring 1991): 1, 4–5, 12.

———. "The Third Turning of the Wheel: A Conversation with Joanna Macy." Interview by Wes Nisker with Barbara Gates. *Inquiring Mind* 5, no. 2 (Winter 1989): 1, 10–12.

———. "Embracing the Tiger." Interview by Mackenzie Stewart. *Tai Chi Journal* (Fall 1987): 3.

———. "Joanna Macy: The Eroticism of Deep Ecology." Interview by Charlene Spretnak. *Creation Spirituality* (May/June 1987): 29–31.

———. "Despair and Personal Power in the Nuclear Age: A Conversation with Joanna Macy." Interview with Stephan Bodian. *Yoga Journal* no. 60 (January/February 1985): 22–29.

———. "Notes from an Interview on 'Womanpower.'" Interview by Bobbi Lev. *Woman of Power,* no. 1 (Spring 1984): 10–13.

———. "Interview with Joanna Macy." Interview by Liz Campbell. *Association for Humanistic Psychology Newsletter* (July/August 1982): 15–18.

ABOUT JOANNA MACY

Kaza, Stephanie. "Joanna Macy: Fierce Heart-Mind Warrior." In *Green Buddhism: Practice and Compassionate Action in Uncertain Time*s, 139–48. Boulder, CO: Shambhala Publications, 2019.

Hathaway, Mark D. "Activating Hope in the Midst of Crisis: Emotions, Transformative Learning, and 'The Work That Reconnects.'" *Journal of Transformative Education* 15, no. 4 (December 14, 2016): 296–314.

Egger, Michel Maxime. *Soigner l'esprit, guérir la Terre* (Care for the spirit, heal the Earth): *Introduction à l'écopsychologie.* Geneva, Switzerland: Labor et Fides, 2015.

Leighton, Taigen Dan. "Maitreya: Bodhisattva as Future Buddha." In *Faces of Compassion: Classic Bodhisattva Archetypes and Their Modern Expression*, 270–74. Somerville, MA: Wisdom Publications, 2012.

Sponsel, Leslie. "Reconnecting, Joanna Macy." In *Spiritual Ecology: A Quiet Revolution*, 107–14. Santa Barbara, CA: ABC-CLIO Books, 2012.

Plotkin, Bill. *Nature and the Human Soul: Cultivating Wholeness and Community in a Fragmented World.* Novato, CA: New World Library, 2008.

"Aus der Tiefe." Portraits of Joanna Macy and Dolores LaChappelle. *Natur und Kosmos* (July 2003): 42–43.

Ingram, Catherine. "Joanna Macy." *In the Footsteps of Gandhi: Conversations with Spiritual Social Activists*, 133–56. Berkeley, CA: Parallax Press, 2003.

Graham, Barbara. "The Feminine Face of the Buddha." *Common Boundary* (March/April 1996): 28–35.

Baker, Christopher, and Hans Joachim Ehlers. *"Wir Mussen Lernen, Den Shit Zu Begreifen, Den Wir Fabriziert Haben." Raum & Zeit* 73 (1995).

Biegert, Claus. *"Eine Stimme der Erde." Natur* 7 (1995): 109–13.

Barrows, Anita. "From Despair to Empowerment." *Resurgence*, no. 63 (March/April 1994): 40.

Bancroft, Anne. *Weavers of Wisdom: Women Mystics of the Twentieth Century.* New York: Penguin, 1990.

Boucher, Sandy. *Turning the Wheel: American Women Creating the New Buddhism*, 271–76. San Francisco: Harper and Row, 1985.

About the Contributors

DAVID ABRAM, PHD, is a cultural ecologist and geophilosopher based in New Mexico who lectures and teaches widely on several continents. Director of the Alliance for Wild Ethics (AWE), he is the author of *The Spell of the Sensuous: Perception and Language in a More-than-Human World* and *Becoming Animal: An Earthly Cosmology*. David's creative work and writing have helped catalyze the emergence of several new fields of thought, including ecopsychology.

BOBBI ALLAN is a Buddhist teacher and activist. She has been facilitating the Work That Reconnects since 1985, when Interhelp Australia first brought Joanna to Australia. She later developed four-day "Stillness in Action" retreats, combining Buddha Dharma, meditation, and the Work That Reconnects. She is currently focused on ending Australia's deplorable policy of detaining asylum seekers and refugees indefinitely in offshore detention centers, while encouraging a kinder, more compassionate world through teaching mindfulness in elementary schools.

A. T. ARIYARATNE is the founder of the Sarvodaya Shramadana movement of Sri Lanka that emphasizes Gandhian ideals, Buddhist philosophy, and ecumenical spirituality. He conducted the first Shramadana work camp in 1958, which eventually led to the establishment of the largest NGO in the country. He is the father of six distinguished adult children and has led tens of thousands of "family gatherings" and meditations with millions of people throughout Sri Lanka and the world.

ANITA BARROWS, PHD, is an internationally published poet and translator, as well as a clinical psychologist at the Wright Institute in Berkeley, California. She is the author of *We Are the Hunger, Exile*, and translator of fourteen books, including three books of Rilke translations with Joanna Macy.

OLEG BODROV is an engineer-physicist and ecologist who worked in the nuclear industry testing nuclear submarines and studying the ecological impact of nuclear facilities. After a research visit to the Chernobyl contaminated area in 1986, he established an environmental NGO and in 1994 left the nuclear industry. He has served as chairperson of the Green World Council and in 2004, was named Russia's "Green Person of the Year." He currently leads an international project to promote the safe decommissioning of Russian nuclear power plants and final disposal of radioactive waste and spent nuclear fuel.

JEANINE M. CANTY, PHD, is professor and chair of Environmental Studies at Naropa University with specialties in ecopsychology, ecological and social healing, transformative learning, climate justice, and systems of oppression. Her work situates racism, sexism, and ecological devastation within larger systems, combined with the power of mindfulness, nature, and the transpersonal. She is the editor of and contributor to *Ecological and Social Healing: Multicultural Women's Voices* and *Globalism and Localization: Emergent Approaches to Ecological and Social Crisis.*

HELENA TER ELLEN, PHD, is of Dutch origin and has lived in Colombia since 2018. She is the co-founder of Terr'Eveille, a Belgium organization that has helped spread the Work That Reconnects in Europe since 2009. She translated *Coming Back to Life* into Dutch and since 2013 has been offering WTR-inspired Peace and Reconciliation work in Colombia. In 2018 she and a Colombian team initiated *Re-Conectando*: Laboratories of Truth and Reconciliation in the Womb of Mother Earth to accompany the Colombian Truth Commission peace process.

SHERRY ELLMS is an associate professor at Naropa University in resilient leadership, environmental studies, and ecopsychology, where she has helped to create the Joanna Macy Center to "empower present and future generations in building a more resilient world that works for all."

She works at the intersection of nature, contemplative practice, and social and ecological justice.

HIDE ENOMOTO is a graduate of the California Institute of Integral Studies in San Francisco and founder of CTI Japan, promoting coaching in Japan. He played a key role in spreading the Work That Reconnects, the Transition movement, and Awakening the Dreamer in Japan. Through his business, Yoku-ikiru Kenkyusho (Institute for Right Livelihood), he offers talks and workshops. He is the author of *Empower Your People by Coaching*, *The Real Work*, and *Living Your Authentic Life*.

ANDY FISHER, PHD, is a central figure in ecopsychology, having tracked the development of the field since its beginnings in the 1990s. Author of *Radical Ecopsychology: Psychology in the Service of Life*, he is best known for his critical scholarship and holistic vision of the ecopsychological project. Fisher keeps an active schedule of teaching and writing while also working as a rites-of-passage guide and psychotherapist in private practice.

PAT FLEMING lives in the UK and has led workshops in the Work That Reconnects and deep ecology since 1983 in many countries, while also supporting and training facilitators. She currently teaches and mentors on the Call of the Wild course at Schumacher College. She also works in conservation botany and set up the Dartmoor Conservation Garden, a wild-planted public education resource within Dartmoor National Park, Devon, UK. She co-authored *Thinking Like a Mountain* with Joanna Macy, Arne Naess, and John Seed.

MATTHEW FOX, PHD, is a spiritual theologian, Episcopal priest, and activist who was expelled from the Dominican Order after thirty-four years for teaching about the divine feminine, creation spirituality, and liberation theology. He has devoted forty-five years to creation spirituality, recovering great Western mystics such as Hildegard of Bingen and Meister Eckhart. Among his many books are *Original Blessing*, *Creation Spirituality*, *The Reinvention of Work*, and *The Lotus & The Rose: A Conversation Between Tibetan Buddhism & Mystical Christianity*. He is a visiting scholar at the Academy for the Love of Learning in Santa Fe, New Mexico.

PAULA GREEN, EdD, has forty years of experience as a psychologist, peace educator, consultant, and mentor in intergroup relations and conflict resolution. In 1994, she founded the Karuna Center for Peacebuilding, focused on international conflict transformation, intercommunal dialogue, and reconciliation. She is professor emerita at the School for International Training in Brattleboro, Vermont, where she founded the Conflict Transformation across Cultures Program. Currently she develops and facilitates dialogues across divides between polarized groups in the US.

TOVA GREEN is a Zen priest who lives and and teaches at San Francisco Zen Center and received dharma transmission from Eijun Linda Cutts in 2015. She cofounded the SFZC Queer Dharma Group and the group Unpacking Whiteness—Reflection and Action. She has worked for the Buddhist Peace Fellowship and as a hospice social worker. She plays the cello and writes poetry.

GUNTER AND BARBARA HAMBURGER have been involved in Despair and Empowerment work in Germany since the late 1970s. Gunter cofounded the German Holon Training program in Deep Ecology and the Work That Reconnects. The Hamburgers translated the latest edition of *Coming Back to Life* into German, titled *Für das Leben: Ohne Warum.* They are deeply involved in nuclear guardianship, refugee rights in Europe, and rites-of-passage work with young activists.

STEPHAN HARDING, PhD, is senior lecturer and program coordinator for the MSc Holistic Science program and founding faculty of Schumacher College at the Dartington Hall Trust, UK. An expert in Gaia theory and practice, he has taught alongside many of the world's leading ecological thinkers and activists. He is the author of *Animate Earth: Science, Intuition and Gaia* and editor of *Grow Small, Think Beautiful: Ideas for a Sustainable World from Schumacher College.*

LIZ HOSKEN was born in South Africa and active from a young age in environmental issues and the anti-apartheid movement. She cofounded the Gaia Foundation in the UK and has since been building "affectionate alliances" across Africa, South America, Asia, and Europe to support the revival of indigenous knowledge and ecological governance systems, and restore respectful relationships with the Earth. Inspired by the Work that Reconnects, she has developed experiential trainings in Earth Jurisprudence, especially in African countries.

DAHR JAMAIL is an award-winning independent journalist who went to Iraq to report on the war and occupation. In 2007 he was awarded the Martha Gellhorn Award for his Iraq war reporting, and in 2018 he won an Izzy Award for excellence in independent media for his climate crisis reporting. He is the author of *Beyond the Green Zone*, *The Will to Resist*, and *The End of Ice: Bearing Witness and Finding Meaning in the Path of Climate Disruption*.

CATHERINE JOHNSON is the author of *Finding Mercy in This World*, the winner of the 2018 Sarton Women's Book Award for memoir. Her essays have appeared in *Face to Face: Women Writers on Faith, Mysticism, and Awakening*, *Scent of Cedars*, *Teaching with Fire*, and *Nature of an Island*. The former dean of the Leadership Institute of Seattle, she homesteads with her wife, Dana, on Vashon Island, Washington.

WENDY JOHNSON is the author of *Gardening at the Dragon's Gate* and writer of the long-running Gardening column in *Tricycle* magazine. She teaches engaged ecological Dharma at Green Gulch Farm and Upaya Zen Centers and serves as an organic gardening mentor for the national K–12 Edible Schoolyard Project.

KAYE JONES is an educator, homesteader, and mother of three young children in the Columbia River Gorge. Kaye completed her graduate work in holistic science from Schumacher College, trained extensively with Joanna Macy, and continues to be a student of nature, complexity, and relationships as understood through the lenses of dharma and natural systems.

STEPHANIE KAZA, PhD, is professor emerita of environmental studies, University of Vermont, and former Director of the UVM Environmental Program. Her books include *Green Buddhism: Practice and Compassionate Action in Uncertain Times*; *Dharma Rain: Sources of Buddhist Environmentalism*; *Mindfully Green*; *Hooked! Buddhist Writings on Greed, Desire, and the Urge to Consume*; and *Conversations with Trees: An Intimate Ecology*. She currently works on climate issues in Portland, Oregon, where she pursues her love of trees, tides, and deep time.

SEAN KELLY, PhD, is a professor of philosophy, cosmology, and consciousness at the California Institute of Integral Studies in San Francisco, where he has collaborated with Joanna Macy teaching courses on the Great Turning. He is the author and editor of several books including *Coming Home: The Birth and Transformation of the Planetary Era* and *The Variety of Integral Ecologies: Nature, Culture, and Knowledge in the Planetary Era*.

TAIGEN DAN LEIGHTON, PhD, is a lineage holder and Zen teacher in the Soto tradition of Shunryu Suzuki and is the founder and guiding teacher of Ancient Dragon Zen Gate Center in Chicago, Illinois. He is the author of *Zen Questions: Zazen, Dogen, and the Spirit of Creative Inquiry*; *Faces of Compassion: Classic Bodhisattva Archetypes and Their Modern Expression*; *Just This Is It: Dongshan and the Practice of Suchness*; and *Visions of Awakening Space and Time: Dōgen and the Lotus Sutra*.

SUSAN MOON is a writer, editor, and lay ordained teacher in the Soto Zen tradition. She is the author of a number of books about Buddhism, including *This Is Getting Old: Zen Thoughts on Aging with Humor and Dignity* and, with Norman Fischer, *What Is Zen? Plain Talk for a Beginner's Mind*. For many years she was the editor of *Turning Wheel: The Journal of Socially Engaged Buddhism*.

SUSANNE MOSER, PhD, is director and principal researcher of Susanne Moser Research & Consulting. She is also research faculty in environmental studies at Antioch University–New England and affil-